# ROMANTIC MUSIC
## Sound and Syntax

# ROMANTIC MUSIC
## Sound and Syntax

# Leonard G. Ratner

SCHIRMER BOOKS
An Imprint of Macmillan Publishing Company
NEW YORK

MAXWELL MACMILLAN CANADA
TORONTO

MAXWELL MACMILLAN INTERNATIONAL
NEW YORK   OXFORD   SINGAPORE   SYDNEY

Schirmer Books
An Imprint of Macmillan Publishing Company
866 Third Avenue, New York, N.Y. 10022

Maxwell Macmillan Canada, Inc.
1200 Eglinton Avenue East, Suite 200
Don Mills, Ontario M3C 3N1

Macmillan Publishing Company is part of the Maxwell
Communication Group of Companies.

Library of Congress Catalog Card Number: 92-10566

Printed in the United States of America

printing number
1   2   3   4   5   6   7   8   9   10

**Library of Congress Cataloging-in-Publication Data**

Ratner, Leonard G.
    Romantic music: sound and syntax/Leonard G. Ratner.
        p.      cm.
    Includes bibliographical references and index.
√ ISBN 0-02-872065-2
    1. Music—19th century—History and criticism.    2. Romanticism in
music.      3. Musical analysis.
ML196.R27   1992
781′.09′034—dc20                                          92-10566
                                                              CIP
                                                              MN

The paper used in this publication meets the minimum requirements of American
National Standard for Information Sciences—Permanence of Paper for Printed
Library Materials. ANSI Z39.48-1984. ∞™

*To Ingeborg*

# Contents

# *Acknowledgments*

A study of the sound-syntax relationship in Schubert's Quintet in C major, Op. 163, was the starting point for this book. The reciprocal action of these aspects of Schubert's musical language suggested an approach to the analysis of Romantic music that hitherto had not been fully explored. During the preparation of this book I had many discussions with colleagues, students, and friends. For their interest, which has been of great encouragement, I want to express my deep appreciation and sincere thanks.

Particularly, I should like to thank those whose general comments or specific input have been of special value: Wye Allanbrook, George Barth, Jonathan Bellman, Karol Berger, Hermann Danuser, Laurence Dreyfus, Nina Gilbert, Thomas Grey, George Houle, Janet Levy, William Mahrt, Kimberly Marshall, Leonard Meyer, Herbert Myers, and Jodi Rockmaker. My thanks to Editor-in-Chief Maribeth Payne who was most supportive during the various phases of the writing of the book, to editor Robert Axelrod, and production supervisor Garrett Schure.

I should like to thank Mark Dalrymple and Jodi Gandolfi who gave musical and technical assistance; Annie Sultan who prepared the first version of the manuscript; the music libraries of the University of California and Stanford University for assistance in providing research materials; Diane Westfall and Mimi Tashiro who were helpful in procuring interlibrary loan materials. Last but not least, special thanks go to my wife, Ingeborg, who was deeply involved in every aspect of the book's preparation from its inception onward and whose share in the project was of incalculable value.

# Introduction

This book investigates the interaction of sound and syntax in Romantic music. It considers the ways in which qualities of sound affect the unfolding of form on both large and small scales, and thus it offers an approach in which sound figures as a factor in the analysis of this music.

In the early years of the nineteenth century, profound changes took place in the nature and scope of musical sonority—what we may call the *climate of sound*. Thanks to modifications in the structure of instruments, many dimensions of sound were expanded. The pitch range increased, reaching extremes in the high and low registers with telling effect. Instruments were capable of more extreme dynamics, opening areas of expression at *ppp* and *fff* levels. The palette of timbres grew in richness, in subtlety of shading, and in the variety of effects. Instruments developed greater resonance and sustaining power, while greater precision of intonation gave freer range of action in keys remote from the ancestral C major. Expanded sound resources in instrumentation added new values to harmony by allowing a chord to express itself as a color in addition to acting as a function in a cadential formula.

The effect of these changes—of this new climate of sound—was pervasive. It affected every aspect of musical form and expression. Melody could take a broad, sweeping manner; harmony could intensify in richness and color; rhythm could cover articulations with a steady flow of sound; the more deliberate rate of change arising from the savoring of the new and more colorful sounds allowed, or even demanded, the alteration of musical form. For the listener, colorful sound was an immediate clue to the expressive content of a composition. Broad declamations, misty veilings, brilliant and bold gestures, seductive envelopings, firm stabilities, troubling instabilities— these and other affective qualities and stances were given vivid presence by the great palette of sound available in the Romantic style. Whether the message was intensely emotional, sentimental, or colorfully pictorial, it was carried on a flow of sound that could be generated only by nineteenth-century means.

The new qualities of sound invaded the world of traditional practice. Compositional procedures were being fully codified, in theory and in practice. This codification, based on eighteenth-century models, spelled out all the details of syntax—key-centered harmony, fundamental bass and its laws of root movement, complementary melodic and rhythmic configurations, the shape of phrases and periods—and gave explicit descriptions of what had become standard forms.

The codification of traditional syntax formed the basis of the training of all composers in the nineteenth century. In their studies, in the models they followed, traditional syntax controlled much of the music they wrote, especially the music based on popular song and dance types.[1]

# Interaction of Innovative Sound and Traditional Syntax

While innovative sound and traditional syntax have been recognized as basic processes in Romantic music, heretofore there has been no formal consideration of the action of these two processes upon each other in the music of this era. Studies of nineteenth-century music to date have given scant attention to the question of how sound values operate together with other rhetorical components. This book addresses that question; it factors sound into the rhetoric of nineteenth-century music.

The spectrum of color, both instrumental and harmonic, in Romantic music is so rich and varied in its nuances and gradations that quantification and categorization would require immensely detailed descriptions. Yet when we link sound qualities to firmly established, fixed compositional processes, we have a method by which the fluid play of sound can be evaluated in terms of its effect on syntax. The deployment of sound was an important strategy of composition in Romantic music, equal in significance to strategies and processes that have received attention in analytic studies—layout of themes, organicism, developing variation, harmonic processes, *Ursatz* and *Urlinie*. This book undertakes to explore this aspect of Romantic music, to examine the ways in which the new values of sound can affect the shape and size of structures that were traditional and familiar, such as the phrase, the period, two-reprise form, and sonata form.

The music discussed in this book was written in the period roughly from 1815 to 1900. These approximate time limits enclose the following developments:

circa 1815–1820: the emergence of the new climate of sound as a decisive factor in musical technique and expression

circa 1820–1900: the decisive shift away from traditional syntax as an organizing principle in composition: when cadential harmony loses much of its power to direct musical action—this trend is exemplified by the works of Debussy, Schoenberg, and Stravinsky composed shortly after the turn of the twentieth century

Within these time limits, the interplay of innovative sound and traditional syntax was active and pervasive. Indeed, composers produced works of strikingly diverse character and sharply profiled individual styles; yet they all drew from the palette of tone colors available, and they all proceeded from traditional premises of texture and form. Whatever an individual work may embody—a touch of color and a familiar, easy symmetry, or a bold splash of color and an involuted phrase structure—the distinctive mix of sound and traditional syntax in that work provides a set of clues to its form and expressive content.

Throughout this eighty-five-year period, we find both progressive and retrospective uses of sound and syntax. Both the Sonata in D Major, Op. 53, by Schubert (1825) and the *Italian Serenade* by Wolf (1887), although written more than sixty years apart, recall the lightness of texture and the smooth part writing that characterize Classic music. On the other hand, both Berlioz's *Symphonie fantastique* (1830) and Mahler's Symphony No. 2 (1894), also written more than sixty years apart, manipulate orchestral sound in strikingly innovative ways, with corresponding modifications of traditional syntax.

The material in this book is presented according to the ways in which Romantic composers deployed the compositional processes of scoring, texture, harmony, and phrase and period structure. The points raised herein could be set forth in chronological order or be employed to determine trends in the evolution of style; such approaches imply a diachronic historical point of view. This book, despite the great range of styles among various works, takes a synchronic view: it looks to ways in which music of the middle and late nineteenth century shared common approaches in some basic aspects of rhetoric, and especially in its treatment of sound. Alfred Einstein implies this synchronic view when he writes:

> The unifying principle that links all the composers from Weber and Schubert to the end of the neo-Romantic movement and brings together such seemingly antipodal composers as Wagner and Brahms is this: their relationship to the most direct and perceptible element of music, its sound.[2]

Chronology is relevant, of course, when the material shows historical progress or change. The nationalisms of the later nineteenth century, the influence of Wagner, the political changes during the century, the time lines of musicology—these and other manifestations must find their places in the historical perspective. But in music the phenomenon that retains a basic consistency throughout the century—the affective use of sound qualities in combination with an adherence to traditional syntactical processes—is best viewed in terms of its manifestation in individual works as an expression of the *ars combinatoria,* the ways in which sound and syntax can be combined to make arrangements and permutations.

In this synchronic view of Romantic music, the sense of history is indeed present. Seen from a broad perspective, the Romantic era emerges as a dialect of the eighteenth century, somewhat like Jakob Burckhardt's characterization of the baroque in art as a dialect of the Renaissance.[3] Much of what strikes us as typically Romantic in music was prefigured in the later eighteenth century, then carried over and colored by the new climate of sound, with the result that all terms were modified, all affective stances altered. This study takes cognizance of the stylistic continuum as an integral part of the synchronic historical picture.

The music of Haydn, Mozart, and Beethoven occasionally focuses attention on qualities of sound as primary values (e.g., the Prelude to Haydn's *Creation;* the opening of Mozart's Piano Concerto in D Minor, K. 466; the principal part of the development section in the first movement of Beethoven's Symphony No. 6 in F Major). But their music did not live in the new climate of sound; it was embodied in the thinner, lighter, and more articulate sounds of eighteenth-century instruments. For this reason, earlier music does not enter into the present consideration, although its influence on Romantic sound values can be shown.

# *Physical, Critical, and Internal/Syntactical Evidence*

This book draws on three kinds of evidence which bear witness to the changes in the climate of musical sound that took place around the turn of the nineteenth century. These are physical, critical, and internal/syntactical evidence.

Physical evidence provides a great deal of specific information. It offers descriptions of musical instruments, specifications of their construction, and pictorial representations. It gives ranges, indicates what kind of music the instruments could preform, the manner in which they were used, and how they were modified and improved over the years. Full and detailed documentation of such physical evidence is available in encyclopedias and in histories of musical instruments. To this evidence can be added the actual sounds produced by instruments that have survived from the nineteenth century, by their reconstructions, and by their modern replicas.

Still, physical evidence is not sufficiently reliable, especially for the purpose of determining the sound-syntax relationship in a given work. Marked differences among instruments, as well as among performers, can result in widely different readings of a given piece, even to the extent of affecting its overall shape and length. Although we know much about the general climate of sound in the Romantic era, we can only speculate on the specific sounds produced in a performance in the nineteenth century.

Critical evidence reveals contemporary attitudes toward the new values in sound. This kind of evidence appears as incidental comments in reviews of compositions and performances and in surveys of stylistic trends. Critical evidence offers intriguing clues to what music was heard and how it was received. Scattered among journals, reminiscences, treatises, essays, and letters are comments that refer to the pervasive effect of the new qualities of sound (see Chapter 1).

Physical and critical evidence both testify abundantly to the presence of new sound values in Romantic music. But neither type of evidence pinpoints the actual sound-syntax relationship in a given piece or passage. Moreover, we cannot find such evidence in the vast corpus of theoretical writings on music in the nineteenth century. While entire sections of theoretical treatises during the century deal with details of orchestration and their effects at particular moments, the actual incorporation of sound values into formal processes was left to the composer.

To pinpoint the sound-syntax relationship in a given work, we turn to internal/syntactical evidence, the actual notation of the music, the score itself. This notation is a set of instructions given by the composer for the realization of a work of musical art. Of the three types of evidence cited here, the internal/syntactical evidence is the most exact. The score is the blueprint of the music; from this set of symbols all performances proceed, whatever differences in musical instruments or circumstances of performance there may be. From the blueprint we can extrapolate a whole series of decisions made by the composer; we can see how sound and syntax have worked on each other in specific details of composition. Internal/syntactical evidence, therefore, provides the basic material for the analysis in this book. It is the clue to the composer's conception of sound.

The analysis itself proceeds along familiar lines. It examines textures, harmonies, phrase and period structures, and typical formal plans, with the addition of one component—the new sounds. The addition of this factor alters the relationships among the basic components of the eighteenth- and nineteenth-century musical language; it gives them a different coloring and affects the very sense of the passage of time within a phrase or period.

## *Rhetorical Reduction*

From time to time in the course of this book, a process of reduction is applied wherein sound is thinned to two-part textures, with melody, harmony, and texture simplified to match popular song and dance types of the nineteenth century. Then, by extrapolation and reconstruction, we can pinpoint the specific decisions of the composer regarding texture and gesture that distinguish the original from which the reduction was made. Thus we can put the unique features of the original into sharp relief; we can appreciate these unique touches and turns of the original against the simplified common-places of the reduction. This process is here designated *rhetorical reduction.*

Rhetorical reduction is precisely that: the reduction of the melodic-rhythmic continuity (the rhetoric) of a passage in order to isolate the principal figures and to locate the places where they appear in the periodic continuity.

In this manner, rhetorical reduction draws on the analytic processes of traditional rhetoric. Whether or not this reduction reflects or approaches the original concept of the composer is immaterial. Such reductions enable the observer (analyst, performer, listener) to identify the unique processes and gestures that characterize the original.

Rhetorical reduction differs from other reductive procedures, such as *Urlinie*, thematic derivation, and harmonic analysis, in that it retains something of the quality of the original—its melodic manner, its affective stance, its integrity as a musical statement. Such a reduction addresses itself to the rhetorical content of the original, its musical persuasiveness. In examples where the figured material is reduced to simple alla breve melody, the lines themselves represent patterns typical of eighteenth-century alla breve counterpoint—conjunct lines, cadential formulas, sequential configurations. These formed the foundation on which so much eighteenth- and nineteenth-century figured music was built.

## *Modus Operandi*

The analysis in this book addresses the questions: to what extent and in what manner do sound qualities of a given excerpt or work represent traditional or innovative procedures? how does innovative sound affect syntax?

This approach reflects traditional rhetoric in that it deals with the two basic aspects of rhetorical communication—the establishment of coherence, represented by the heritage of the eighteenth century's common musical language, and the promotion of eloquence, to which sound made a significant contribution in the nineteenth century. Since it proceeds along rhetorical lines, the analysis focuses attention on the relationship of figures. It shows how sound can affect syntax and how syntax can channel sound in measure-to-measure and phrase-to-phrase continuities. This approach differs from methods of analysis that bring to light overarching configurations but leave sound itself out of the analytic picture.

Chapter 1 surveys critical comments that deal with qualities of sound and shows the extent to which sound was a concern of composers, performers, and listeners in the nineteenth century. Chapter 2 demonstrates the continuity that existed between Classic and Romantic textures. These textures form the basis for the samplings of scoring for piano, orchestra, and chamber music in the Romantic era, illustrated in Chapters 3–5. Chapter 6 explores the uses of harmonic color in the nineteenth century. Chapter 7 reviews the tradition of the period form in Western music and its continuity in Romantic music. Chapter 8 deals with rhetorical reduction. The succeeding chapters discuss period structures and musical forms.

Briefly, the modus operandi of this book involves characterizing the sound of a given example by range, texture, scoring, and harmonic color, and analyzing the effect of these sound values on the expressive implications and the syntax of a given example. The perimeters of phrase and period structure are used as points of reference. The basis of this approach is in the procedures that define the idiom of Romantic music. Those procedures reflect the language of that time, the materials and syntax used by Romantic composers. By extrapolation, by induction, this analysis arrives at the consideration of the individual work of musical art, the choices made by the composer to achieve unique, felicitous arrangements from music's common materials. In this process, sound quality plays a vital part; whether by subtle touch or by profound saturation; it colors every configuration and affects the extent and import of every gesture. To approach Romantic music by way of its qualities of sound enables us to focus either on affective stance or on structure; indeed, it effectively coordinates these two aspects.

# PART ONE

# *NEW SOUNDS*

# CHAPTER ONE

# *Sound as Criterion*

Sound qualities became a major area of attention in nineteenth-century writings about music. Critical comments, letters, essays, concert reports, biographies, and theoretical and technical studies offer a substantial body of evidence for the importance of sound as a special value in Romantic music. This was a new emphasis in the history of Western music. While earlier writers had considered sound in various ways—temperament, instrumental and vocal qualities, even pictorialism—they made few comments directly focused on sound as a special attribute. Before the nineteenth century, critical concern with this aspect of music was incidental to matters of style, form, and expression.

With the change in the climate of sound, we find writers giving special attention to the effects that tone color can produce. Berlioz's comments reflect this change in emphasis. His *Treatise upon Modern Instrumentation and Orchestration* begins with the following statement:

> At no period in the History of Music has there been greater mention made of *Instrumentation,* than at the present time. The reason of this is doubtless to be found in the completely modern development which has taken place in this branch of the Art; and perhaps, also, in the multitude of criticisms, opinions, different doctrines, judgments, rational and irrational arguments spoken or written, for which the slightest productions of the most inferior composers form a pretext.[1]

The theorist Adolph Bernhard Marx (1795–1866) had a strongly negative view of the trend toward fuller scoring current in the mid-nineteenth century:

> With the increase of the mass [of sound] all relationships are changed. We artists "are subject to what we create." When voices are introduced they demand participation. As soon as they are heard, their weight of sound affects every motion; the amount, increase, and decrease of sound (from few instruments to more and vice versa) becomes broader; the finer working-out of the active dialogue of the instruments is made to recede; the spiritual yields to the massive; the orchestra yields its absolutely inspired drama, that precious heritage of Haydn and Beethoven, in order to allow that mighty barrel organ [*Leier*] to ring out.[2]

As is often the case, negative comments such as those of Marx, point sharply to the practice being criticized. They are strong indicators of what was actually taking place.

While individual responses differ widely, the very fact that they were articulated bespeaks a general concern with sound qualities as prominent values in nineteenth-century music, a concern not manifested in eighteenth-century writings about music. For composers, performers, and listeners, sound quality emerged as one of the chief appeals in Romantic music, with an aesthetic value in its own right.

This chapter surveys the considerable breadth of coverage and the various ways in which sound qualities were interpreted in nineteenth-century critical attitudes. Those attitudes point to the importance of sound quality as an aspect of the Romantic musical experience.

## *Tone Color*

Comments on the tonal qualities of instruments and instrumental music appear throughout the nineteenth century. An 1807 article in two installments in the most comprehensive music periodical of the first half of the nineteenth century, the *Allgemeine musikalische Zeitung (AmZ)*, is one of the first of its kind to direct attention to the aesthetic character of musical instruments. The presence of the article therein and its considerable scope reflect the increasingly prominent position of instrumental music at that time. The article introduces the subject as follows:

> Music has within itself a great means for powerful effectiveness: various instruments that can be used not only for different works but also within a single composition. . . . How varied are the musical instruments in their character, their expression, their range, their strength, their charm![3]

It later refers to the "range, richness, and tonal variety of the flute . . . the lively, charming color of the clarinet and oboe . . . the rich, song-like quality of the bassoon . . . the stirring, noble quality of the hunting horn."[4]

Carl Maria von Weber, an active music critic as well as a composer, made several comments about tone color. His review in 1817 of an adaptation of

André Grétry's *Raoul Barbe-bleue* (1789) recognizes the then-current preference for colorful scoring:

> The demands of today's taste have been thought here [Dresden] as in Vienna to justify a richer and more piquant orchestration in order to make the music more effective.[5]

Weber's recognition that such a demand can be met by inferior music is evident in his *AmZ* article of the following year on the music of Friedrich Fesca:

> The four voices . . . can win our attention only by the nature of their relationship to one another, whereas in symphonies, etc., comparatively insignificant melodies can be made effective and ornamental by skillful orchestration and the charms of variety. In quartets mere noise can never masquerade as strength.[6]

Ignaz Moscheles, in reporting a rehearsal of Felix Mendelssohn's overture *Die schöne Melusine* in 1834, told the composer, "I hope to bring out the lights and shades still better at the performance."[7] Light and shade were also a concern of Franz Liszt when he wrote to Louis Kohler in 1856 about attempting to score his symphonic poem *Tasso* for pianoforte: "I soon gave up the project on account of the unadvisable mutilation . . . without tone and colour and *orchestral light and shade*. . . ."[8] In 1858, in a letter to Basil von Engelhardt, Liszt complimented Mikhail Glinka's *Jota Aragonesa* (1845): "What fine *nuances* and colouring divided among the different *timbres* of the orchestration!"[9] Later, in 1876, Liszt wrote to Camille Saint-Saëns concerning his piano transcription of Saint-Saëns's *Danse macabre*, begging to be excused for "unskilfulness in reducing the marvellous colouring of the score."[10]

Criticisms of Piotr Ilyich Tchaikovsky's music call attention to his handling of sonority. César Cui's comments on a performance in 1876 of Tchaikovsky's Symphony No. 3 speak of. "The only charm of the fourth [movement] being its sonority, for the musical contents are poor."[11] Tchaikovsky's *Francesca da Rimini*, was characterized as displaying "much interesting, but glaring tone colour" and "harshest discords."[12] His First Piano Concerto, Op. 23, elicited the following reaction:

> The first movement conceals its very primitive formal structure under an overpowering rush of harmonic effects, of dazzling kaleidoscopic passages, of intricate treatment of the subjects and of orchestral colour.[13]

Further contemporary critical remarks on Tchaikovsky's music use such terms as "dazzling," "brilliantly orchestrated," "picturesque," and "originality of rhythm, harmony, and orchestration."[14]

Tchaikovsky, in a letter of January 12, 1883, complained about the obscurity of meaning in *Tristan und Isolde*, while approving its orchestration:

> To compel people to listen for four hours at a stretch to an endless symphony which, however, rich in orchestral colour, is wanting in clearness and directness

of thought . . . is certainly not the ideal at which contemporary musicians should aim.[15]

Along the same lines is his comment in a letter of January 20, 1879, to Nadezhda von Meck:

But all the German composers of the present day write laboriously, with pretensions to depth of thought, and strive to atone for their extraordinary poverty of invention by exaggerated colouring!"[16]

Toward the end of the nineteenth century, the pianist Elisabet von Herzogenberg, a sensitive and knowledgeable observer, touched upon details of composition that showed her appreciation of special tone color. In a letter to Johannes Brahms, she observed of his Sonata in D Minor for Violin and Piano, Op. 108:

What a fine contrast those clashing chords form to the broad flowing line and how beautiful it *sounds*. . . . The piano part is so charmingly written, a pleasure from first to last, and so playable, with all its colour effects.[17]

She responded in 1890 to the texture of the Quintet in G Major by noting "how beautiful, how impressive it is, how entirely satisfying in *sound*, how luminously clear by virtue of its neat proportions."[18] In 1885 she noted the "novel combinations" and "the arresting, overpowering effect" in the finale of Brahms's Symphony No. 4.[19]

The tonal qualities of individual instruments are often described in critical comments. The 1807 *AmZ* article mentioned above covers the principal instruments in use at that time. Carl Maria von Weber's valuation of instrumental tone color is evident in his review of Gottfried Weber's *Gang nach Eisenhammer* (1812), where he speaks of "the characteristic sonority of trumpets and drums" and "pure trumpet sound."[20] In his contribution to the *Allgemeine Enzyklopädie der Wissenschaften und Kunst* (1821), Weber compared the traditional organ to the then-current orchestra:

The organist was the directing spirit [in the church], and the world of sound that is locked up in the organ for the creative artist to release was a plentiful source of the material that a composer today must look for in the rich field of the orchestra.[21]

Czerny, in his *School of Practical Composition*, 1848, made a similar observation:

The resources of no musical instrument are yet so exhausted that *all* the effects of which it is susceptible, have been already discovered and used. Even on the Piano-forte and on the Violin, as is well known, new effects are constantly being invented, of which we formerly had no idea.[22]

Elisabet von Herzogenberg pointed to special instrumental effects in Brahms's Symphony No. 4. In the finale she singles out the trombones, who "played their E-major variation superbly and the flute its lovely monologue likewise."[23] She was particularly struck by the "two pulsations on B for the drum at the end" of the second movement, which were "deliciously thrilling."[24]

Tchaikovsky made prominent use of the harp at times, as in the "Waltz of the Flowers" from *The Nutcracker*. Yet he wrote in 1883 to Madame von Meck:

> You ask why I never write anything for the harp. This instrument has a beautiful timbre and adds greatly to the poetry of the orchestra. But it is not an independent instrument, because it has no *melodic* quality, and is only suitable for harmony. . . . Chords, arpeggios—these form the restricted sphere of the harp, consequently it is only useful for accompaniments.[25]

Treatises on instrumentation (see Chapter 4) explore a major new area of music theory in the nineteenth century. Their descriptions of instrumental tone color are, of course, more specific and extensive than the comments we find in critical writings. Both criticism and theory present evidence for instrumental tone color in Romantic music as a prominent and, at times, autonomous value.

## *Mood and Imagery*

The rich and varied palette of tone color in Romantic music evoked responses that related the music to states of feeling and pictorial imagery, often involving comparisons and analogies with poetry and painting. In an article written in 1816, for instance, Weber provided a lengthy description of the sequence of events in his cantata *Kampf und Sieg* (1815), a celebration of Wellington's victory at Waterloo. The article begins:

> The mood of the musical introduction (D minor, strings with four horns, bassoon and timpani) is abrupt—stormy—lamenting—vehemently accented.[26]

It later characterizes Ludwig Spohr's opera *Faust* (1816) as

> this dark, Romantic spirit-world . . . ideally matched with the composer's inmost musical character. Owing to this fact the work as a whole is marked by great aptness of colour—big musical and dramatic effects of charm and tenderness alternating with shatteringly powerful effect in the ensembles and choruses.[27]

Responses to Frédéric Chopin's music include some particularly fanciful imagery. In 1833 Berlioz wrote of Chopin's performance:

> There are incredible details in the *Mazurkas*; he has discovered the means of rendering them doubly interesting in executing them with the utmost degree of softness, with a superlative *piano*, the hammers skimming over the strings, so

that one is tempted to incline the ear as though one were attending a concert of sylphs and sprites.[28]

Ferdinand Hiller's, recollection of Chopin's music in 1877 is equally vivid:

"What in others would be elegant ornamentation, in his music was the effect of a multicolored bouquet of flowers. . . . What in others was technical dexterity was in his performance the flight of a swallow. . . . his performance was like the light of a marvelous meteor."[29]

On another occasion Berlioz wrote of the second movement of the Piano Concerto No. 1 in E Minor, Op. 11, by Chopin:

This andante (*sic*) immerses the listener in an ecstatic calm; [ . . . ] the last note drops like a pearl into a golden vase . . . after having followed the harmonious diminution of the half-tints of an evening's twilight, one remains motionless in the obscurity, the eye ever fixed upon the point of the horizon where the light is about to disappear.[30]

Comparisons and analogies between music, poetry, and painting have been made from the Renaissance to the present. Before the nineteenth century, such connections involved expression and rhetoric—what feelings or images the arts had in common and the ways in which they were set down to show common elements of order.[31] In the nineteenth century sound became a vehicle of comparison, especially with painting. As we have seen above, terms used to describe effects of tone quality were often borrowed from the lexicon of art appreciation or criticism.

Czerny, in 1848, compared the tone qualities of instruments to hues in painting:

The different instruments are to the composer, what colours are to the painter; and the instrumentation of a musical idea, bears a perfect analogy to the colouring of a picture. As therefore, each great painter has a particular mode of employing and blending his colours, by which the connoisseur immediately recognizes his pictures; so, each of the above-named composers (Haydn, Mozart, Cherubini, Beethoven, Weber, Meyerbeer, and Rossini), possesses a certain peculiarity, in the application of the different sounds which the manifold resources of the orchestra present.[32]

Adolph Marx, in 1873, decried the nineteenth-century search for novelty in the arts, comparing harmony, color, and prosody:

When a Berlioz succeeds in discovering new varieties of tones, when another stumbles upon a new harmonic combination or hazards a new melodic progression, it signifies no more than a new mixture of colors in painting, or a new word or combination in language. It is not this that makes the composer, the painter, or the poet; but each invents or applies whatever he requires, and wherever he requires it.[33]

Weber made a similar comparison when, in speaking of his personal style, he wrote that "the many descriptive adjectives in a language closely resemble the instrumentation of a musical idea."[34]

Particularly striking in the foregoing comments is the range of individual responses, a reflection of the individualism that characterizes the Romantic era in general. Also characteristic is a sensitivity not only to harmonic and instrumental color but also to the sheer amount of sound produced.

## *Amount of Sound*

One of the most impressive changes that took place in the nineteenth century was an increase in the compass, dynamic range, and timbral intensity of virtually all instruments. These innovations, along with the trend toward larger performing forces, led composers at times to use amount of sound as a primary expressive value. (See Chapters 3 and 4 for discussions of this trend in piano and orchestral textures.)

This aspect of Romantic music was more often than not looked upon unfavorably, but the presence of such negative views bespeaks the widespread exploitation of fullness of sound for musical effect. As early as 1810, there appeared this comment in *AmZ:*

> How often are the carefully chosen tones [of the composer] so completely drowned out by the turmoil and din of the trumpets, timpani, and trombones, reinforced by a group of other wind instruments, that one can hardly perceive the brilliantly figured part of the first violin.[35]

Marx, in 1873, made the following comment on the condition of music, focusing his attention on sound itself:

> It must then be acknowledged that music is, in our days, spread more widely than it was ever before; that our whole existence is immersed in the playful waves of sound, and completely overwhelmed and stunned by this noisiest, most intrusive of all arts . . . [which] with the united strength of rival orchestras, and through excess and over-zeal, destroys its own efficacy.[36]

A review of Tchaikovsky's *Francesca da Rimini* in the *Berliner Fremdenblatt* of September 17, 1878, says that

> the first and last allegros, which depict the whirlwinds of hell, have neither subject nor ideas but only a mass of sounds, and these ear-splitting effects seem to us . . . too much even for hell itself.[37]

Tchaikovsky himself turned critic to complain in 1879 that "Wagner's orchestration is too symphonic, too overloaded and heavy for vocal music";[38]

later, in 1884, he referred to "the deafening clamour of the orchestra" in Wagner's *Parsifal.*[39]

On the other hand, Weber, in 1814, complimented Gottfried Weber on the scoring of his *Te Deum:*

> In view of the circumstances of this composition, he chose to write with a maximum of concision and effectiveness, brilliance, strength, volume of sound and mass effect. To achieve this he has used all valid means, especially loud and resonant instruments.[40]

For better or worse, the capabilities of nineteenth-century instruments to produce louder, fuller, and more resonant sounds than their eighteenth-century predecessors became a standard resource for all composers.

## *Harmonic Color*

Harmony contributes its own color to the palette of Romantic sound qualities. (Chapter 6 examines this topic in detail.) Many nineteenth-century writers commented on Romantic composers' novel and rich harmonic progressions and colorful manner of presenting individual chords or keys. For instance, Berlioz, comparing past and present usage in 1858, referred to the new approach to modulation:

> Then came the turn of modulations. At the period when the habit was to modulate only in relative keys, the first who ventured to pass into a foreign key, was treated with contumely,—as might have been expected. Whatever the effect of this new modulation, masters severely objected to it. The innovator vainly pleaded:—"Listen to it; observe how agreeably it is brought in, how well worked, how adroitly linked with that which precedes and succeeds, and how deliciously it sounds!" *"That's not the question!"* was the reply. "This modulation is prohibited; therefore it must not be made!"[41]

In an 1812 review of a song from Gottfried Weber's *Twelve Four-Part Songs,* Carl Maria von Weber spoke of the

> unusual and effective harmonic progressions in the middle section . . . too much rather than too little ingenious harmony throughout[42]

Four years later, he commented on a duet by a popular Italian composer of the early nineteenth century, Giuseppe Farinelli: "This empty tinkling seemed very jejune amongst the luxuriant wealth of German harmony."[43]

François-Joseph Fétis, in a review of Chopin's Piano Concerto No. 2 in F Minor, Op. 21, printed in the *Revue musicale* of March 3, 1832, complained of "too much extravagance in the modulation,"[44] Liszt, a more progressive musician, praised Albert Fuch's *Hungarian Suite* for orchestra, noting "rather much new employment of harmonies and always a national colouring."[45]

An 1885 letter from Elisabet von Herzogenberg to Brahms uses imagery to describe instrumental and harmonic color in the third movement of Brahms's Symphony No. 4:

> How beautiful the soft C-sharp minor passage is at the end when all the gay apprentices slouch home from work, and the peace of evening sets in, while the reminiscence of all this merriment becomes lyrical (*that* subject lyrical!) in D flat; and, most beautiful of all, the soft entry of the horns and trombones at *poco meno presto!*[46]

This passage is remarkable in the way it encompasses instrumental tone color, imagery, and harmonic color to add a poetic touch to a passage that has no pictorial or programmatic implications.

In a similar vein Elisabet von Herzogenberg writes of Brahms's choral work *Nänie:*

> How vividly it stands out in my memory, each part for itself and the whole in its wonderful unity! One is loth to pick and choose,—but oh, the sweet Aphrodite part in F, the bewitching passage at the splitting of the Eber, the splendid seething of the wave-triplets in F sharp when the goddess rises from the sea, the syncopated weeping of the gods, and the breathless suspense at the words, *"Dass das Schöne vergeht,"* where it dies away! One would like to mention everything, but above all the blissful ending, for which you deserve every blessing! How thrilling are the different voice entries, and how splendidly it works up and lingers on the dominant—passing with the more refreshing effect into D major at the words, *"im Mund der Geliebten"*[47]

An especially fanciful set of images evoked by the sounds of individual harmonies appears in E. T. A. Hoffmann's vignette "Kreisler's Musico-poetic Club," from *Kreisleriana* (1814–15). In this episode, Kreisler tells how he is stirred to intense feelings and colorful visions simply by striking chords and allowing them to resound and fade away. The harmonies themselves are simple triads and sevenths in various positions and degrees of strength; they encompass A-flat major, A-flat minor, E-major chords in several positions, A minor, F major, B-flat major, then B-flat major with its seventh, E-flat major, G-major seventh in the 4-3 position, C major, and finally C minor. The entire progression can be worked out with the smoothest traditional part writing, but the focus on the actual sound of each chord as it extends in time and then shifts to another effect is a Romantic way of experiencing traditional processes, a new absorption in sheer sonority.[48]

The foregoing comments express subjective attitudes, personal reactions to sound qualities in Romantic music. The technical and theoretical writings discussed in Chapters 3 and 4, by the very substantial treatment they give to instrumentation, tone production, acoustics, and psychological aspects of sound perception, bear witness to the objective importance of these aspects of Romantic music. One of the most important scientific works on music in the nineteenth century, Hermann von Helmholtz's *On the Sensations of Tone* (1863), is concerned with the physical properties of tones and with the physiological responses within the ear. Its comprehensive coverage and its sharply focused direction parallel the preoccupation with sound values found in the music itself and in views about the music.[49]

# *Historical Views*

At the end of the nineteenth century, Hugo Riemann looked back on Romantic music to take note of its emphasis on tone color:

> In recent times, however, the use of the esthetic impressions [created] by tone colors moves to the foreground in such a manner that one may speak of *Kolorismus* [colorism] as a distinct tendency in today's art.[50]

Riemann warned against the danger of this tendency, saying that "it becomes only too easy to overlook the mediocrity of the content because of its brilliant setting."[51]

Twentieth-century historians have taken cognizance of sound as an important aspect of Romantic musical style. Alfred Einstein in *Music in the Romantic Era,* says:

> with the first Romantics, sound took on a new meaning. It was a stronger factor in the body of the music than it had ever been before; it won a higher value in and for itself.[52]

Jacques Handschin, referring to both piano and orchestra, writes, "Generally speaking, we can ascertain an increase in sound volume for the music of the nineteenth century."[53]

Arthur Loesser, in *Men, Women, and Pianos,* contrasts sound qualities in the pianos of the eighteenth and nineteenth centuries:

> A gulf lies between these two ideals of sound. The former belongs to a philosophy that values logic, that wants to control the world by dividing it into neat, tight, inviolable categories, orders, and ranks. The latter is characteristic of a fluid, pietist, libertarian cast of thought, which has little respect for what it regards as contrived boundaries or limits—a frame of mind harboring the mystical suspicion that anything might merge into everything. The former was gratified more by the distinctness—that is, the separateness—of tones; the latter, more by their fusion and their blend. Taken literally, the above dichotomy may be an oversimplification: it is intended as a mere hint of the truth. Still, its obvious social and political allusions seem to have their significance. The shift of tone-ideal was gradual; it had taken about eighty years to accomplish. It seemed to have been completed, as we have suggested, by about 1830, the time that also marked the final political triumph of the money-wielding classes over the older landed aristocrats, and the general acceptance of their habits of mind as social ideals.[54]

Loesser's comments point out a notable correspondence between the differing piano mechanisms and differing worldviews of the eighteenth and nineteenth centuries; the differences are symbolized by the change in what he calls "tone-ideal." For the eighteenth century, sound gave body and color to action; for the nineteenth century, sound became a primary musical value, an ambience in which action stirred.

Carl Dahlhaus and Ernst Kurth have both seen in the nineteenth-century focus on color values the roots of a historical development that culminated in the twentieth century. Dahlhaus writes:

> Sophistication of local color interacted with a relaxation of functional harmony to become one of the decisive evolutionary features of the age. Ultimately, around 1900, it led to a reformulation of the notion of timbre, one of the crucial features of fin-de-siècle musical modernism. This "emancipation of timbre," initiated by Berlioz, freed tone color from its subservient function of merely clarifying the melody, rhythm, harmony, and counterpoint of a piece, and gave it an aesthetic raison d'être and significance of its own.[55]

In what still stands as the most important study of Romantic compositional processes, Kurth's *Romantische Harmonik und ihre Krise in Wagners "Tristan"* (1923), Kurth describes the relationship between Romantic harmony and the aesthetic of musical impressionism:

> Whoever has understood the essential features of impressionism, its limitlessness and the flexible capacity of the musical sensibility to move back and forth momentarily among these values, will see immediately that the entire Romantic period is filled with details that are oriented in this direction [toward impressionism] even when they have not yet evolved to an individual and clearly defined style.[56]

# *Conclusion*

The foregoing cross-section of responses to tone color and sound quality in Romantic music shows several distinct tendencies. Most of the reactions expressed therein are subjective, personal manifestations of a specific listening experience; they indicate in general terms the strong effect that sound itself had on the listener. Other comments characterize personal styles of composers or national styles. Still other approaches in both the nineteenth and twentieth centuries take sociological or historical views.

The comments themselves have been selected from a wide range of material—letters, essays, treatises, histories covering more than a century. Whether early or late, each recognizes the vital role that sound played for composers, performers, and listeners in the nineteenth century. Despite individual differences in taste, these comments imply a common factor—

sound as a principal aesthetic value. They thus support the synchronic view taken in this book.

Sound qualities have received considerable attention in the past two centuries. They have been approached as effects in their own right. They have been described, reacted to, analyzed, measured, and subjected to an unbroken chain of experiments, modifications, improvements, and inventions, right down to the present day.

Yet sound is but one part of what makes music coherent and eloquent. Its role in conveying music's meaning to the listener meshes with every other aspect of musical action, as Dahlhaus acknowledges in the passage quoted above. When Dahlhaus says Berlioz's "emancipation of timbre . . . freed tone color from its subservient function of merely clarifying the melody, rhythm, harmony, and counterpoint of a piece," he implies an interaction between tone color and other aspects of musical syntax. This emancipation was not so much a freeing as a shifting of priorities: melody, harmony, rhythm—and, we may add, structure—maintained much of their coherence, so that they could operate in a back-and-forth, give-and-take relationship with sound qualities.

One of the difficulties in assessing this relationship is the elusive aspect of nineteenth-century sounds. As values in their own right, often to the detriment of more traditional aspects of musical composition, the sounds are difficult to describe except in metaphorical terms.

This book offers criteria by which the effect of sound qualities on the compositional process, through the decisions made by the composer, can be assessed. To that end, two types of musical configurations must be distinguished:

1. Vertical, or simultaneous, configurations, which represent texture. This criterion is applied to ways in which nineteenth-century composers adapted traditional eighteenth-century textures in piano and orchestral music to create innovative effects of sound.

2. Horizontal, or time-lapse, configurations, which represent syntax. This criterion is applied to ways in which nineteenth-century composers adapted traditional phrase and period structures and traditional musical forms to incorporate the effects and values that innovative sound generated.

Vertical configurations—texture—are taken up in Chapters 2–6. Horizontal configurations—syntax—are the subjects of Chapters 7–13.

# CHAPTER TWO

# *Texture*

*Texture* here signifies the action of the component voices, parts, or instruments at a given moment or in a particular segment within a composition. Texture thus offers a "vertical sight line" as its principal orientation, as against the "horizontal sight line" offered by the syntax of phrase and period structure.

Deployment of sound in Romantic music—tone color, range, amount of sound—is based on textures carried over from the eighteenth century. By viewing Romantic textures as modifications and elaborations of traditional layouts, we can assess effectively the changes in the climate of sound that took place during the nineteenth century. The process by which this assessment is made involves two procedures:

1. Establishing traditional types of texture as bases for analysis
2. Determining to what extent such textures are modified or elaborated by tone color, range, or amount of sound

This chapter reviews traditional textures as a point of departure for the exploration of nineteenth-century adaptations in Chapters 3–6. The evidence for traditional textures is drawn partly from theoretical treatises and partly from scores. The considerable material cited from music theorists reflects general compositional practice; the treatises themselves represent a consensus of what composers found effective among musical processes. Seen in this light, the music theorist is a link between the composer and the student, and in rare cases what is transmitted to a gifted student may become a part of a future composer's language, or even a platform from which a fresh stylistic or expressive direction may take off. Thus theoretical explanations reflect, rather than rule, general procedures in music.

Texture, when it encompasses more than a single voice or line, sets up a polarity between lower and upper levels of action. This polarity governs most textures throughout the eighteenth and nineteenth centuries. However fanciful a texture may be, its lines of action work around the interplay of bass and treble, regardless of actual register.

## *Figured Bass*

In pedagogy and in free composition of both eighteenth and nineteenth centuries, the polarity of outer lines is manifested commonly in figured-bass textures. Most exercises in treatises and a great deal of free composition embody the typical layout of figured-bass texture, which derived from continuo practice; that is, a single bass line supporting two or three close-position voices in the treble. Figured bass itself was current in teaching throughout the nineteenth century; its methods differed little from those established in the eighteenth century.

Example 2-1 illustrates typical layouts for figured-bass realization—a single bass line with three voices in the treble. Example 2-1a, 2-1b is taken from a late eighteenth-century treatise; Examples 2-1b and 2-1c are taken from nineteenth-century manuals. Each example is laid out according to a typical harmonic sequence current during the eighteenth and nineteenth centuries

EXAMPLE 2-1.  Figured-bass realizations.
a. Koch, *Versuch*, 1782, vol. 1, pp. 192–93.

b. Logier, *System,* 1827, p. 106.

122.

c. Sechter, *Grundsätze,* 1854, part 2, p. 372.

—descending circle of fifths in Examples 2-1a and 2-1c, descending thirds in Example 2-1b. While Roman numerals are used in Example 2-1c instead of figured bass, the material presented is entirely consistent with figured-bass practice.[1]

Although more than seventy years separate Koch's example from that of Sechter, the approaches to the realization of a bass are the same in texture and chord formation. Indeed, the dates could be juggled among these three examples without loss of continuity. Such layouts form the "backbone" of harmony instruction throughout the nineteenth century and play a prominent role in free composition.

Examples 2-2a and 2-2b show a similarity in layout that also bespeaks an unbroken tradition in the application of figured-bass procedures to practical music making. Each presents an elaborate bass that might accompany an

EXAMPLE 2-2.  Continuo.
a. Paisiello, *Regole*, 1782, p. 15.

b. Lobe, *Lehrbuch*, vol. 1, revised by Kretschmar, 1900, pp. 190–91.

actual melody, while the right hand of the keyboard would fill out the harmony.

Composers occasionally refer to figured bass in their writings. Berlioz wrote in his memoirs that, in 1819, as a youth, he knew little music beyond flute solos and *"solfeggios* accompanied by a figured bass."[2] Tchaikovsky, in discussing his methods of composition, wrote to Madame von Meck in 1878: "When the harmony is quite simple, I only put in the bass, or a figured bass."[3]

# Duet Layout

Continuo texture, reduced to its simplest embodiment, becomes a duet between bass and treble. These two parts delineate a musical passage by line alone, much as a cartoon will indicate the shape of a figure. Sketches, analyses, and examples from teaching manuals demonstrate that such duet textures constitute a significant step in the realization of fuller sounds. Moreover, such textures, elaborated by figuration, appear from time to time in Romantic keyboard music as a contrast to fuller voicings.

Example 2-3 embodies a simple polarity of outer lines, illustrating the continuity that existed in the teaching of duet layouts. Example 2-3a is a typical minuet of the late eighteenth century. The two-voice setting establishes the outer perimeters of action, defining the uppermost and lowermost ranges. It also invites reinforcement of either or both of the essential lines by doublings in thirds, sixths, or octaves, as in Example 2-3b. Example 2-3c, from a mid-nineteenth-century treatise, could well have been written in the later eighteenth century; rhythmically, it is a bourrée. All three dances employ typical continue procedures: quick rates of chord change and active, melodic basses.

Example 2-4 illustrates an elaborate treatment of duet texture, in which the broken-chord figures imply a full harmony, yet are so deployed that we hear only two tones at any time. The reduction in Example 2-4b incorporates the bass tones that provide the firmest progression, i.e., G sharp–A–G natural–F

EXAMPLE 2-3. Polarity of outer voices in duet texture.
a. Türk, *Klavierschule,* 1789, "Zwölf Handstücke," p. 4.

sharp; accordingly, the G sharp–A that reaches an apex in the melody does not make the best counterpoint with the bass. This may appear to be an inconsistency in reduction but it demonstrates the flexibility possible in the deployment of structural lines. The arrival at a 6 chord in measure 208 is a critical moment in this progression and should be approached by the parallel-sixth motion.

Figured-bass texture constitutes a principal source for textural elaboration in eighteenth- and nineteenth-century music. Examples in contemporary treatises on harmony and composition illustrate many of the textures then in use;[4] yet the points made in these examples, drawn extensively from Classic and Romantic music, generally deal with harmony, melodic behavior, rhythm, and phrase syntax. Texture itself is not directly addressed, as a rule.

EXAMPLE 2-3.  *(continued)*
b. Türk, *Klavierschule*, 1789, p. 5.

An exception is Johann Logier's *System der Musik-Wissenschaft* (1827), the latter half of which introduces many examples of elaboration, creating various kinds of texture from straightforward figured-bass models. (See Examples 2-7c and 2-8b). Adolph Marx, in the third volume of his *Lehre von der Musikalischen Komposition* (1848), pages 26–43, discusses the keyboard etude, with several illustrations of elaborate texture. Both Logier and Marx demonstrate various kinds of arpeggiation and broken-chord accompaniment figures idiomatic to the keyboard.

c. Sechter, *Grundsätze*, 1854, part 2, p. 63.

EXAMPLE 2-4.    Elaborate treatment of duet texture.
a. Schubert, Sonata in D Major, Op. 53, 1825, first movement.

Schubert, *Sonatas for the Piano.* Copyright © G. Schirmer, Inc. Used by permission.

b. Reduction with figured bass.

Examples 2-5 through 2-9 illustrate prototypical textures in Classic and Romantic music: melody and accompaniment, arpeggiation, full-chord texture, and polyphony.

## *Melody and Accompaniment*

The simple opposition of melody and accompaniment is the most familiar and frequently used type of texture in both eighteenth- and nineteenth-century music. The examples given represent the alpha and omega of elaboration for the accompaniment. Examples 2-5a and 2-5b require the minimum of dexterity, since the simple accompaniment figures encompass no more than a sixth; Examples 2-5c and 2-5d spread their accompaniment figures over a much wider range, calling for considerable keyboard skill.

Early examples of melody-accompaniment texture are the Bourrée from J. S. Bach's English Suite no. 2, first reprise, and Domenico Scarlatti's Sonata in E Major, K. 381, second reprise. Nineteenth-century examples are innumera-

EXAMPLE 2-5. Melody and accompaniment.
a. Koch, *Lexikon,* 1802, pp. 721–22.

b. Mozart, Sonata in C Major, K. 309, 1777, finale.

c. Lobe, *Lehrbuch*, 2d ed., 1858, vol. 1, p. 394.

d. Liszt, Sonata in B Minor, 1854, mm. 153–55.

ble; two instances in the music of Brahms are the finale of his Sonata in F Minor, Op. 5 (1854), measures 39–62, and the eleventh variation of his *Handel Variations*, Op. 24 (1862). Other variants of melody-accompaniment texture include full chordal support (see Example 2-7), punctuating bass, bass and offbeat chords (as in a waltz pattern), *trommelbass* (repeated tones in the bass), pedal tones, continuotype bass (active melodic bass line). Combinations, variants, and mixtures of these prototypical melody-accompaniment textures enrich the palette of eighteenth- and nineteenth-century scorings.

# Arpeggiation

In arpeggiation, broken-chord figures become the focus of interest, in contrast to their supporting role in melody-accompaniment textures. Throughout much of the eighteenth century, arpeggiation had been a way to spread out a full-chord texture, in the procedure called *Brechung*, where voices in a chord alternate so as to expose a contrapuntal action, as in Bach's suites for solo violoncello. While proper voice leading and implied counterpoint still control arpeggiation in late eighteenth- and in nineteenth-century music, the principal interest shifts toward sound and color. Marx aptly described this trend:

> The arpeggio, in all its manifold forms, from the monotone to full chords, from the softest murmur to the loudest thunder tones on the instrument—this arpeggio (either by itself or in connection with a melody, which it supports or surrounds as with a flowing and transparent drapery) has become the fundamental element of the new school.[5]

Example 2-6, a typical eighteenth-century use of arpeggiation, illustrates the coordination of brilliant keyboard elaboration and the clear voice leading of

EXAMPLE 2-6.    Arpeggiation. Mozart, Allegro in F Major, K. 533, 1788.

Theodore Presser Company. Nathan Broder, ed. used by permission.

*Brechung.* Example 12-5 offers a corresponding example of nineteenth-century procedure.

## Full-Chord Texture

A texture of four or more voices sounding simultaneously to form full chords represents the opposite pole from arpeggiation, where one or two voices sound together. Like arpeggiation, full-chord texture is idiomatic to the keyboard, while it also can imitate the tutti of an instrumental ensemble. Example 2-7 illustrates full-chord textures in the late eighteenth and early nineteenth centuries. Example 2-7a, as well as the others in Türk's *Klavierschule,* were intended primarily for performance on the clavichord. Although the sonata shown in Example 2-7b was specifically written for fortepiano, its

EXAMPLE 2-7.  Full-chord texture.
a. Türk, *Klavierschule,* 1789, ninth example.

b. Haydn, Sonata in E-Flat Major, Hob. XVI:52, 1795, first movement.

EXAMPLE 2-7.  *(continued)*
c. Logier, *System*, 1827, p. 274.

low, rolled chords are suggestive of the harpsichord, while its air of grandeur
is orchestral in effect.

Logier precedes Example 2-7c with the following comment:

> The following exercise, written for the pianoforte, contains . . . sequences in
> various forms, rising and falling; they are written principally in three voices, in
> order to clarify the effect . . . when they are set as contrast to the other
> harmonies, which are set forth with the fullest possible voicing.

The second half of this excerpt represents another kind of texture, the *stile
legato* (see below).

Full-chord texture is used extensively throughout the nineteenth century.
It characterizes much of the music of Schumann (see Ex. 3-7) and Brahms, as
for example, the Rhapsody in E-flat Major, Op. 119, No. 4 (1893).


# *Polyphony*

Polyphonic procedures, a central area of pedagogy and composition throughout the eighteenth and nineteenth centuries, formed an unbroken continuum
in the music theory of that time, with relatively little change in the basic rules
and precepts. The various aspects of polyphony—strict counterpoint, the
*stile legato* or bound style, canon, fugue, and free counterpoint—occupy
major sections in the most important treatises of the nineteenth century.[6]

EXAMPLE 2-8. *Stile legato.*
a. Mozart, Rondo in F Major, K. 494, 1786.

Theodore Presser Company. Nathan Broder, ed. Used by permission.

b. Logier, *System*, 1827.

The influence of the *Gradus ad Parnassum* (1725) by Johann Joseph Fux was strong and pervasive throughout the eighteenth and nineteenth centuries with respect to the theory and practice of the *stile legato*. Mozart and Haydn studied the work; later theorists modeled their treatises on the *Gradus*, which went into many editions, including modern versions.

With few exceptions, the teaching of contrapuntal composition in the nineteenth century was concerned with harmony, voice leading, and formal structure. Texture, a distinctive aspect of polyphonic composition, seems to be regarded as an outcome of contrapuntal procedures, rather than as an aspect that has its own value. Two types of polyphonic texture are illustrated here, the *stile legato* (incorporation of suspensions) in Example 2-8 and *imitation* in Example 2-9.

A continuity of textural procedures connects the musical practices of the eighteenth and nineteenth centuries. Though Romantic composers varied and expanded on the categories set forth here, they added no new categories. The following chapters explore how they adapted these textures to the richer resources of sound available to them, resources of tone color, scoring, and

EXAMPLE 2-9.  Imitation.
a.  Mozart, Allegro in F Major, K. 533, 1788.

b.  Brahms, Variations and Fugue on a Theme by Handel, Op. 24, 1861, fugue.

dynamics. We can easily hear in Romantic music the opposition of soprano and bass, the play of figure, the contrasts of full and light scoring that supported the action of eighteenth-century music. But the incorporation of striking, often seductive values of instrumental color works profound changes in textural relationships, so that action yields much of its boldness and salience to ambience. In Romantic music a condition of sound, rather than a process of action, can establish the premise of expression.

# CHAPTER THREE

# The Piano: Texture and Sound

During the period 1800–1830, the piano underwent a profound metamorphosis. More changes were made in this instrument than in any of the other standard Western instruments. Also during this time, the piano solidified its central role in the musical life of the Western world.

These developments have been documented in a number of comprehensive studies.[1] This chapter first cites from these studies, summarizing the principal changes that took place in the physical makeup of the piano from the eighteenth to the nineteenth centuries. It also offers critical comments of the time on the piano's tone, technique, and expressive capabilities. Then, as internal evidence, a number of examples are analyzed to show how piano textures in Romantic music modify the various prototypical textures described in Chapter 2. It also considers the piano as a surrogate for the orchestra.

## Physical and Critical Evidence

Arthur Loesser, in *Men, Women, and Pianos*, sums up the changes in piano structure:

> Few, if any, significant fundamental developments of the pianoforte can be said
> to have taken place after the first third of the nineteenth century. During the

following thirty years, its range was increased from six and a half to seven octaves, still later to seven and a third; and a very important improvement in stringing and tension bracing was achieved by American makers shortly before 1860. Otherwise, the piano of the 1830's was substantially that of today.

> One could maintain that the modern piano had practically completed its growth before 1830. The agraffe [a reinforcing device for strings] goes back to 1808, the practical double escapement to 1821, the metal plates and bracing bars to 1822 or 1823, the felt hammer-covering to 1826, the use of tempered steel wire to 1826, the low oblique-strung upright to 1827, the round-pin method of continuous stringing likewise to 1827. A seven-octave grand was played in concert as early as 1824.[2]

Together with these features came improvements in the sustaining pedal and the use of heavier, thicker strings. These changed the tone quality of the piano from that of the fortepiano of the eighteenth century in virtually every respect—range, tone color, dynamics, sustaining ability. Presently, thanks to research into earlier piano construction, we can get a fair idea of what the Classic fortepiano sounded like. Through recordings and reproductions of instruments, listeners have become familiar with the light, piquant sound of the fortepiano and can easily make comparisons with earlier and later instruments.

Loesser describes the distinctions between the eighteenth- and nineteenth-century instruments:

> The metal frame permitting a stronger blow and therefore greater volume, the rapid double-escapement action making for more delicate stroke-responsiveness combined with speed, the thickly felt-covered hammers giving a "rounder" tone than those formerly used—all these developments converged into one trend: the making of an instrument suitable for use by a person who could project piano music commandingly, fascinatingly, in a large room, a concert virtuoso in other words; a piano that could be played louder and faster, with more sensitive shading, more violent contrast, and a richer, more "singing" quality than had been possible previously. It was about 1830 that this newer ideal of piano making and piano playing was taking definite shape; it was fully realized a few years later. By then the last echoes of the eighteenth century were being stilled: the conception of what was desirable in a tone quality had completed its long period of change, and the fading ghost of the harpsichord was finally laid to rest. A sharp, bright sound—a clear, well-defined, unambiguous statement of individual tone—such as the earlier eighteenth century had liked, was no longer wanted. The yearning was for a vague, mellow tone-cloud, full of ineffable promise and foreboding, carrying intimations of infinity.[3]

William Newman, in *The Sonata since Beethoven*, provides a similar description of the improvements introduced into piano construction and tone in the early nineteenth century.[4] Edwin Good has made a comprehensive survey of piano technology—construction and action—in *Giraffes, Black Dragons, and other Pianos*.

Among the changes that took place in the life of the nineteenth-century piano, one of the most profound in its effect was the pedal. Several comments of the time, directed to its use and abuse, reflect on both content and performance. In 1841 the following remarks appeared in the *Neue Zeitschrift für Musik* (NZM):

> With the pedals one obtains the marvelous effects of harmony, from the wildest uproars and dins to the delicate fading away of sound. Similarly, it is possible for the melody to emerge with versatility and richness, to match the voice in long-sustained tones and to master boldly the usurping flow of the accompaniment.[5]

Czerny wrote in the 1830s:

> With the proper use of the forte or damper pedals, the performer can produce such effects that it would seem four hands were playing. Used inopportunely, however, the pedal produces an unintelligible din, which is as offensive to the ear as script on wet paper is to the eye.[6]

These two comments describe the versatility of the pedal for the nineteenth-century piano. It can build to great power, clothe a melody with rich sound, and create the lightest, most evanescent effects.

Newman notes that the bolder, more dramatic nineteenth-century piano "could be brilliant, stentorian, daemonic, overpowering, as the many descriptions of Liszt's playing make abundantly clear.[7] At the other end of the expressive spectrum is Robert Schumann's impressionistic description of Chopin's "Aeolian Harp" Etude (Etude in A-flat Major):

> Imagine an aeolian harp possessing all the scales, and an artist's hand combining these with all kinds of fantastic embellishments, but always with an audible deep ground bass, and in the treble, a softly flowing cantilena—and you will have some idea of his playing. . . . But it would be a mistake to suppose that he allowed us to hear every one of its small notes. It was rather an undulation of the A-flat major chord, brought out more loudly here and there with the pedal.[8]

The piano as a surrogate for ensemble music, a versatile role that it had played in the later eighteenth century, was described in 1853 by Schumann in reference to the playing of Brahms:

> He is a player of genius who can make of the piano an orchestra of lamenting and loudly jubilant voices. There were sonatas, veiled symphonies rather; songs the poetry of which would be understood without words . . . single piano pieces . . . again sonatas for violin and piano, string quartets . . . all united by him into a single waterfall the cascades of which were overreached by a peaceful rainbow.[9]

These comments touch upon three aspects of the nineteenth-century piano's sound capabilities—utmost power, delicate tracery, and persuasive, eloquent declamation.

The following comment in *AmZ*, (1813) also points to the versatility of the pianoforte:

If the fantasy of the master has created a complete tone picture with rich clusters [of sound], brilliant lights and deep shadowings, so can the player call these [effects] to life from the pianoforte, so that [the tone picture] emerges colorfully and brilliantly from the inner world.[10]

Czerny in 1848 attributed this versatility to

the means by which an effect is produced on the pianoforte, as for instance, the great compass of the instrument, the fullness of the accompaniment and of the chords, brilliant passages, great fluency, the frequent and striking use of the pedal, arbitrary passing notes and singular harmonies.[11]

In another observation Schumann, writing in 1835, pointed to three special styles of performance suited to the piano of his time:

The older I grow, the more convinced I am that the piano expresses itself mainly in the following three styles: (1) richness of sound and varied harmony progressions (made use of by Beethoven and Franz Schubert); (2) pedal effect (as with Field); (3) volubility (Czerny, Herz, and others). In the first category we find the expansive players; in the second, the fanciful ones; and, in the third, those distinguished by their pearly technique. Many-sided, cultured composer-performers like Hummel, Moscheles, and, finally, Chopin, combine all three, and are consequently the most beloved by players; those writers and performers who neglect to study any of these fall into the background.[12]

Physical and critical evidence testify abundantly to the improvements in the structure, tone, and action of the nineteenth-century piano. They also make clear that these improvements were certainly not uniform, that they varied with individual makers and with individual instruments. William Newman notes various preferences among virtuosi of the nineteenth century:

Hummel preferred the light, clean, yet solid touch of the Streicher-Graf piano made in Vienna, for his concert playing. Moscheles was another early Romantic who took a keen interest in the piano's development. In the 1820's and 1830's he preferred the lightness of touch, clarity of tone, and "more supple mechanism for my repeating notes, skips, and full chords" on the Clementi piano as against the heavier touch, yet fuller, more resonant tone of the Broadwood. The Erard's repetition also appealed to him, but not its tone at first. Chopin seems to have been satisfied with the piano as he found it, regarding the still delicate, wood-frame Pleyel as "perfection" and always preferring it to the Erard (which Thalberg and Liszt used) or the Broadwood.[13]

A comment in *AmZ* (1829) compares the tone qualities of English and German pianos:

Now the tone of English pianos clearly inclines toward that of most orchestral instruments: the German [pianos] differentiate themselves from this tone quality.[14]

Jean-Jacques Eigeldinger quotes a comment from the periodical *Le pianiste* (1834):

> You will give an *Erard* piano to Liszt, to Herz, to Bertini, to Schunke; but you will give a *Pleyel* piano to Kalkbrenner, to Chopin, to Hiller; one needs a *Pleyel* piano to sing a romance by Field, caress a mazurka of Chopin, sigh a nocturne by Kessler; one needs an *Erard* piano for the great concert. The brilliant *sound* of this maker carries, not further, but in a more sharp, more incisive, more distinct fashion than the soft *sound* of the *Pleyel* piano, which circulates and loses some of its intensity in the angles [recesses] of a large hall.[15]

As Robert Winter points out, the present-day image of the tone quality and action of nineteenth-century pianos is clouded by problems of the reconstruction of old instruments or their replication by modern makers. The result is often a distorted, unpleasant effect, very different from the sound referred to by Mendelssohn, as quoted by Winter: "there be none of Beauty's daughters with a magic like Érard's.[16] When we add to the variables cited above the variations among present-day manufacturers of pianos and among individual styles of performance, we arrive at a wide range of readings for any given work.[17]

Still, among the many variable features that characterize nineteenth-century pianos, several can be taken as "common denominators." We can assume a greater compass than that of the eighteenth-century piano, as well as an improved sustaining pedal action. These two features build resonance. The greater compass engages a broader complex of harmonics to reinforce the middle and upper registers in addition to increasing the actual pitch resources of the instrument. The sustaining pedal introduces a richness of resonance as well as a potential for songlike declamation. Example 3-1 gives sample ranges of eighteenth- and nineteenth-century pianos. For the latter, the clusters of notes show variations in actual range among a group of instruments.

Along with its mechanical improvements, the piano developed a vastly expanded presence in the musical, social, and commercial life of the earlier nineteenth century. Piano making was a profitable business.[18] The market included a wide and varied clientele—reigning virtuosos of the day,[19]

EXAMPLE 3-1.  Changes in piano compass.
a. Eighteenth-century pianos.　　　　b. Nineteenth-century pianos.

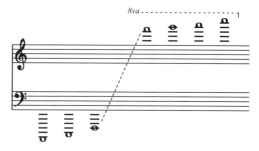

aristocratic and affluent bourgeois customers seeking instruments for their elegant establishments, and middle-class music lovers furnishing their homes.

## Internal Evidence

Internal evidence of the piano's changing musical role may be seen in the shifting emphasis of keyboard tutors, that is, manuals of instruction. In the eighteenth century, exercises for fingering and passagework constituted a relatively small part of a keyboard manual; these exercises were principally directed to clarity of declamation, reflecting what was then called the brilliant style. The principal concern in these manuals was musicianship—correct harmony, good sense of style, ornamentation, clear rhythmic articulation, realization of thorough-bass. Exercises consisted principally of small pieces in various styles and forms—dances, rondos, arias, sonata movements, and the like.[20]

The most demanding of the keyboard pieces included in J. G. Witthauer's 1791 edition of Georg Simon Löhlein's *Clavier-Schule* is illustrated in Example 3-2. The degree of difficulty involved here is modest. There are a few touches of the brilliant style, easily managed by a competent student. The actual amount of sound is minimal, except for a few reinforced intervals and chords. The piece would be equally effective on harpsichord, clavichord, or fortepiano, of whatever make might be available.

In contrast, the tutors of the early nineteenth century became increasingly concerned with technical agility, specifically at the piano. Exercises of progressive difficulty were laid out for the student pianist; these reached the level of transcendental difficulty, epitomized by Carl Czerny's manuals.[21] Example 3-3, from Friedrich Kalkbrenner's piano method (1830), illustrates

EXAMPLE 3-2.   Elaborate Classic keyboard texture. "Alla polacca." from Löhlein, *Clavier-Schule*, 5th ed., 1791, part 1, p. 79.

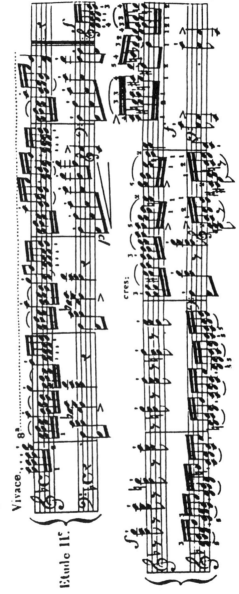

EXAMPLE 3-3. Elaborate nineteenth-century keyboard texture. Kalkbrenner, *Méthode*, 1830, p. 76.

the higher levels of skill attained and the kind of sound that pianos of the 1830s were expected to produce. The range only slightly exceeds the eighteenth-century piano's five-octave compass, but Kalkbrenner fills that space with clusters of notes—rapid parallel thirds, full chords and octaves in the left hand, and rapid changes of chord in the right hand (mm. 8–9). An 1830 piano in top condition, with its quick escapement action, felt hammers, and heavy strings, would allow a scintillating performance of this piece, which represents a characteristic genre of the era—a simple, singsong tune loaded with elaborate embellishments, a typical Biedermeier object. The brilliance of Kalkbrenner's etude is relatively modest compared to the extreme virtuosity displayed in other piano tutors and studies, as, for example in Czerny's *Die Schule der Geläufigkeit*, Op. 299, (n.d.) and Liszt's *12 études d'exécution transcendante* (1851).

Examples 3-4 through 3-8 represent nineteenth-century modifications of prototypical keyboard textures: melody and accompaniment, arpeggiation, full chords, and polyphony. In addition, Examples 3-9 through 3-12 demonstrate the piano as an instrument for declamation and the fantasia style and as a surrogate for or emulator of the orchestra. These examples display a spectrum of color and elaboration ranging from the subtle nuance of eighteenth-century keyboard texture to the brilliant effects of nineteenth-century sound quality and figuration. While sound and texture are the principal points of focus in this chapter, some consideration is given to the action of the music, that is, ways in which characteristic styles are embodied.

The tune of Franz Schubert's rondo in Example 3-4 is reminiscent of the

EXAMPLE 3-4.   Melody and accompaniment. Schubert, sonata in D Major, Op. 53, 1825, finale.

Schubert, *Sonatas for the Piano*. Copyright © G. Schirmer, Inc. Used by permission.

eighteenth-century gavotte. It has that dance's rhythmic regularity and a comparable gracefulness, with the hint of *romanza* that often appears in eighteenth-century gavotte topics. The light melody-accompaniment texture recalls a typical late eighteenth-century keyboard texture, somewhat fuller than that of Example 5-2a.

One element is new: the one-and-one-half-measure curtain, or vamp, that precedes the tune. This curtain creates a climate of sound for the tune; it draws attention to the ambience it establishes so that the tune appears to follow its accompaniment, to chime in, rather than to lead the action. This curtain represents a minimal addition of sound as a controlling element, yet its trace effect, with the slight shift of declamatory emphasis that it provokes, places the rondo theme squarely in the early Romantic piano world. Curtains do not appear in the sonatas of Joseph Haydn and Wolfgang Mozart; their music sets out immediately to say something melodic.[22] The very sound of the piano in Schubert's time, whatever it might have been, was different from that of the instruments for which Haydn and Mozart wrote. With its resonant, perhaps more "aggressive" sound, it could impart a piquant character to the strumming accompaniment, as if Schubert were imitating a mandolin.

Chopin's Prelude in E Minor, Op. 28, No. 4 (1838) (Ex. 3-5), also has a simple melody-accompaniment texture. Both right and left hands are laid out in narrow ranges. Apart from the octave leap that begins the melody, the right hand (to m. 12) remains within the compass of a diminished fifth, C–F sharp (the D and E in measure 9 are incidental ornaments). The left hand retains its close-position texture as its three-note chords slowly descend in an ancient gesture of descending parallel-sixth chords—a touch of the traditional ecclesiastical practice in the suspension-laden *stile legato*. The bass descends slowly, at whole-note and double-whole-note intervals, in the manner of the alla breve of the *stylus gravis*. Yet the prelude has a typically Romantic flavor. Within the traditional framework, Chopin has saturated the harmony with dark glints of color. We hear suspensions of sevenths, sliding shifts of harmonic meaning, a steady give-and-take of restless dissonance, an irregular set of counterrhythms in the middle voices contradicting the regular movement of the outer voices. The first eight measures contain twenty-two different harmonic combinations; most of these appear as subtle shifts rather than bold juxtapositions of contrasted colors.

While the eighteenth-century fortepiano could manage the text of this prelude, its light, detaché declamation would contradict both the sound and the expressive stance of the piece. Here a legato style of performance is called for, with a full, sustained tone for each instant of the music. An effective sustaining pedal is essential, both for the legato and for the sympathetic resonances it stimulates, resonances that clothe the struck tone with an aura of richness. The harmony of this piece, steadily reinforced by the repeated eighths in the left hand, together with the resonance of the piano, creates the sound that marks it truly as a Romantic song without words.

EXAMPLE 3-5.    Melody and accompaniment. Chopin, Prelude in E Minor, Op. 28, No. 4, 1838.

# *Arpeggiation*

At the beginning of the nineteenth century, the arpeggio, long a characteristic idiomatic figure in keyboard music, moved to a spectacular central role in piano textures. The tonal features of the Romantic piano—broader range, fuller tone, and especially the sustaining or damper pedal—provided a broad scope for arpeggiation both in range and in duration. An arpeggio could, by itself, make a bold, complete statement, extending its resonance and its harmonic color over the entire gamut, or intensifying a specific segment of the pitch range. It could also carry the sound forward through a significant stretch of musical time. In the passage quoted on p. 24, Marx pointed to the role of the arpeggio creating a new school of composition.

Of all composers in the Romantic era, it was Chopin who exploited the possibilities of the arpeggio most imaginatively. The opening measures of the

Etude in C Major, Op. 10, No. 1 (1830) (Ex. 3-6), exemplify some of the more spectacular steps taken by the Romantic piano over its eighteenth-century predecessors in the use of the arpeggio. Greater strength of construction allows an even, strong tone throughout the entire range, which, supported by an effective sustaining pedal, permits the chord of C major to soar brilliantly over a span of over five octaves within the first two measures. Moreover, the pedal opens the full harmonic series of C major into sympathetic resonance as the upper strings are stirred into vibration by the powerful octaves in the bass, creating an aura of sound. The figuration builds an impressive rush of sound that cascades upward and downward some forty times during the etude to provide the entire melodic facade of this study. With its virtuoso demands, the figuration departs from the ornamental patterns of eighteenth-century keyboard music; it becomes driving, substantive, with a sharp cutting edge.

Arpeggios are the most prominent of an extensive battery of virtuoso figures cultivated in Romantic piano music. A review of Liszt's *Grand Fantasia on Motives from Meyerbeer's "Robert le Diable"* in AmZ (1842) lists some of these figures, noting that

> Liszt [has] exhausted virtually every resource from that art of his, which has attained the highest level. These octave and tenth passages, his chromatic runs, his boldest leaps, double trills, etc., must be seen as well as heard so that one can believe that only a single player is performing.[23]

Chopin and Liszt were the greatest masters of the art of piano figuration. The varied configurations they shaped have their own particular qualities of eloquence and brilliance, often tightly substantive in the various convolutions they traverse. At the other end of the spectrum are Berlioz's comments on pianism in 1819 and his good fortune in avoiding its pitfalls:

> My father did not wish me to learn the piano, otherwise I should doubtless have swelled the ranks of the innumerable army of famous pianists . . .

EXAMPLE 3-6.    Arpeggiation. Chopin, Etude in C Major, Op. 10, No. 1, 1830.

Chopin, *Etudes.* Copyright © G. Schirmer, Inc. Used by permission.

I have often felt the want of this accomplishment, and it might have been of the greatest use to me; but when I consider the appalling number of miserable musical platitudes to which the piano has given birth, which would never have seen the light had their authors been confined to pen and paper, I feel grateful to the happy chance which forced me to compose freely and in silence, and has thus delivered me from the tyranny of the fingers, so dangerous to thought, and from the fascination which the ordinary sonorities always exercise on a composer, more or less. Many amateurs have pitied me for this deprivation, but that does not affect me much.[24]

# *Full Chords*

With the substantial resonance of the Romantic piano itself, and the reinforcement by means of the pedal, full-chord textures with as many as six or seven notes can produce a massive effect of sound. Throughout the nineteenth century, this resource was frequently exploited in piano music, as in Brahms' Rhapsody in E-Flat Major, Op. 119, No. 4 (1893); Chopin's Prelude in C Minor, Op. 28, No. 20 (1838); and the *grandioso* section in D Major of Liszt's Sonata in B Minor (1854). In contrast to arpeggiation, where the uppermost tones of arpeggio figures hint at simple, rhythmically regular melodic lines, full-chord textures often support broadly scaled, sharply profiled melodies, as if the piano were emulating homophonic choral declamation.

Example 3-7, the opening measures of the Préambule from Schumann's *Carnaval* (1834), calls for the power of the nineteenth-century piano, a fortissimo that builds to even greater strength through a broad crescendo. Six- and seven-note chords create a massive sound that amplifies a traditional texture—bass and soprano polarized moving in first parallel then contrary conjunct motion.

EXAMPLE 3-7.    Full chords. Schumann, *Carnival*, 1834, Préambule.

Kalmus.

# Polyphonic Texture

Each of the textures described above involves some aspect of polyphony, be it opposition of contrasting melodies, registers, or points of articulation (that is, action overlapping or opposing in point of time). The most formal embodiment of polyphony, the fugue, was a standard area of study in musical composition in the nineteenth century; a composer had to complete a course in fugue in order to qualify for professional status.

Some important Romantic piano works include fugal sections: for example, Schubert's *Wanderer Fantasia*, Op. 15 (1822), Liszt's Sonata in B Minor, and Brahms's *Variations and Fugue on a Theme by Handel*, Op. 24. Texture provides a clue to the way in which fugal procedures are adapted to nineteenth-century piano sound. In each of these works, the fugue begins traditionally, voice added to voice as entries follow one another. As the fugues progress, other piano textures begin to assume increasingly important roles until, toward the end of each of these sections, virtuoso pianism overwhelms formal polyphony. Grand arpeggios, massive chords, augmented two-part action (several tones on each strand) provide the kind of expansive climax toward which the Romantic fugue is propelled.

Example 3-8, a characteristic nineteenth-century adaptation of polyphony to piano sonority, is taken from the middle of the fugue that closes Brahms's *Handel Variations*, the subject and answer of which have been shown in Example 2-8b. Although four "voices" are scored, the texture is best

EXAMPLE 3-8. Polyphonic texture. Brahms, Variations and Fugue on a Theme by Handel, Op. 24, 1861, fugue.

understood as two lines reinforced in sixths and thirds for maximum resonance. Polyphony yields much of its character to sonority.

## *The Piano as Orchestra*

The piano, like its keyboard predecessors, was a musical clearing house. Being a complete ensemble in its own right, the piano incorporated styles, textures, and topical materials from the solo and ensemble music of church, theater, and chamber. Operatic arias, concertos, and symphonies were arranged for piano in the later eighteenth century, with or without the accompaniment of a violin, violoncello, or flute. For many listeners, the piano was the only way in which they could come to know such a composition, by performing it or by hearing it in a keyboard arrangement.

Symphonies, especially those by Haydn, were popular items in two-hand keyboard arrangements.[25] These symphonies retained many elements of chamber music texture. Indeed, much of the content of these works is characterized by the interplay of figures typical of chamber music (see Example 4-1). Tutti passages are set against this interplay in a vigorous but moderately full texture. Example 3-9 illustrates both textures in an early nineteenth-century two-hand pianoforte setting by William Crotch.

The keyboard's imitation of larger ensembles is not limited to transcriptions. Many of the piano sonatas of Haydn and Mozart, as well as those of their contemporaries, imitate operatic, orchestral, and wind music. Mozart's Sonatas in D Major, K. 284 (1775) and K. 311 (1777), open in the manner of the Italian opera sinfonia; Haydn's Sonata in E-Flat Major, Hob. XVI:52 (1795) begins with a powerful quasi-orchestral march theme. Mozart's Sonata in E-Flat Major, K. 282 (1774), has vivid suggestions of wind serenade behavior in all of its three movements.

In the nineteenth century, the physical improvements in piano construction had a profound effect on the piano's ability to serve as a surrogate for the orchestra. A review by G. W. Fink in *AmZ*, 1840, of Franz Liszt's transcription of Ludwig van Beethoven's Symphony No. 5 in C Minor, Op. 67 (1807), speaks to the brilliance and breadth that the piano could achieve in this role:

EXAMPLE 3-9. Classic piano transcription. Haydn, Symphony in E-Flat Major, Hob. I:74, 1781, first movement.

The poorest lithograph, the faultiest translation gives an idea, however unclear, of the genius of a Michelangelo, a Shakespeare; in the most incomplete keyboard adaptation on can perceive, here and there, even though half hidden, the mark of the inspiration of the master. In this connection, it is now possible to achieve more and better [results] than was heretofore possible, through the expansion in technical fluency and mechanical improvement that the piano has recently developed. Through the immense increase in its harmonic power, the piano seeks constantly to approach orchestral compositions. In its range of seven octaves, it can, with few exceptions, reproduce all passages, all combinations, all configurations of the most basic and profound tonal ideas, and concedes to the orchestra no more advantage than the variety of tone color and the massive effect—actually, a tremendous advantage [for the orchestra].[26]

Example 3-10 illustrates the richness and complexity that Liszt was able to incorporate into his transcription of Beethoven's symphony. Rapid alternations of figures at contrasting pitch levels, a kind of latter-day *Brechung*, aided by the sustaining power and resonance provided by the pedal, enables Liszt to capture much of the drive and intensity of Beethoven's declamation.

Liszt's arrangements were recognized by his contemporaries as works of art in their own right. His imaginative adaptations of orchestral textures into brilliant, idiomatic tours de force for the piano became the exception rather than the rule in piano transcriptions of orchestral music. The limitations Fink mentioned—the piano's relative paucity of tonal variety and incapacity for massive effect—elicited in 1828 the criticism of Berlioz, the first great orchestral colorist. His comments on piano transcriptions in his *Mémoirs* draw a distinction between eighteenth-century scoring and that of his time:

Can anyone conceive the absurdity of trying to judge of the merits of an orchestral work thus mutilated? The piano can give an idea of an orchestral work to anyone who has already heard it played by an orchestra, because memory supplies what is lacking and recalls the full performance. But in the present state of music it is utterly impossible to convey any adequate idea of a new work in that way.

A score such as Sacchini's *Oedipe,* or any work of that school in which there is no instrumentation, loses very little by being heard on the piano. But with any modern music—that is supposing, of course, the composer has availed himself of the means now at his disposal—it is quite another matter. Take the Communion march from Cherubini's *Mass du Sacre,* for example. What would become of those wonderful prolonged notes of the wind instruments which fill you with mystic ecstasy? or of those delicious interlacings of flutes and clarinets to which almost the whole effect is due? They would disappear completely, because the piano can neither hold nor swell a note. . . . The piano, for the orchestral writer, is a guillotine that severs the head of noble and of churl with the same impartial indifference.[27]

On the other hand, Berlioz recognized the potential of the piano to project its own color values in a orchestral ensemble, or to become a complete orchestra by itself. He says in his *Treatise upon Modern Instrumentation* (1848):

EXAMPLE 3-10. Romantic piano transcription. Beethoven, Symphony No. 5 in C Minor, finale, transcribed by Liszt, 1837.

Reproduced by kind permission of Gregg International.

The pianoforte, at the point of perfection to which our skillful manufacturers have brought it now-a-days, may be considered in a double point of view: as an orchestral instrument, or as forming a complete orchestra in itself.[28]

The piano becomes "a complete orchestra in itself" in such works as Brahms's ballade *Edward,* Op. 10 (1856), and the opening of Schubert's *Wanderer Fantasy,* Op. 15. Liszt, in a statement credited to him, although not verified, described his piano in orchestral terms:

In the circumference of its seven octaves, it embraces the entire circumference of the orchestra . . . enough to render the harmonies which in an orchestra are only brought out be the combination of hundreds of musicians. . . . We can give broken chords like the harp, long sustained tones like the winds, staccati and a thousand passages which before, it seemed only possible to produce on this or that instrument. . . . The piano has on one side the capacity of assimilation; the capacity of taking into itself the life of all [instruments]; on the other it has its own life, its own growth, its individual development.[29]

The coda of Liszt's Sonata in B Minor, (Ex. 3-11) has the effect of an epilogue, a reminiscence, a reconciling final utterance that serves to bring all the turbulence of the work to rest in a beatific mood of resignation. Here the piano suggests an orchestra, imitating massed horns and woodwinds against the bassoons in the first eight measures of the example; later a solo oboe is suggested, then violoncellos, eventually contrabasses, and again massed winds. The crescendo, measures 755–756, impossible on the piano, is a nice hint of orchestral dynamics.

The opening measures of this coda create the greatest textural contrast in the entire sonata—sustained treble chords against a percussive bass. The harmony reinforces the contrast: as the bass drums out the tonic, B, the diminished-seventh chords transform to become Neapolitan harmonies, totally separated from their underpinning. The wide textural separation hints of polychordality, B versus C, yet the harmonic tug-of-war is resolved as a Phrygian cadence measures 732–733. In this passage the sound of the piano is critical; it must resound pervasively, though softly, both in the sustained chords and in the pithy repeated notes of the bass. While the entire epilogue has a convincing quality of closure, it contains not one authentic cadence (see pp. 213–14).

Rather, the cadential effect is plagal, afterthoughts themselves ingeniously devised—though, there are no traditional plagal cadences. The last measures epitomize both the pianistic and harmonic elements of color explored so adventurously throughout the sonata. The final progression juxtaposes harmonies a tritone distant—F major and B major. Neither is in a root position; F major, is set as a $\frac{6}{3}$ chord, B major floats as a $\frac{6}{4}$ chord. The high register, voice leading by half step, and full-chord texture at a *ppp* dynamic level combine to suggest a final dissolution of feeling, an otherworldly effect. Yet at the very end we hear the decisive B, five and one-half octaves below, that heard alone puts a period, however subtle, to the harmony, as it touches

EXAMPLE 3-11.   Orchestral style. Liszt, Sonata in B Minor, 1854, coda.

the lowermost range of the piano—again, a sound effective only on the Romantic piano.

The opening measures of this sonata (Ex. 3-12) have the quality of an improvisation, a fantasia, with strong dramatic color in the powerful, sudden contrasts.

The sonata opens with a series of improvisatory gestures idiomatic to the

EXAMPLE 3-12. Improvisatory style. Liszt, Sonata in B Minor, 1854.

piano of Liszt's time. Three of these gestures, highly contrasted yet hinged on the note G, are encompassed in the first thirteen measures:

1. Octave Gs (no melodic profile), mm. 1, 4, 7
2. Descending scales (conjunct melodic profile), mm. 2–3, 5–6
3. Leaps and arpeggios reinforced in double octaves (disjunct, convoluted melodic profile), mm. 8–13

Each of these gestures draws on some unique capacity of the "grand" piano. The terse opening Gs, although *sotto voce*, are somewhat percussive, with a heavy, resonant, yet understated core of sound. The descending scales, covered by the sustained Gs, exploit the piano's capacity for legato, while the damper pedal provides an enveloping curtain of sound. Both gestures have an air of great portent, intensified by the silences that separate individual notes and figures and draw the listener into the sonata's fantastic sound world.

In boldest contrast, the leaps and arpeggios demand a ringing, brilliant, percussive sound from the piano. Here, too, silence sets off gestures, this time melodramatic in their intensity. These first thirteen measures have something of the quality of a *recitative obligé*—figures charged with high pathos, alternating accompaniment (mm. 1, 4, 7, 8–13) with solo (mm. 2–3, 5–6).

The sonata in its entirety traverses a tremendous gamut of textures and expressive stances. The piano must produce powerful unisons, dark massive chords, passages of transcendental brilliance, grand chorales, lyric songs, convoluted counterpoints, and ethereal harmonies (see Ex. 13-12). Often these are closely juxtaposed in a vast musical tableau.

In a letter to Liszt of 1843, Berlioz took the liberty to imagine what Liszt might say about his pianism:

> With a slight modification of the famous *mot* of Louis XIV, you may say with confidence: "I myself am orchestra, chorus, and conductor. I can make my piano dream or sing at pleasure, re-echo with exulting harmonies, and rival the most skilful bow in swiftness. Like the orchestra, it has its harmonies of brass; and like it, though without the smallest apparatus, it can throw on the evening breeze a cloud of fairylike chords and vague melodies. Neither theatre nor set-scenes are needed, no vast rows of benches, nor long and fatiguing rehearsals, for I want neither musicians nor music. Give me a large room and a grand piano, and I am at once master of a great audience."[30]

Eigeldinger contrasts the styles of the two greatest pianists of the nineteenth century, Liszt and Chopin, in terms of their relation to the orchestra and to the voice:

> Pianistically, Liszt finds his place between Beethoven and Ravel, in a line that essentially wishes to extract the symphonic color from the piano. Chopin, he, is the heir of Mozart and the precursor of Debussy. The only musical genius of the nineteenth century in which the piano does not reflect the orchestra of its time, he is placed at the heart of a trajectory that is essentially vocal, in which the refinements of the touch excel.[31]

Eigeldinger's reference to Chopin's essentially vocal style touches upon the influence of Italian opera upon Chopin, notably Bellini, with his graceful, spun-out melodies. In Chopin's music, this vocal style moves in a flow of glowing sound, arpeggiated or chordal, but always singing.

The broad sound spectrum of the Romantic piano, by enabling the composer to suggest symphonic and vocal styles as well as exploit uniquely pianistic effects, encouraged the juxtaposition of contrasting melodic figures, textures, and harmonies that had long been part of the fantasia genre. These varied effects, under the control of a single performer, combine to project the sense of improvisation and free declamation that distinguishes much Romantic piano music.

# CHAPTER FOUR

# The Orchestra: Texture and Sound

The sound of the Romantic orchestra had already begun to emerge in the later eighteenth century. Its characteristic tone colors—its richness, variety, and intensity in both light and full scorings—were already prefigured in the scoring of Classic music.[1]

## The Classic Orchestra

Instruments of the Classic orchestra—strings, winds, and brass—took over the role of harmonic amplification in the middle register from the traditional keyboard continuo. Wind instruments came to the fore from time to time in solos to show their characteristic timbres and styles, rather than simply to double and reinforce the strings, as in the earlier orchestra. Orchestral textures thereby, already in Classic music, developed a new horizontal, or antiphonal, dimension of strings against winds to complement the traditional vertical dimension of bass and treble that constituted the layout of Baroque orchestral texture.

At first, in Classic scoring, the new orchestral sounds gave a more vivid coloring to a traditional chamber music texture. Orchestral music not intended for use in theater and church was subsumed under the category of chamber music, and indeed, orchestras in the eighteenth century, with some notable exceptions, were rather small. Their textures were built with lines of action rather than with masses of sound. Berlioz, in 1827, characterized the symphonies of Haydn and Mozart as being "of an essentially *intimate* character" and therefore unsuited for performance in a large hall.[2]

The textures of chamber music predominate even in such grand symphonies as Mozart's "Jupiter" (1788) and Haydn's "Drumroll" (1796). The clarity and deft play of figure, colored by a variety of timbres, provides most of the appeal of those works. With a typically small Classic orchestra, a tutti passage can be bold in effect, but not massive; it serves to mark off and provide contrast to the prevailing chamber music texture.

Example 4-1 illustrates the play of winds and strings in Classic orchestral texture. Such passages have the lightness, the deft give-and-take of chamber music.

Beyond their ability to give color to the play of figures, wind and brass instruments can sustain tones effectively as a support and background for melodic action, as in measures 165–69 of Example 4-1. Their capacity to sustain harmony became a critical factor in the emergence of the Romantic orchestral sound. This sustaining power promoted drastic changes in declamation; the active interplay of bass and treble in continuo texture gave way to a broadly scaled set of gestures, often songlike, in the treble. Moreover, the seductive beauty of a sustained tone in the strings as well as in the winds and brass often became the means by which a listener's attention was captured. Events spin out deliberately, taking considerable time. The slow introductions to many Classic symphonies exploit this ability of orchestral instruments, especially winds, to create a mood, an ambiance generated by sustained, slowly moving sounds, as in the introduction to Haydn's Symphonies No. 102 in B-Flat Major and No. 104 in D Major ("London"), or Mozart's Symphonies No. 38 in D Major ("Prague") and No. 39 in E-Flat Major, and Beethoven's Symphonies No. 2 in D Major, Op. 36, and Symphony No. 4 in B-Flat Major, Op. 60.

By these means, and by such effects as the Mannhein crescendo, orchestral scoring eventually elevated sound quality to a primary position in the compositional processes of Romantic composers. This trend got under way much earlier in orchestral music than in piano music. Listeners were hearing brilliant orchestral sounds in Classic symphonies long before they encountered a comparable brilliance in piano music.[3] Charles Burney credited Johann Christian Bach with a significant contribution to this trend. He wrote, in his *A General History of Music*, 1789:

> Bach seems to have been the first composer who observed the law of *contrast* as a *principle*. . . . His symphonies seem infinitely more original than either his songs or harpsichord pieces, of which the harmony, mixtures of wind instruments, and general richness and variety of accompaniment, are certainly the most prominent features.[4]

In his Overture to *Lucio Silla* (1776; also listed as Symphony in B-Flat Major, Op. 18, No. 2) Bach distributes the figures of an elegant gavotte melody in the

EXAMPLE 4-1. Winds and strings in dialogue. Haydn, Symphony No. 92 in G Major, 1788, first movement.

Haydn, Symphony No. 92, Eulenburg Edition. Used by kind permission of European American Music Distributors Corporation, agent for Eulenburg Editions.

first movement among pairs of winds—flutes, oboes, clarinets, horns—to create a delightful play of instrumental color worthy of a Mendelssohn or Schubert.

Thanks to the growing richness of tone qualities in late eighteenth-century orchestral music, Classic symphonies were important items in the concert repertory of nineteenth-century orchestras and opera houses. On the other hand, the sonatas of Haydn and Mozart, fitted texturally to the fortepiano of the late eighteenth century, were rarely heard in piano recitals of the Romantic era.[5]

## *The Romantic Orchestra*

Changing roles among instruments of the orchestra went hand in hand with trends that focused on sound qualities. By the late eighteenth century, strings had developed a richer tone quality and greater resonance, thanks to mechanical adjustments such as lengthened necks, raised bridges and fingerboards, and the perfection of the Tourte bow. Profound improvements in wind instruments provided composers with a much wider palette of tone colors than had previously been available. These improvements—including adjustments in hole size and bore, as well as Theobald Böhm's development of the ring-key mechanism 1830s and 1840s—aimed for improved tone quality, more precise intonation, greater facility in performance, and an increase in range (see below, p. 71 for a summary of the improvements in brass instruments).[6]

A significant trend was the increase in the size of orchestras. During the later eighteenth century the average personnel of orchestras in the more important centers—Paris, London, Mannheim, Berlin, for example—would include about sixteen violins (in two sections), four violas, three to four each of violoncello and bass, and two (occasionally four) flutes, oboes, bassoons, and horns. Some groups had clarinets and trumpets. By the mid-nineteenth century these numbers had increased notably in larger orchestras. For example, the Berlin Court Opera orchestra in 1849 had twenty-seven violins, eight violas, eleven violoncellos, and seven double basses. In the same year, the orchestra of Her Majesty's Theatre in London had an equally large group of strings.[7] Clarinets, trumpets, and trombones became standard additions to the pairs of winds and brass of the Classic orchestra. The increased amount and strength of sound allowed a greater exploitation of color values. Moreover, the larger number of strings on a melodic line increased measurably the intensity of tone; a melodic line or an accompaniment figure projected a presence more compelling than was possible in the Classic orchestra.

Other instruments often included in nineteenth-century scores were the piccolo, English horn, bass clarinet, contrabassoon, tuba, and harp, as well as a variety of percussion instruments in addition to the traditional timpani. Instruments now obsolete—serpent, sarrusophone, and ophicleide—were sometimes prescribed. The application of efficient valve systems to the brass instruments—trumpets, horns, cornets, and the newly invented saxhorns (c. 1845)—contributed to the palette of available colors and opened doors to far wider harmonic explorations involving the full orchestra (see Examples 4-10 and 4-11).

Liszt wrote, "In my orchestral works I have taken the larger measure of instrumentation (Paris, Vienna, Dresden . . . ").[8] The score of his *Tasso*, 1849, for instance, includes piccolo, bass clarinet, fourth trumpet, tuba, harp, and a battery of percussion instruments in addition to a standard nineteenth-century complement. On a trip to Berlin in 1843 Berlioz encountered a representative large orchestra:

> 14 first and 14 second violins, 8 violas, 10 cellos, 8 double-basses, 4 flutes, 4 oboes, 4 clarinets, 4 bassoons, 4 horns, 4 trumpets, 4 trombones, 1 kettle-drummer, 1 big drum, a pair of cymbals, and 2 harps.

But even this did not meet the description of his ideal orchestra in his *Treatise upon Modern Instrumentation:*

> But the finest concert orchestra, for a room scarcely larger than that of the Conservatoire,—the most complete, the richest in gradations, in varieties of tone, the most majestic, the most powerful, and at the same time the most soft and smooth, would be an orchestra thus composed:—

| | | |
|---|---|---|
| 21 First Violins. | 2 Hautboys. | 3 Trombones (1 Alto, 2 |
| 20 Second do. | 1 Corno Inglese. | Tenors), or 3 Tenors |
| 18 Violas. | 2 Clarinets. | 1 Great Bass Trombone |
| 8 First Violoncellos | 1 Corno di Bassetto, or | 1 Ophicleide in B-flat |
| 7 Second do. | one Bass-Clarinet. | (or a Bass-Tuba). |
| 10 Double-Basses. | 4 Bassoons. | 2 Pairs of Kettle- |
| 4 Harps. | 4 Horns with Cylin- | Drums, and 4 Drum- |
| 2 Piccolo Flutes. | ders. | mers. |
| 2 Large Flutes. | 2 Trumpets with Cylin- | 1 Long Drum. |
| | ders). | 1 Pair of Cymbals.[9] |
| | 2 Cornets à Pistons (or | |
| | with Cylinders). | |

As a final commentary on instrumentation in his *Treatise* Berlioz described some of the effects he envisioned with his ideal orchestra:

> But in the thousand combinations practicable with the vast orchestra we have just described, would dwell a wealth of harmony, a variety of qualities in tone, a succession of contrasts, which can be compared to nothing hitherto achieved in Art; and above all, an incalculable melodial, expressive, and rhythmical power, a penetrating force of unparalleled strength, a prodigious sensitiveness for gradations of aggregate and of detail. Its repose would be majestic as the slumber of ocean; its agitations would recall the tempest of the tropics; its explosions, the outbursts of volcanos; therein would be found the plaints, the murmurs, the mysterious sounds of primeval forests; the clamours, the prayers, the songs of triumph or of mourning of a people with expansive soul, ardent heart, and fiery passions; its silence would inspire awe by its solemnity; and organizations the most rebellious would shudder to behold its *crescendo* spread roaringly,—like a stupendous conflagration![10]

The changing circumstances of public performance influenced the size of orchestras, as Adam Carse points out:

When orchestra concert-giving was further expanded during the second quarter of the 19th century, and the general public were being admitted by payment, still larger halls and consequently larger orchestras were necessary. The wind and percussion could then hardly number less than from eighteen to twenty, and the strings from forty to fifty players. So it seems that although the increase in the size of string orchestras was largely the outcome of the growing power of the wind band, a contributing factor to the growth in size of concert orchestras was also in some measure due to the development of concert performances before larger audiences in larger halls.[11]

Larger halls have more space for sound to reverberate. Sound, in these immense rooms, can make its point through texture and color; musical effects are often enhanced by slowing down the pace of declamation. Sustained tones can pervade the expanses through which they travel (see Examples 4-4, 4-7, and 4-14).

# Orchestration Treatises

Although orchestration became elevated to a formal branch of music theory only in the earlier nineteenth century, writers as early as the 1770s made comments on scoring such as the following, from Johann Friedrich Daube's *Der musikalische Dilettant* (1773):

> It is certain that harmony has many effects. A chord that has wide intervals creates an entirely different impression than a chord in close position . . . a chord sounds best in the middle range. Its effect is good on the organ, *Flügel,* or *Klavier,* even better when played by two violins and violoncello. Played by wind instruments of similar and different classes, with or without string instruments, again the effect is quite different . . . two oboes sound better in thirds, flutes in sixths . . . a complete chord, assisted by horns, has a magnificent sound. . . . When the violins are muted, and the winds blow softly, a doubled chord sounds delicate. When the oboe plays an octave above the violin, this unusual setting creates an excellent effect. The truth is: the tone quality of each instrument contributes much to the expression of the affects.[12]

John Marsh's *Hints to Young Composers* (1800) is a brief sketch that describes current orchestral instruments and includes an analysis of an orchestral march. August Kollman[13] and Jérôme-Joseph de Momigny[14] provide comments on scoring that reflect Classic practice of assigning roles to strings, winds, and brass principally according to ranges, with some consideration for tone color. C. Michaelis's essay in *AmZ* (1807) deals especially with the tone qualities of musical instruments and the kinds of passages they can best manage.[15]

Carl Czerny, Adolph Marx, and Johann Christian Lobe each devoted a substantial portion of his composition treatise to orchestration,[16] but the first important work devoted entirely to orchestration is Berlioz's *Treatise upon Modern Instrumentation and Orchestration* (1844). This comprehensive survey of all the orchestral instruments extant at that time, replete with examples and commentary on the capacities and tone qualities of each instrument, describes the art of instrumentation as follows:

> The employment of these various sonorous elements [strings, winds, brass, percussion] and their application—either for *colouring* the melody, harmony, and rhythm, or for producing peculiar impressions (originating or not in an intention of expression) independently of all aid from the three other great musical powers—constitutes *the art of instrumentation.*[17]

Physical and critical evidence testifies abundantly to the richer sounds of Romantic orchestral music. The many surviving instruments document the changes in their physical properties; letters and memoirs comment on the size of orchestras and on orchestration; and treatises on orchestration bear witness to the increasingly significant role this aspect of musical composition played in theory and practice.

Still, the climate of orchestral sound, rich as it was, was by no means uniform. Orchestras differed widely in their size and makeup, as well as in skills and leadership. The gap between a composer's image of his music and the actual performance could be frustratingly wide. Richard Wagner, in his essay *Über das Dirigieren* (1869) complained,

> I am not aware that the number of permanent members of an orchestra, in any German town, has been rectified according to the requirements of modern orchestration.[18]

Whatever the local circumstances may have been, the spectrum of orchestral sound values was nonetheless different from the typical eighteenth-century sound. This evidence is clearly marked in the actual scorings specified by the composer; they indicate the composer's concept of sound, however well or poorly it may have been realized in performance.

## *Romantic Orchestral Scoring*

### Adaptation of Traditional Scoring

Much of Romantic orchestral music adapts textures established in the Classic style to the fuller instrumentarium of the nineteenth century. This reflects a contemporary practice, the performance of older music by forces larger than those for which the works were conceived. For instance, Berlioz in 1845 attended a concert in Vienna in which works by Haydn, Mozart, and Beethoven were performed by a chorus of six hundred and an orchestra of four hundred. He comments upon this practice:

It is true that the programmes of these music festivals are almost always made up of the best known works of the old masters. . . . No doubt, grand music like the oratorios of Handel, Bach, Haydn, and Beethoven gains very much by being thus performed (with an immense body of performers); but after all, it is only a question of more or less doubling the parts.[19]

While Baroque and Classic music can sustain the augmented forces of nineteenth- or twentieth-century ensembles, the reverse is untenable: a Brahms or Tchaikovsky symphony played by a Haydn orchestra!

Czerny's *Treatise on Instrumentation*, volume 3 of his *School of Practical Composition* (1848), without going into the detail that Berlioz, Marx, and Lobe provide in their treatises, gives a compact, useful list of textures that he considers to be "ordinary" in instrumentation. Czerny's designation of these textures as "good effects" reflects the nineteenth-century concern for sound values:

Good effects are best ensured by an observance of the following rules:—

1. Broad and suitable progressions.
2. Vigorous passages in unison.
3. A noble and well conceived melody, which requires no embellishments to render it interesting.
4. A grand, and sometimes melodious progression of the bass, so that it may not always seem to be merely accompanying.
5. The alternate and also conjoint employment of the two full masses, provided that it neither continues too long, nor degenerates into mere noise.
6. Little, but not would-be-brilliant solo passages for single wind instruments, with an interesting accompaniment.
7. Great care in the use of passing notes in the accompanying inner parts, so as to avoid harshness in the harmony.
8. A just and proportional disposition of the inner parts, as well in open, as in close harmony.
9. Fullness is attained rather by doubling the quartett parts, than by a heterogeneous addition of inner parts in the upper octaves.
10. Too quick a succession of many constrained and dissonant harmonies must be avoided.
11. A due alternation and union of the *Staccato* and *Legato*, particularly in the quartett.
12. The moderate use of the *Pizzicato* in connection with the wind instruments.
13. The introduction, in the proper place, of the brass instruments and drums.
14. The avoidance of too difficult times and divisions, which render the exact entry of the instruments uncertain.
15. In quick passages assigned to the Violins, a clear and well attuned accompaniment, which neither obscures nor confuses the same. &c:

The combinations of the Quartett with one or more wind instruments are very numerous, each of which produces a different effect.

1. When a wind instrument is added to some one of the Quartett parts (most frequently to the first Violin) which it doubles either in the unison, or in the octave above or below.

2. When this wind instrument is treated differently from the Quartett, and receives either an essential part, or long sustained notes, or even quicker passages.
3. Lastly, when a decided *Solo* is assigned to the wind instrument, to which the quartett performs an accompaniment.

Thus, for example, the first Bassoon may double the bass either in the unison or in the octave above. In like manner, it may be made to proceed in unison with one of the inner parts, or still better, to double the first Violin in the octave below. And lastly, it may either perform sustained notes in harmony with the Quartett parts, or else a decided Solo.

The like is admissible with the first Clarionet and Hautboy, only that these never proceed with the bass, but move probably in unison with the inner and upper parts of the Quartett. In gentle melodies we avoid setting the acute Hautboy in unison with the first Violin: it is preferable in the octave above.

The Flute is well adapted to proceed with the first Violin either in the unison or in the octave above, as it agreeably mollifies the tone of the Violins. All these instruments may likewise receive little solo passages.[20]

Giuseppe Verdi's *Il Trovatore* was completed in 1852, only four years after the publication of Czerny's rules. The instrumentation in Manrico's aria (Ex. 4-2) departs from Classic convention in only one detail: three horns, not two,

EXAMPLE 4-2.   Reinforcement of traditional scoring. Verdi, *Il Trovatore*, 1853, "Di quella pira."

augment pairs of winds and the usual strings. The traditional texture opposes the outer voices with a middle-level support of full chords. Yet the horns in close-position harmony, along with the second violins and violas, create an unmistakably nineteenth-century curtain of sound against which the tenor melody is set in bold relief. Moreover, Verdi's emphatic doubling of the third of the triad, the highest note of the chord, gives a glow, an intense ring, to a familiar sound, an active rather than a stable effect. Interpolated touches of color in parallel thirds and sixths in the winds point up the simple tune. With its energetic bolero rhythm, its high solo tessitura, and its insistent yet familiar harmony, the aria conveys a vivid emotion—fury—across the theater to listeners in the galleries, rather than to those in the boxes.

The closing measures of Weber's *Euryanthe* Overture (1823) (Ex. 4-3) illustrate the fuller, more powerful sound achieved by joining three trombones and an extra pair of horns to the traditional wind and brass pairs. The stunning, martial effect of E-flat major harmony in fortissimo holds the listener by virtue of its brilliance and intensity. The action, however, is quite conventional: first fanfares in the winds, then sustained wind chords against brilliant string figures and concitato cellos and basses, then all together in incisive march rhythms and a final sustained chord. It is the amplification of traditional scoring that gives this excerpt its Romantic aspect.

The opening tutti of Brahms's Symphony No. 1 in C Minor, Op. 68 (1876) (Ex. 4-4) seems far removed from the eighteenth-century sound world, yet its texture reaches back beyond Haydn and Mozart to the Baroque trio sonata. Two treble lines (one doubled in thirds) crisscross in contrary motion while a firm pedal point on C anchors the shifting harmonies. The doubling of each line in three octaves aims for mass rather than color; the effect is of a great organ with full registration. The opening Cs in five octaves build a towering lattice of sound that becomes denser as the harmonies grow more active.

Example 4-5, from the finale of the symphony, also deploys three lines. This time the active components are the outer voices moving in contrary motions within unstable harmonies. The middle voices are spread over three to four octaves; they reinforce, with repeated notes, the hectic syncopation of the two outer parts, which move in first contrary then parallel motion. Here, the orchestra realizes Brahms' penchant for sprung rhythms with massive, virtually percussive attacks upon the syncopations after breath-catching instants of silence. The effectiveness of melodic and rhythmic action in this example rests largely on the massive sound generated by the full orchestra.

## Innovative Scoring

The two examples from Brahms's First Symphony indicate the extent to which Romantic composers expanded upon traditional textures to create sonorities entirely unlike those of the eighteenth century. A complementary aspect of Romantic orchestral music is the search for novel instrumental effects, which became a preoccupation of critical and theoretical writings.

Berlioz was the leading figure in this quest, and his role was quickly

EXAMPLE 4-3. Three trombones, two horns added to traditional scoring. Weber, *Euryanthe* Overture, 1823.

Payne.

recognized in his own time. An anonymous reviewer in *AmZ* conceded in 1846 that Berlioz

> is reproached for requiring many instruments for his orchestra; but truly, he does not use them to create empty noise. We cannot deny that he also has made new discoveries in instrumental music, of which his predecessors had no idea,

EXAMPLE 4-4.   Doublings. Brahms, Symphony No. 1 in C Minor, Op. 68, 1876, first movement, introduction.

that through these discoveries he has brought forth the most wonderful, virtually indescribable effects, and that he makes use of the great number of rarely used instruments only to produce these effects.[21]

Two years later, Czerny made some practical suggestions for what he called "Unusual Combinations of Different Instruments":

We have hitherto spoken of the ordinary combinations which are employed in every orchestral composition. But in works where the composer can depend on having a large and numerous orchestra (in the Opera, for instance), he must also *occasionally* allow himself even an unusual employment or combination of certain instruments, for the attainment of particular effects. Thus, for example

EXAMPLE 4-5. Doublings. Brahms, Symphony No. 1 in C Minor, Op. 68, 1876, finale.

the Violoncelli may not only be divided into two, but even into three parts, so as to form with the double-basses a four-part harmony.

In like manner, three or four Horns may be combined, and which, either alone or in conjunction with the bassoons and other instruments, may perform various harmonized melodic phrases. Furthermore, as the two Violins may each be divided into two parts, we can by this means, in connection with the Viole (also divided), produce a six-part harmony in the upper parts. The three Trombones may likewise be employed alone, or in union with the other noisy instruments, for particular effects.

A single and powerfully sustained note by the Trumpet or Horn *solo*, is sometimes productive of great effect. Even the Drums may receive a Solo either in measured beats or in a roll, *piano* or *forte*.

The employment of such effects, or the creation of new ones, depends on the fancy and the talent of the composer; who has merely to observe, that the same unusual combinations are only to be introduced rarely and with moderation, and also that the ideas which give rise to them are deserving of such means, by reason of their beauty and originality: for, otherwise, the hearers must regret to see them expended on ordinary, mean, or ugly thoughts.[22]

By the third quarter of the century, a reaction to orchestral experimentation had set in. Verdi, the consummate Italian melodist, complained in an 1878 letter to Giulio Ricordi that "everything is supposed to be based on orchestration and harmony."[23] He also refers to what he called "German artistic methods" in which "fashion, love of innovation, and an alleged scientific spirit tempt us to surrender the native quality of our own art."[24]

By the end of the century a member of the British Royal Musical Association would sum up the conservative position:

The tricks on instruments are offensive, partly because they soon become formulae and mannerisms, and partly because in nine cases out of ten they are introduced to cover some passage which musically is bald and has nothing in it. Their name is legion, and they are sensationalisms of a bad kind.[25]

Though there is no doubt some substance to such complaints, in the best instances novel scoring not only enhances expressive melody and harmony, but can itself become a means of conveying musical ideas.

*Strings.* Paradoxically, some of the most effective uses Romantic composers made of the expanded string sections of the nineteenth-century orchestra involved the softest reaches of the dynamic spectrum. The passage from Bedřich Smetana's overture to *The Bartered Bride* (1866), quoted in Example 4-6 is effective only with substantial string sections, sections that can attack a fortissimo powerfully and then maintain a body of sound in the pianissimo. While the first impression is that of a fugato as the sections enter in imitation, the counterpoint soon dissolves into a harmonically static "beehive" buzzing suggestive less of Bach than of the impressionists or even the minimalists.

In the opening measures of the finale of Berlioz's *Symphonie fantastique*, Op. 14, (Ex. 4-7), the strings ring the changes on a single harmony, the diminished seventh chord.

Berlioz's prescription at the beginning of the symphony for at least fifteen first violins and a full string complement of at least fifty ensures a substantial core of sound, with five or more players on each strand, even among the threefold divisi of the violin sections. The eight upper parts form a shimmering curtain for the interpolations of cello, bass, and timpani.

EXAMPLE 4-6.   String instruments. Smetana, Overture to *The Bartered Bride*, 1866.

Reproduced with the kind permission of Boosey & Hawkes, Inc.

Reading down the left-hand side of the score, we can see the powerful arsenal of instrumentation waiting in the wings to join in the celebration of the Witches' Sabbath.

Verdi draws his listeners into the poignant mood of his opera *La Traviata* (1853), by the subtlest of means. Sixteen solo violins begin the Prelude (Ex. 4-8) in a high register, on a close-position B-minor harmony. With a purity of intonation not possible with massed strings, their sound has an inner intensity despite the *ppp* dynamics.

EXAMPLE 4-7.  Strings: innovative scoring. Berlioz, *Symphonie fantastique*, Op. 14, 1830, finale.

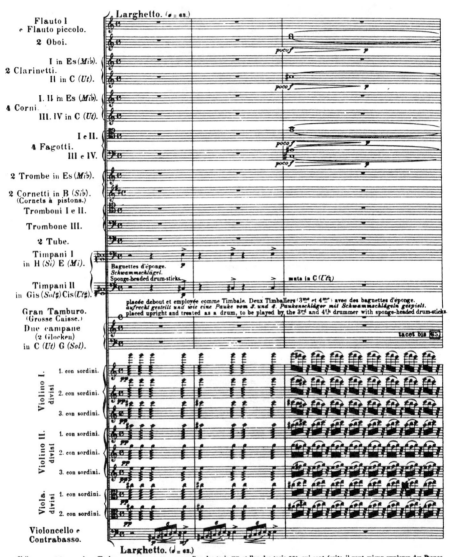

Used by permission of Dover Publications, Inc. Reproduced from: *Werke von Hector Berlioz*, Vol. 1, ed. Charles Malherbe and Felix Weingartner. Breitkopf & Härtel (1900–1910).

Harmony is a major actor in this slowly-moving pantomime. It winds its way circuitously through chromatic chords, eventually to prepare the tonic key of E major by measure 15. Only in retrospect is the opening chord understood as the dominant minor; for the listener attuned to key, this turn of harmonic events contributes to the tentative, elusive quality of the passage. Then, in a wide three-octave range, the harmonic action stabilizes in E major with the melody of Violetta's love song, "Amami, Alfredo," accompanied simply and resonantly. For the first time the entire string section is heard, creating a subtle textural contrast with the preceding solo violins.

EXAMPLE 4-8.   Eight solo violins. Verdi, Prelude to *La Traviata*, 1853.

EXAMPLE 4-8.  (*continued*)

Reproduced by arrangement with the publisher, Broude Bros., Ltd.

The listener becomes an active participant in this exquisite episode. In order to move with the pianississimo, the listener must virtually hold breath; silence must be assured so that no thread of sound be broken. Despite the richness of harmony and the fineness of texture, understatement is the magnet that draws the listener in preparation for the tragic story of Violetta and Alfredo.

Strings also create a rare mood in the second movement of Chopin's Concerto in E minor, Op. 11, (1830). In one of the few comments he made on scoring, Chopin wrote:

> The *Adagio* of my new concerto is in E major. It is not meant to create a powerful effect; it is rather a Romance, calm and melancholy, giving the impression of someone looking gently towards a spot which calls to mind a thousand happy memories. It is a kind of reverie in the moonlight on a beautiful spring evening. Hence the accompaniment is muted: that is, the violins are stifled by a sort of comb which fits over the strings and gives them a nasal and silvery tone.[26]

***Winds.*** In Classic music winds doubled string melodies, performed brief solo passages, participated in tutti, and from time to time recreated their indigenous roles in military bands and wind serenades. As their number, variety, and timbre expanded, however, wind instruments became an ever more important and independent part of the spectrum of nineteenth-century orchestral sound. Passages for winds alone became increasingly prominent.

The four chords for winds that open Mendelssohn's Overture to *A Midsummer Night's Dream*, Op. 21 (1830) (Ex. 4-9) have no precedent in the standard repertory as opening sounds in an orchestral piece. The military connotations of the wind and brass chords that open Mozart's *Magic Flute* Overture are entirely absent here. These high, sustained tones, held measurably longer than their whole-note notation by the fermatas, focus attention upon sound. Harmony adds its magic to this moment as it draws out a reverse cadential formula: I, V, minor IV, I. As a result we tend to hear each harmony as a color effect, much as Kreisler does in the Hoffmann tale cited in Chapter 1. Mendelssohn expands the effect progressively by adding instruments and

EXAMPLE 4-9. Wind harmonies. Mendelssohn, Overture to *A Midsummer Night's Dream*, Op. 21, 1830.

Mendelssohn, *A Midsummer Night's Dream*, Eulenburg Edition. Used by kind permission of European American Music Distributors Corporation, agent for Eulenburg Editions.

widening the spacing to a four-octave sonority for ten winds, while maintaining the firmness of each sonority by means of root positions. The effect is incantatory, as if to prepare us for the elfin scamper that gets under way during the body of the overture. Kurth describes these chords:

> The seventeen-year-old Mendelssohn knows how to evoke the romantic world of elfland with four woodwind chords that lead into the overture to *A Midsummer Night's Dream* by a simple cadence with major dominant and minor subdominant [harmony].[27]

At the opposite end of the wind-color spectrum is the sombre, lugubrious color of clarinets in their chalumeau register and bassoons at the opening of Tchaikovsky's *Romeo and Juliet* (Ex. 4-10).

Harmony contributes to the effect. Of the twenty-two chords in the first nine measures, only four are major triads; one is a half-diminished seventh chord (in measure 9) while the rest are minor triads circling around F-sharp minor, the home key. The dark minor sounds join with the lower resonant tones of the clarinets and bassoons to convey a sense of fateful events to come. The piece itself is a solemn march. With its lack of leading tones, it has a strong flavor of archaic ecclesiastic modality, to indicate the presence of Friar Lawrence in the story of the two lovers, Romeo and Juliet.

Verdi employs a similar scoring in the first *ombra* scene, Act III, of his opera *Macbeth* (revised version, 1865), when the ghosts of the eight kings return to haunt Macbeth (Ex. 4-11). Verdi comments on this moment in his letters:

> This little orchestra, two oboes, six clarinets in A, two bassoons, and a contra-bassoon, produces a strange, mysterious, almost quiescent body of sound which no other instruments could duplicate. It must be arranged under the stage, but under an open *trappe* wide enough to enable the sound to spread through the whole theater—only it must seem to come from a mysterious distance.[28]

EXAMPLE 4-10. Wind harmonies. Tchaikovsky, *Romeo and Juliet*, 1880, Overture-Fantasia.

EXAMPLE 4-11. Wind harmonies. Verdi, *Macbeth*, Act III, 1865.

Kalmus.

**Brass.** Some of the most spectacular improvements and refinements in orchestral instruments during the nineteenth century took place among the brass instruments. Improvements in the efficiency of valve construction led to two important developments: (1) trumpets and horns, the traditional orchestral brass instruments, became fully chromatic, and (2) a series of new instruments came into use. These included the saxhorns, standardized by Adolph Sax, circa 1845, in which features of various brass instruments were combined to achieve a greater homogeneity of tone, and the conical-bored Wagner tubas, invented by Richard Wagner for the *Ring* cycle and later used by Anton Bruckner (see Ex. 4-13) and Richard Strauss to bridge the gap between horns and tuba with a similar warm sound. These two developments altered the way brass instruments were used individually, as a separate choir, and in combination with other instruments. Also, nineteenth-century orchestras in France included the cornet, used by Berlioz in the *Symphonie fantastique* and the *Damnation of Faust,* by Bizet in *Carmen,* and by Rossini. While the cornet was rarely used as a soloist in the orchestra, it served a useful purpose for color and mass as it doubled the trumpet or joined lower wind or brass.

Unlike Examples 4-3 and 4-5, in which the brass provides a core of full, simple harmony against active figures in the winds and strings; the brass in Example 4-12 doubles the chromatic figures in winds and strings in an amplified two-part texture. The full participation of the brass creates a powerful piercing sound, with a sense of heavy, rather frantic movement.

EXAMPLE 4-12.   Chromatic melodic lines with tenfold brass amplification. Tchaikovsky, Symphony No. 4 in F Minor, Op. 36, 1878, first movement.

Kalmus.

Bruckner, in Example 4-13, uses a choir of five tubas—pairs of tenor and bass Wagner tubas with contrabass tuba—in a pseudovocal texture. The soft, "closed" quality of tuba sound creates an impression of remoteness as well as a homogeneity of which a mixed ensemble of horns and trombones would be incapable.

That mixed ensemble is used to good effect, however, in the fourth movement of Schumann's *Rhenish* Symphony (1850) (Ex. 4-14), where

EXAMPLE 4-13. Tubas and strings. Bruckner, Symphony No. 7 in E Major, 1884, second movement.

Bruckner, Symphony No. 7, Eulenburg Edition. Used by kind permission of European American Music Distributors Corporation, agent for Eulenburg Editions.

EXAMPLE 4-14.   Winds in motet style. Schumann, Symphony No. 3 in E-Flat Major, Op. 97, 1850, fourth movement.

Reproduced with the kind permission of Boosey & Hawkes, Inc.

Schumann depicts the grandeur of the Cologne Cathedral by taking up an archaic motet style. The traditional use of the trombones to imitate choral textures is made unmistakably Romantic by the addition of fully chromatic valve horns.[29]

In the finale of Berlioz's *Symphonie fantastique* (Ex. 4-15) the brass are again summoned to perform their ceremonial duties.

EXAMPLE 4-15.   Bells, bassoons, and brass. Berlioz, *Symphonie fantastique*, Op. 14, 1830, finale.

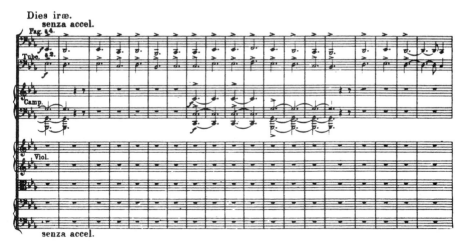

Here the reference is to plainsong, not motet, and the ritual of worship is diabolic, not holy. Berlioz created his air of parody by scoring, register, and rhythm. He assigned the *Dies irae* first to the low brass[30] and four bassoons in long, *alla breve* notes. The middle brass answer, doubling the melody in thirds and halving the time values. In turn the strings and winds mock the lower instruments in a high-pitched caricature of the plainsong melody, quickened again, this time to a saltarello-cum-tarantella manner. Against these antiphons, the seldom-heard large bells ring out tonic and dominant harmonies.

When Berlioz visited Berlin in 1843 he heard, as a guest of the Crown Prince of Prussia, a wind transcription of his overture to *Les francs-juges*, Op. 3 (1826), a work that had already many striking effects of instrumentation. Astonished by the "marvellous exactness" and "furious fire" with which the 320 wind players performed the work, he found the solemn pronouncement of the death sentence in the introduction

> startling, performed by fifteen bass trombones, eighteen or twenty tenor and alto trombones, twelve bass tubas, and a host of trumpets.[31]

Such physical amplification of sound prefigures the electronic amplification of our time; each is addressed to the same purpose—to create an overpowering effect of sound.

*Contrasts.*  Just as the large string band of the Romantic orchestra encouraged composers to subdivide the sections into smaller units, so the increased size of the full orchestra encouraged the division of musical material among small, highly contrasting instrumental combinations. These small groups, often at a considerable distance from one another owing to the sheer physical size of the orchestra, might engage in antiphonal dialogue or constantly

EXAMPLE 4-15.   (*continued*)

Used by permission of Dover Publications, Inc. Reproduced from: *Werke von Hector Berlioz*, Vol. 1, ed. Charles Malherbe and Felix Weingartner. Breitkopf & Härtel (1900–1910).

recombine to create a pointillistic effect. The Romantic preoccupation with programmatic references nourished the coloristic use of contrasting timbres.

The fairyland setting of Weber's opera *Oberon*, for instance, gives rise to the overture's give-and-take of suave fragments assigned to solo horn, strings, winds, and brass in a texture that allows each color to make a brief appearance and then recede (Ex. 4-16). Solo horn and muted strings alternate in single-measure units, then combine to form a single group opposite twittering flutes and clarinets. Distant martial brass and an elfin string figure alternate, again in single-measure units, then combine for two measures before giving way to an eloquent alto melody in the high cellos supported by

EXAMPLE 4-16.  Pointillistic contrasts. Weber, Overture to *Oberon*, 1825–26.

Adagio sostenuto.

| | |
|---|---|
| 2 Flauti. | |
| 2 Oboi. | |
| 2 Clarinetti in A. | |
| 2 Fagotti. | |
| 4 Corni  in D | Solo. *dolce* |
| in A | |
| 2 Trombe in D. | |
| Timpani in D.A. | |
| Tromboni. { Alto. Tenore. | |
| Basso. | |
| Violino I. | con Sordino. *p* con Sordino |
| Violino II. | *p* |
| Viola. | *pp* *pp* |
| Violoncello. | *pp* *pp* |
| Contrabasso. | |

EXAMPLE 4-16.    (continued)

chalumeau clarinets. The entire section of twenty-one measures remains within a dynamic range from *p* to *ppp*. A critic in *AmZ* (1827) acknowledged this introduction's special color qualities:

> Overture. Introduction: extremely delightful Adagio. The horn of Oberon begins alone; the string instruments follow with light, gently melancholy melody and harmony, sweetened several times by the short figures of the flutes and clarinets, which suggest the light mood of the spirits—until, following a

Weber, *Oberon*, Eulenburg Edition. Used by kind permission of European American Music Distributors Corporation, agent for Eulenburg Editions.

pause, the clear D major of the trumpets and horns rings out with a bright gallantry—and so forth: all of which had previously not existed.[32]

Instruments rarely featured in orchestral music, harp and tympani, are given salient roles in the two final examples in this chapter, from the *Symphonie fantastique*. Example 4-17 invokes the vision of a great ball as the chromatic harmonies slide upward. Each stage of the chromatic rise is given a glitter by the arpeggios of the two harps, cutting across the shimmering tremolos and concitatos of the upper strings, and answering the sweeping figures of the lower strings. All elements converge on the excitement that builds as the image of a gala emerges bright and grandiose on the cadential $^6_4$ of A major, a stunning bit of pictorialism given a sharp edge by the brilliance of the harps.

EXAMPLE 4-17. Strings and harps. Berlioz, *Symphonie fantastique*, Op. 14, 1830, second movement.

Used by permission of Dover Publications, Inc. Reproduced from: *Werke von Hector Berlioz*, Vol. 1, ed. Charles Malherbe and Felix Weingartner. Breitkopf & Härtel (1900–1910).

Berlioz brings the third movement of the *Symphonie fantastique* to a close with a subtle bit of musical pointillism (Ex. 4-18). Each section of the orchestra projects a characteristic tone color in the musical counterpart of a collage in which individual colors are placed in subtle juxtaposition rather than blended. The woodwind section is represented by the English horn, as it trails off in the last notes of the *ranz des vaches*. The percussion is represented by a unique sonority, three timpani sounding on a $^6_3$ chord of F-minor, A flat, C, F. The brass is represented by the single sustained tone of the horn. The strings enter on the horn's C, a soft yet massive sound, then move to short, cadential F-major chords but leave the fifth of the chord, C, to the horn. The distant horn is the last sound we hear in the movement, undermining the tonic chord's sense of resolution. The separation of players, the separation of phrases by silence, and the tonal separation of the F-minor timpani and the F-major strings, all make tangible the program's "distant sound of thunder— loneliness—silence." Although phrasing and harmony play their parts, the passage's affective content is expressed primarily through its scoring. It is this ability to use the colors of the nineteenth-century orchestra to convey meaning directly that distinguishes Romantic composers such as Berlioz from their predecessors.

Finally, the Romantic orchestra, thanks to its physical setup, added a significant new component to the climate of sound created by its wide range of pitch and its rich palette of tone colors. That component was *space*, encompassing dimensions of breadth and depth. The very size of the orchestra, its deployment on a larger stage than that of its eighteenth-century predecessor, the larger theaters and the greater number of listeners—these offered many possibilities for the effective play of sound emerging from left

EXAMPLE 4-18.   Minimal texture. Berlioz, *Symphonie fantastique*, Op. 14, 1830, third movement.

Used by permission of Dover Publications, Inc. Reproduced from: *Werke von Hector Berlioz*, Vol. 1, ed. Charles Malherbe and Felix Weingartner. Breitkopf & Härtel (1900–1910).

or right, from foreground or background. This spatial dimension had dramatic and pictorial potential; it lent itself particularly well to music with programmatic implications—Berlioz's *Symphonie fantastique*, Mendelssohn's Overture to *A Midsummer Night's Dream*, Weber's Overture to *Oberon* (see Examples 4-7, 4-9, 4-16).

Riemann, looking back upon the Romantic era from 1895, says:

> The art of instrumentation in the modern sense is not that of the proper use of the instruments in respect to their range and technique, but in the proper use of the characteristic tone colors, indeed of the variety of sounds among the registers of these instruments.[33]

Riemann's comments echo those of Becker, in 1840, as he compares the arts of painting and music. Becker says:

> Color itself is represented in music by instrumentation, and the secrets of the palette are like those of scoring [Instrumentation]. Just as the mixing of colors promotes manifold effects and the finest nuancing, so does the combination of individual instruments [provide] an endless variety of effects. . . . If I were to compare individual instruments to individual colors, I would liken the flute to violet, the clarinet to orange-yellow, the string instruments to blue, the trumpets to fiery red, the trombones to purple, the piccolo to sulphur-yellow.[34]

While Becker's comparisons may be subjective and fanciful, the very notion of comparing scoring to color has a validity for nineteenth-century instrumentation, a comparison more vivid and compelling than would have been the case a century earlier.

CHAPTER FIVE

# *Chamber Music: Texture and Sound*

Chamber music reached its apogee in the string quartets of Haydn, Mozart, and Beethoven. Conditions in the later eighteenth century were optimum for the attainment of this level of excellence. String instruments had been refined to very nearly their present degree of tone quality, flexibility, capacity to blend, and range. The texture of the string quartet was capable of fullness and at the same time of buoyancy; the delight of composer, performer, and listener was the active give-and-take of figures among the four instruments. Stylistically, the string quartet had a polished, beautifully meshed language with which to work, firm in its harmonic and rhythmic underpinnings yet amazingly flexible in the combinations it could produce. It drew continually from the comic and galant genres—dance, opera buffa, and low styles— deploying them skillfully with controls drawn from the serious styles— learned and legato. Indeed, chamber music of the eighteenth century represented the textural paradigm for all instrumental music of that era. The interplay of solo and tutti in the eighteenth-century concerto and symphony show the lightness, even the transparency of chamber-music textures (see Ex. 4-1).

In the nineteenth century this relationship reversed. Piano and orchestra established a heavier norm for sound and texture. Tilmouth, in the *New Grove Dictionary,* comments upon this change:

> The vivid colours and great contrasts of timbre and dynamics sought by the Romantics could not easily be achieved in the context of conventional chamber music forms and arch-Romantics like Liszt and Wagner scarcely entered the field.[1]

One result of this shift of emphasis was a less prominent position for chamber music among the concerns of composers in the nineteenth century. Some important works were produced—the quartets of Brahms, Schumann, and Schubert, some quintets, sextets, and such—but these represented a smaller fraction of the total output of these composers than was the case with most eighteenth-century composers. Moreover, the texture of Romantic chamber music tended to become richer and fuller, as if the ensemble were trying to achieve the weightiness of pianistic or orchestral sound. Significantly, more than half of the chamber music works of Schumann and Brahms, the most important Romantic composers in this genre, include piano, treated idiomatically in the Romantic fashion (see Ex. 5-12).

Other composers—Chopin, Liszt, Berlioz, Verdi, Wagner, Bruckner, Mahler—produced little or nothing at all in the field of chamber music, especially for the elite ensemble, the string quartet.

Chamber music received little attention in nineteenth-century manuals of music theory, compared to the extensive coverage given piano and orchestral textures. Marx, in 1851, dispatched various chamber ensembles (trios, quartets, quintets, etc.) in a few short paragraphs. He extolled ensembles of strings alone as the most tasteful of all combinations because they are composed of instruments of similar construction, able to blend perfectly and share idiomatic figures.[2]

Czerny's *School of Practical Composition* (1848) quotes excerpts from quartets by Haydn, Mozart, Beethoven, and only one contemporary, George Onslow. The first three

> have alike exerted all the powers of their genius in *this* form; and the numerous quartetts of these masters, which alone would secure their immortality, remain imperishable models for all time.[3]

A unique approach to the study of composition is taken in the first volume of Lobe's *Lehrbuch* (1858), which presents the materials of composition—harmony, meter, part writing, melody, form—solely in the context of the string quartet, with special emphasis on the quartets of Beethoven. One section, pages 78–101, quotes seventy-five examples taken from string quartets by Haydn, Mozart, Beethoven, Mendelssohn, and Schumann, though with no specific comments on texture. Lobe recommends to the student to imitate the layouts illustrated, adding personal and original touches where they might be effective.

Critical and theoretical evidence makes it clear that the nineteenth century's orientation to chamber music was retrospective. The high esteem in which chamber music was held was based on an admiration for the works of

Haydn, Mozart, and Beethoven, which retained a prominent position in the chamber music repertoire. The index of the *AmZ* for 1829–48 lists more than three hundred performances of the quartets of Haydn and the quartets and quintets of Mozart and Beethoven.[4]

Many different ensembles are subsumed under the general category of chamber music. They may involve from two to twelve or more performers, one to a part. In this chapter examples of chamber music for strings, for winds, and for piano with strings are cited to illustrate two characteristic trends: (1) a retrospective orientation as in the scoring of Classic chamber music, that is, an emphasis on the play of figures in a light texture, and (2) the influence of the sound climate of Romantic music to produce more massive color values.

## *Chamber Music for Strings*

The effect of the new climate of sound in Romantic chamber music is especially evident in larger ensembles—quartets, quintets, sextets, and octets. Examples 5-1 through 5-8 illustrate various aspects of traditional and innovative scoring in string chamber music of the nineteenth century.

Hugo Wolf's *Italian Serenade* (1887) is remarkable for the lightness and deftness of its part writing, the kind we associate with Classic string quartet texture (Ex. 5-1).

Sustained notes and rests make room for the concise figures, suggestive of a saltarello, to pass among the four instruments in much the way they would in a string quartet by Haydn. Measures 82–95 exemplify this quicksilver-like interplay.

Only the flickering harmonic nuances, such as the passing clash of F natural and F sharp in measure 77, which color the light-hearted play of figure and rhythm with a poignancy that is decorative rather than structural, intimate that this work appeared at the end of the Romantic era.

In the coda of the second movement of his Quartet in A major, Op. 41, no. 3 (1842) (Ex. 5-2), Schumann balances fullness of sound with lightness of texture; broad range with gentle dynamics. This section shows the influence of piano and orchestral textures in a Romantic vein. The suaveness of the traditional quartet sound is maintained throughout, but the widely-spaced scoring, the unusual pairing of outer voices versus inner voices and the unbroken flow of texture and rhythm suggest that the quartet is acting as a tiny orchestra, an orchestra that, in turn, seems to transcribe a typical Romantic piano texture of broadly scaled melody and rustling accompaniment. Harmony contributes to the coloristic effect; following the *agitato* mood that pervades the principal section of this movement the F-sharp major and E-flat major of Example 5-2 alternate to provide a calming, smoothing effect. Just before the close, F-sharp major is darkened momentarily by the minor third, A. The fading close itself is a typically Romantic gesture.

EXAMPLE 5-1. Traditional quartet texture. Wolf, *Italian Serenade*, 1887.

Wolf, *Italian Serenade*, Eulenburg Edition. Used by kind permission of European American Music Distributors Corporation, agent for Eulenburg Editions.

EXAMPLE 5-2. Coloristic scoring. Schumann, Quartet in A Major, Op. 41, No. 3, 1842, second movement.

Payne.

Examples 5-3 and 5-4, from the Double Quartet in D Minor (1823), of Ludwig Spohr, illustrate at once a continuation and negation of Classic textural values. Spohr is generally thought to be a link between Classic and Romantic styles. In his chamber music he is generally retrospective, both in the layout of parts and in the concentration upon chamber-music genres in his oeuvre. In his concertos and operas, he displays Romantic features— virtuoso tours de force and striking harmonic gestures. The melodic material and distribution of voices is typically Classic: the opening figure (Ex. 5-3) takes up the traditional "pathetic" motive heard often in fantasias, recitatives, and works of high and serious import in the eighteenth century.[5] This figure is thoroughly worked over, set in contrast against short, well-turned motives, typical of Classic declamation. But the massive sound of eight string instruments, which approaches that of a string orchestra, jeopardizes the interplay of voices that characterizes Classic chamber music. Spohr consistently skirts this danger by means of antiphonal layouts (Ex. 5-4). Much of the time we hear only one quartet. Still, this division itself creates a scope for sound that did not exist for the Classic string quartet; it promotes a strategic back-and-forth, either within an eight-instrument group or between two separate quartets. While usually less than eight instruments are playing, when the antiphonies link we hear, at moments, a mass of sound far beyond that which the string quartet can produce (see measure 6 of Ex. 5-3). Thus, the presence of a rich, sonorous body is manifested as an element in the climate of sound, even though it sparingly comes to the fore.

Spohr designated this work as a double quartet, not an octet. The deft part-writing, the light scoring, and the antiphonal layouts justify the unusual title. This work retains the integrity of the quartet units and keeps the potentially rich sound of eight string instruments under strict control. Paradoxically, in his string quartets, Spohr sometimes masses sounds in a melody-accompaniment texture that is much more colorful than we can hear in this double quartet.

Mendelssohn's Octet in E-flat Major, Op. 20 (1830), scored for the same eight instruments, is a true octet, not a double quartet. The violins, violas, and violoncellos are each treated as a group within their own range and action, not aligned into two four-part (quartet) groups (see Examples 5-5 and 5-6).

A comparison of the opening measures of the Spohr Double Quartet and the Mendelssohn Octet, Example 5-5, puts salient features of each work into sharp relief. Spohr begins with an arresting unison figure, compressed into one octave, with shifting harmonies, intense sound, and incisive rhythms. Mendelssohn, on the other hand, expands his sound, spread-eagling his E-flat-major chord over three octaves. He fills in every interstice within the alto and tenor range with rippling rhythmic action embodied in a variety of patterns. The result is a vibrant, restless personification of the E-flat harmony, given an edge by the arpeggiated principal theme. The theme itself seems mainly to give the underlying harmony a special sparkle, rather than to have the motivic importance that Spohr assigns to his principal theme. Added

EXAMPLE 5-3.    Varieties of scoring. Spohr, Double Quartet in D Minor, 1823, first movement.

Payne.

touches of color in the theme are the gaps in the arpeggios, between the G and the E flat, and the B flat and the G, respectively, that give a hint of yodel to the melody. This passage is unique in string chamber music; it embodies to the fullest the capacity of chamber-music strings to produce a sound that matches the nineteenth-century piano and orchestra in richness and fullness. When Mendelssohn divides his ensemble into smaller units, he assigns material to these units that retains something of the rich color of the tutti. Example 5-6 illustrates this procedure; parallel thirds and sixths, parallel sixth chords, suave contrary motions—these form vibrant bands of Romantic

EXAMPLE 5-4.    Separation of groups. Spohr, Double Quartet in D Minor, 1823, finale.

Payne.

color, the full spectrum of the entire ensemble. The interplay of figures typical of Classic chamber music is here given a nuance of color and texture that has a genuine nineteenth-century Romantic quality.

Another work that expands upon the sound of the traditional quartet is Schubert's Quintet in C Major, Op. 163 (1828). Most quintets add a viola to the usual quartet complement; Schubert adds an additional cello, which, as

EXAMPLE 5-5.  Fullness of texture. Mendelssohn, Octet in E-Flat Major, Op. 20, 1830, first movement.

Mendelssohn, Octet, Eulenburg Edition. Used by kind permission of European American Music Distributors Corporation, agent for Eulenburg Editions.

EXAMPLE 5-6.   Doublings. Mendelssohn, Octet in E-Flat Major, Op. 20, 1830, first
movement.

Mendelssohn, Octet, Eulenburg Edition. Used by kind permission of European
American Music Distributors Corporation, agent for Eulenburg Editions.

an alternating solo voice at times with the first violin, projects a richer, fuller, more intense quality of sound on its higher strings than would a viola. In the full ensemble, the three lower instruments produce a particularly resonant, massive sound in their lower registers. Schubert's choice of an additional violoncello was critical for the expressive and, as Chapters 10 and 13 indicate, the structural aspects of this work.

The first six measures (Ex. 5-7) set the qualities of tone we hear in different arrangements throughout the work. The Tourte bow, with its concave camber, permits the strings to build a gradual crescendo over two measures, upbow, then subside gradually, downbow, in a composed *messa di voce*. The vibrant, close-position C-major chord conveys an intense, immediate, yet unspecified expressive content, a poignant feeling that compels the participation of the listener.

A similar close-position major harmony occurs in Example 5-8. The E-major chord, set in a resonant "hunting horn" register, has the sweet, vibrant sound characteristic of the major triad in second inversion. Above and below this stream of sound is room for Schubert to add touches of color in the hocket-like alternation of Violin I and Violoncello II. Whereas the previous example uses a dynamic swell and ebb to animate the deliberate harmonic movement, here Schubert employs pointillistic accompaniment figures for the same purpose. Throughout the work elaborate accompanying figures, powerful massing of forces, juxtapositions of registers, incisive rhythmic profiles, bold tangents, even strategic silences are among the means Schubert employs to create his climate of sound.

EXAMPLE 5-7. *Messa di voce.* Schubert, Quintet in C Major, Op. 163, 1828, first movement.

Used by permission of Dover Publications, Inc. Reproduced from: *Franz Schubert's Werke*, Breitkopf & Härtel, Series 4, 1890, ed. Eusebius Mandyczewski.

EXAMPLE 5-8.   Pointillism. Schubert, Quintet in C Major, Op. 163, 1828, second movement.

Used by permission of Dover Publications, Inc. Reproduced from: *Franz Schubert's Werke*, Breitkopf & Härtel, Series 4, 1890, ed. Eusebius Mandyczewski.

A final example of string chamber music texture shows Brahms building a massive flow of compact sound on the G-major triad, emulating the upper strings of an orchestra (Ex. 5-9). The measured tremolo of the violins and violas rapidly exchange the notes of the triad and emphasize the third, creating an especially intense vibrancy.

The foregoing examples of Romantic chamber music for strings bespeak the individualism that characterizes the expressive attitudes of that era. At the same time, the limitations of string chamber music with respect to breadth of gesture, intensity and variety of tone color did not attract Romantic composers so strongly as did other genres with their more powerful, more flamboyant possibilities.

## Chamber Music for Winds

Chamber music for groups of winds, alone or in combination with strings, developed a small repertory. This music, like its eighteenth-century counterparts, has the flavor of the serenade, of outdoor music, made very effective by the improved mechanisms of nineteenth-century wind instruments—range, intonation, tone color, and efficiency of operation.

EXAMPLE 5-9. Orchestral effect in chamber music. Brahms, Quintet in G Major, Op. 111, 1891, first movement.

Textures reflect the procedures of the earlier *Harmoniemusik.* Compact, powerful tuttis, parallel thirds, transparent melody-accompaniment textures —these frame march, song, and popular dance topics. The improved instruments of the nineteenth century, give a brightness and fullness to familiar devices.

In the very limited repertoire of nineteenth-century wind ensemble music, the Serenade in D minor, Op. 44, by Antonin Dvořák stands out with its effective use of textures and solo instruments.[6] Dvořák presents the wind ensemble as a tutti, a solid wind-band sound in a vigorous march rhythm (Ex. 5-10). While the chordal layout that supports the tune has a traditional look, its sound places the music in the nineteenth century, thanks to the doublings of winds, the three horns, and the optional contrabassoon; these add up to a much fuller, more powerful sound than in the wind ensembles of the eighteenth century, except for Mozart's Serenade in B-flat major, K. 361 for 13 winds.

In other instances (Ex. 5-11), Dvořák pits individual instruments against one another with smooth shifts of color and texture against a suave, gently pulsating background. This passage has the quality of an arioso, shared by several soloists. Again, the fuller complement of instruments provides opportunities for the play of color in shifting groups within the ensemble.

## *Chamber Music for Piano and Strings*

Works for piano and strings constitute a significant part of the Romantic chamber music repertoire. In these works the piano, with its increased scope,

EXAMPLE 5-10.  Wind ensemble. Dvořák, Serenade in D Minor, Op. 44, 1879, first movement.

Dvořák, Serenade in D Minor, Eulenburg Edition. Used by kind permission of European American Music Distributors Corporation, agent for Eulenburg Editions.

played a different role than it did in Classic chamber music. Earlier, although the keyboard instrument presided, it invited string instruments to join the action, either as *ad libitum* or *obbligato* participants. At times the fortepiano became a soloist, backed up by a tiny orchestra; at other times, it took part in a give-and-take or provided a discreet accompaniment. Whatever the texture, the spirit of the ensemble was that of chamber music—light and active. In Romantic chamber music, the expanded capabilities of the piano put a heavy burden on the participating strings. The piano, itself an orchestra in effect, challenges the string instruments to match it in weight and intensity of sound. Hence, we hear often, in the piano chamber music of Schumann and Brahms, for instance, a driving, striving effect. An effort to extract as much sound as possible from the strings is evident in order to match the mass of piano sound.

This potential for fuller, more powerful sound in chamber music is realized in the Trio in B Major, Op. 8 (1889), by Brahms (Ex. 5-12). Against the piano's driving, virtuoso figuration, punctuated by heavy chords, the strings "dig in" with rhythmic unisons of quarter and half notes, exploiting the maximum tone-producing capacities of the Tourte-style bow. A big, penetrating sound is created, as if the ensemble were trying to become an orchestra. The light-handed give-and-take of earlier chamber music is abandoned. Much Romantic chamber music with piano reaches similarly for maximum sonority, using massed effects and drawing lines as broadly as possible.

EXAMPLE 5-11.   Wind ensemble textures. Dvořák, Serenade in D Minor, Op. 44, 1879, second movement.

Dvořák, Serenade in D Minor, Eulenburg Edition. Used by kind permission of European American Music Distributors Corporation, agent for Eulenburg Editions.

EXAMPLE 5-12. Piano and strings. Brahms, Trio in B Major, Op. 8, 1889, first movement.

Homer Ulrich comments in a similar vein concerning the role of the piano in Schumann's Quintet in E-flat Major, Op. 44 (1841):

> In many evaluations of this quintet one finds references to its orchestral quality, to the dominance of the piano, and to other factors which are taken to be defects. It is true that a large number of sonorous doublings occur and that the piano part is worked out in fuller detail than are string parts. But a criticism that considers the piano as merely *one* of five equal instruments is wide of the mark. As a matter of fact, the piano opposes, or balances, or contrasts with the quartet as a unit; it represents not one fifth but one half of the entire tonal body. From this point of view, the quintet takes its high place among true chamber-music works and provides a sonority and effectiveness unmatched in the earlier literature.[7]

Chamber music in the Romantic era was in an equivocal position. Elevated to a status of great dignity above its mid-eighteenth-century role as house music, it had become music for connoisseurs. Yet its prestige, ironically, came from its Classic repertoire, and its influence in the nineteenth century was much less than it had been in Baroque and Classic music. Where before it had served as a model for the play of texture and topic in other genres, it now tended to imitate the more powerful piano and orchestra.

Still, the number of important Romantic chamber works, though relatively small, shows that the medium was congenial to some composers—challenging in formulation, serious in import. Music would have to wait until the nineteenth century had run much of its course, until the rich climate of sound had begun to pall, before chamber music textures would again become central in the compositional process. Paradoxically, it was Gustav Mahler, a composer of no significant chamber music, who would become a pivotal figure in the trend toward chamber music textures. Much of his orchestral music, though mammoth in scope, has the transparency, the play of figure, the generally high tessitura, and the sharply etched polarity between treble and bass that characterize eighteenth-century chamber music.

# CHAPTER SIX

# *Harmonic Color*

The increased capacities of nineteenth-century instruments were used by Romantic composers to explore and expand the world of harmonic color. Already in the preceding chapters harmony has figured in the discussion of instrumental effects.[1] The coloristic use of harmony had little to do with traditional notions of individual key characteristics. Calling that tradition a "chimera" Richard Wagner, in 1852, noted the interdependence of key and timbre in a letter to Theodore Uhlig:

> On the other hand, [referring to what he calls a 'chimera', that is, the traditional tendency to assign individual characteristics to keys], instruments and the human voice when singing words impart individual character to keys and tones; thus the individuality of key (E major or E-flat major) is very different when sounded on a violin or a wind instrument and it is an uncritical superficiality to regard the key in its own right without considering its instrumental setting, or to use the instrument solely for its own sake.[2]

The effects of color achieved in Romantic harmony were produced with the traditional chord forms codified in the eighteenth century—triads and seventh chords—along with the familiar nonchord tones—suspensions, appoggiaturas, and other tones of figuration. In eighteenth-century music, harmony was marshaled almost entirely to embodiments of key through cadential action; rarely was the actual color of a chord an object of expression or affective stance. In nineteenth-century music, the spacing and register of a chord and the timbre of the instrument or instruments producing the sound often became matters of immediate, compelling attention. The urgency of cadential action, a fundamental characteristic of eighteenth-century harmonic rhetoric, was often relaxed in favor of the striking, delectable, piquant, overpowering, expansive effects that harmonic color could produce with the instrumentarium of the nineteenth century. This trend was deplored by some, as an item in *NZM* (1841) indicates:

> You find the difference between the modern and the earlier (so-called Classic music) principally in this decline of harmonic usage. Yes, in the unhealthy, weak and overladen growth of harmony. . . [3]

In this chapter three characteristic treatments of harmony in Romantic music are examined: (1) the amplification of a single chord by duration and scoring; (2) harmonic progressions that exploit the color values of their chords; and (3) modal harmony. This approach differs from extant treatments of Romantic harmony in texts, analyses, and critical studies.[4] Essentially, such works have a historical point of view; they are based on eighteenth-century codifications of harmony—key plans, chord identity, cadences and other typical progressions, voice leading—with consideration for the richer, more elliptical procedures of the Romantic era. Rarely is there any reference to the color of a chord as a significant factor in the compositional process or as a contribution to the affective stance of a piece.

While most of the examples in this chapter embody harmonic color in the form of chords, nevertheless, melody, when it shows clear harmonic configurations, can project color values effectively, as in Examples 6-21, 22, and 26, as well as in the overture *La grande pâque russe*, Op. 36 (1888) by Nicolai Rimsky-Korsakoff (see p. 127).

## Amplification: Duration and Scoring

The effect of a single tone or chord rests in part on the length of time it is heard, its *duration*. Duration can incorporate an agogic harmonic accent, an emphasis of length. As a tone or chord is amplified by being sustained, or elaborated by figuration, it focuses attention on itself; it establishes a period of time within which an expressive stance can be suggested.

Romantic music often exploits this capacity of harmony to project an affective stance or to create a mood through extended duration. A single harmony can be sustained to such length that its function within an ongoing progression recedes and attention is directed to the quality of sound as the focus of expression. Within the duration of a single harmony three main processes can characterize and animate the sound: (1) *tessitura*, or pitch levels; (2) *texture*, the action and timbre of the component voices or parts; and (3) *contour*, the shape outlined by the passage throughout its duration—rise and fall of tessitura, changes of tone color, changes in dynamics. These three processes can be used as criteria to evaluate the effect of harmonies that have substantial duration.

Examples 6-1 through 6-4 illustrate ways in which a single harmony can be drawn out for telling effect. Example 6-1, the opening measures of Wagner's Prelude to *Lohengrin* (1845–48), distributes the sound of the A-major triad among three groups—strings, winds, and solo violins, all set in a high register. The passage remains constant in pitch throughout the first five measures of the Lento tempo, but the section takes on contour as the three groups enter and drop out by overlapping, so that subtle changes of tone color are produced every half measure, as if the component elements were engaging in a hocket procedure. Gentle rises and falls in dynamics accompany these entries and exits in the manner of the *messa di voce* of vocal music. The entire passage, with its sustained A major, fixes, virtually impales the listener's attention on an ambience of quietness, remoteness, mystery, a compelling embodiment of the notion of the Holy Grail that is a central motif in the music drama.

Wagner was a master at deploying broadly scaled harmonies. The most spectacular example of this skill is the Prelude to *Das Rheingold* (1851–54). To symbolize the rise of the Rhine from its source to its fullest flow, Wagner builds a gigantic contour on an E-flat major harmony over a length of 136 measures. The contour begins with the lowermost E flats of which the orchestra is capable, sounded in notes that are four measures of $\frac{6}{8}$ in length. Gradual rise in pitch, quickening of note values, eventual increase in dynamics, fullness of harmony—these set the gigantic time scale on which the four great segments of the *Ring* cycle will carry out their mythic tale. The resonance of Wagner's orchestra, especially the multiple winds and brass, including the tubas, makes of the E-flat major harmony a full, expressive gesture that can hold the listener spellbound.

Sustaining not the tonic but the minor dominant, Chopin's Prelude in A Minor, Op. 28, No. 2 (1838), opens off-center harmonically, with the sound of the E-minor triad maintained for three measures of Lento time (Ex. 6-2). The low register, odd arpeggiation, and prominent A-sharp neighbor tone contribute to the eccentric mood. Only after G-major and B-minor triads do we finally reach A minor. The piece thus opens in medias res, perhaps after a hypothetical beginning in A minor. The texture is standard melody and accompaniment, but the curtain takes over the principal declamatory interest from the slow-moving melody and thus validates the out-of-key beginning by its sheer effect of sound.

Unlike Chopin's oblique approach, Schubert addresses the key of A minor directly at the beginning of his Quartet No. 15 in A Minor, Op. 29 (1824) (Ex. 6-3). Schubert's statement is frankly lyric: gentle, vibrant, in the manner of a musette. The violoncello and viola maintain a drone on the open fifth of the tonic triad while the second violin undulates as a stylized chanter (the melody element in a musette style). Schubert spins out the A-minor sound through the first four measures, but articulates rhythm and texture with

EXAMPLE 6-1.   Chord amplification by sustained tones. Wagner, Prelude to *Lohengrin*, 1845–48.

sharply defined separations, a collage of shapes and motions. We hear three different rhythmic "feet"—in the violoncello and viola, in the second violin, and, in the fourth measure, in the first violin. Texturally, the sound is clearly layered on low, middle, and high registers. These first four measures set a lyric affective stance that emanates from the sound of A minor, a stance that will control all the motions of the quartet to follow. Like the Chopin prelude, from which it differs in terms of expression, direction, and coherence, the quartet uses a single spun-out sound to set a mood, in providing an undulating curtain for its stylized, songlike melodies.

Extended duration of a single harmony can focus attention on color at any time in a movement. Generally, the most striking effects take place at beginnings and endings, when moods are set or prolonged. In Example 6-4, the final five measures of the second movement of the Symphony No. 1 by Brahms extend the tonic harmony, E major, in luminous, widely spaced chords. Within the body of the E-major harmony, various currents sustain, reinforce, and stir the sound. At first, the dotted half notes of the trumpets and bassoons, the broad hemiolas of the flutes, oboes, and horns, the overlapping fragments of arpeggio in the strings, and the triplet pulses in the timpani intertwine to create an inner life within the chord; then the final three measures still the inner motion and allow the sound to float as if transfixed. This broad leveling-off balances and brings to rest the rich chromaticisms that pervade the movement.[5]

A final example illustrates the use of a key rather than a single harmony as an embodiment of harmonic color. The chorus of Hebrew slaves from the third act of Verdi's *Nabucco* (1841) is set in F-sharp major, simply and strophically. The chorus sings the arpeggiated melody in unison, accompanied by orchestral instruments on the tune, supported by a slow, arpeggiated accompaniment. F-sharp major, in the context is a strange and wonderful sound, remote from the other keys of the opera, employed (Ex. 6-5). Moreover, the broadly scaled, symmetrical melody itself lyric tune, stands

EXAMPLE 6-2.   Chord amplification by figuration. Chopin, Prelude in A Minor, Op. 28, No. 2, 1838.

Chopin, *Preludes*, copyright © G. Schirmer, Inc. Used by permission.

out against the agitated declamation that runs through most of the opera. The ambience of F-sharp major and its dominant, C-sharp major, forms an episode of tone color set apart as a single expressive value of distance and nostalgia against the turbulent emotions that surround it. The key of the chorus functions within the opera much as a single sustained harmony might within a single movement.

Given the resources of the improved keyboard and expanded orchestra, the composers of the Romantic period turned quite often to a process of composition which might be called "composing through a sound." A given harmony is extended, elaborated texturally, rhythmically, and melodically so that it creates an ambience. The fullness and richness of tone color of individual instruments or of groups provides a value of expression that emanates from the sound itself, quickened by the inner action within the sound complex.

EXAMPLE 6-3. Chord amplification by figuration. Schubert, Quartet in A Minor, 1824, first movement.

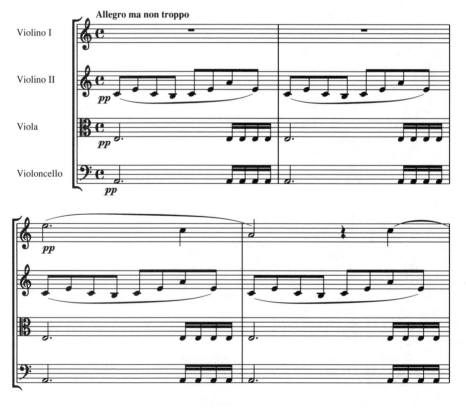

Franz Schubert's *Werke*, Series 5, (1890), ed. Eusebius Mandyczewski and Joseph Hellmesberger, Breitkopf & Härtel. Used by permission.

EXAMPLE 6-4. Varied textures on one harmony. Brahms, Symphony No. 1 in C Minor, Op. 68, 1876, second movement.

Copyright © 1974 Dover Publications. Used by permission. Reproduced from Johannes Brahms, *Sämtliche Werke*, Vol. 1, ed. Hans Gal. Breitkopf & Härtel (n.d.).

EXAMPLE 6-5. Key as harmonic color. Verdi, *Nabucco*, 1841, Act III, "Va pensiero."

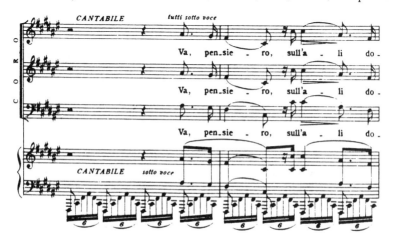

EXAMPLE 6-5.  (*continued*)

Ricordi.

# Harmonic Progressions

In each of the preceding examples, duration and scoring amplify the color value of an individual triad (or key, in the Verdi excerpt). The same devices may be applied to a series of harmonies, setting each chord into high coloristic relief against its adjacent chords, especially when the rate of chord change is deliberate, even slow. All the progressions discussed below operate within a traditional framework of key and are directed to the embodiment of their keys, either clearly or by implication. Still, the emphasis placed on their immediate color impression reduces the urgency of the harmonic drive and undermines the forward propulsion of harmonic progression.

Two general types of progression are considered here: (1) *tangential harmonies,* involving triads related by tritone or third, chromatic bass lines, and interchange of mode, and (2) *tritone harmonies,* progressions in which each chord contains a tritone.

## Tangential Harmonies

As we have seen, the rich timbres of nineteenth-century instruments give a vibrance to a sustained chord, intensifying its harmonic color. When such a chord is followed by another that has a strikingly different tone color, the two chords sharpen each other's effect by a process of relief. Likewise, a distant harmonic relationship tends to isolate each chord as an independent sound object.

*Tritone Relationships.* Example 6-6a, from the fourth movement of the *Symphonie fantastique,* the "March to the Scaffold," is one of the most arresting progressions in the entire Romantic literature. Berlioz sets D-flat major in the winds and brass against G minor, a tritone apart, in the strings. The wide separation of groups and pitches matches the separation of the two triads. The alternation of D flat and G minor is fourfold, compressed by a stretto and accompanied by diminuendo. (Actually, the D-flat major to G minor progression has some elements of a cadential formula; two members of the D-flat major triad can sideslip by half step to members of the G minor triad, in the manner of leading tones, see Ex. 6-6b). Berlioz's separation of the two harmonies by scoring and register obscures any sense of voice-leading and projects the angularity of the progression. Eventually, the harmony converges on a traditional dominant-to-tonic, but not until other harmonic juxtapositions intervene. The entire passage brings the grotesquerie of this movement to a frenzied culmination, a pictorialization of a procession to an execution.[6]

The tritone relationship F major to B major, which Liszt uses for the final harmonic gesture in his Sonata in B Minor, stands at the opposite end of the expressive spectrum from Berlioz's tritone juxtaposition (see Ex. 3-11). Berlioz emphasizes the grotesque disjunction of the two chords, one major and the other minor, by scoring contrasts and remoteness in pitch; doom and the diabolic are symbolized. Liszt's major triads, in contrast, have a strangely beautiful, floating effect as the F-major triad melts into the B major, the progression set in the high register of the piano. The leading-tone motion of F to F sharp and C to B simulates a cadence. These sounds close the turbulent course of the sonata in a mood of transfiguration, perhaps of redemption, a final incantation in the Romantic vein of Wagner and Richard Strauss. (A similar tritone juxtaposition is quoted in Ex. 6-14).

EXAMPLE 6-6.   Tritone progression.

a. Berlioz, *Symphonie fantastique*, 1830, fourth movement, "March to the Scaffold."

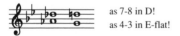

Used by permission of Dover Publications, Inc. Reproduced from: *Werke von Hector Berlioz*, Vol. 1, ed. Charles Malherbe and Felix Weingartner. Breitkopf & Härtel (1900–1910).

b. Sideslip cadential formula.

as 7-8 in D!
as 4-3 in E-flat!

A striking tritone relationship occurs in the "Coronation Scene" from Modeste Mussorgsky's *Boris Godunov* (1868–69). Here the tritone C–F sharp/G flat is a common element that joins two dominant seventh chords whose roots lie a tritone apart A-flat major and D major (Ex. 6-7). Each member of the linking tritone becomes alternately third and seventh of a dominant-seventh-type chord, as perfect fourths and perfect fifths alternate. The progression, reiterated in various guises throughout the scene to suggest bells from two churches answering each other, is scored for massed brass instruments, piano, and percussion for brilliance and exotic effect.

*Chromatic Third Relationships.* When triads whose roots lie a third apart belong to different keys, their relationship is that of a chromatic third as distinct from a diatonic third relationship. As one triad in such a relationship moves to another, a chromatic alteration is made in at least one of the tones. This alteration, along with other inflections, sets the color of one triad in bold relief against the color of its neighbor. Each chord color then takes on a vividness, a personality that does not emerge in diatonic progressions. Romantic music exploits the color potential of chromatic third relationships extensively, although the history of some third relationships—such as the recurrent E major–G minor juxtapositions of Claudio Monteverdi's *Orfeo* (1607)—reaches as far back as the late Renaissance and early Baroque.

Schubert's music comes to mind immediately, since third-related progressions abound in his music. One of the most striking is the sudden appearance of G-flat major after the cadence in B-flat major in the first key area of the first movement of his great Sonata in B-Flat Major, Op. post. (mm. 18–20). Another is the shift from G major to E-flat major in the first movement of the String Quintet in C major (see Ex. 13-2). The introduction to his overture to *Rosamunde* (1823) encloses a constellation of such shifts, from E-flat major via E-flat minor to G-flat major; to A major via F-sharp minor; and finally to return to C major. In all of these progressions, the connections between third-related harmonies are made smoothly by common tones. Characteristically for Schubert, these sudden shifts of harmonic directions form a hinge for two substantial sections in a form.

EXAMPLE 6-7.   Tritone harmonies. Mussorgsky, *Boris Godunov*, 1868–69, Coronation Scene.

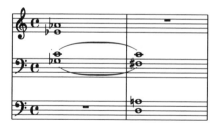

On the other hand, the two examples to follow set triads against each other to highlight the back-and-forth shift of harmonic color. Brahms closes the second movement of his Symphony No. 3 in F Major, Op. 90 (1883), with an alternation of C major and A-flat major triads, for something of the value of a plagal cadence (Ex. 6-8). The final cadence is indeed plagal, as A-flat major drops subtly down to F minor, which then arrives at the final C major. Clarinets, horns, bassoons, and trombones give the progression a richness and fullness of instrumental color that matches the dark-light effect of the harmonic shifts.

An unusual application of a third-related progression is Wagner's music in *Das Rheingold* for the Tarnhelm, the talisman of invisibility. Here, minor triads from keys remote to each other are linked. (Ex. 6-9). Muted horns, pianissimo, add their muffled color to the elusive G-sharp minor–E minor progression, which retains coherence by means of conjunct part-writing and the common tone, B.

EXAMPLE 6-8.   Third-related triads. Brahms, Symphony No. 3 in F Major, Op. 90, 1883, second movement.

EXAMPLE 6-9.   Third-related minor triads. Wagner, *Das Rheingold*, 1851–54, Scene III.

The same relationship of minor chords opens Smetana's String Quartet in E Minor (1879). For sixteen measures we hear a steady undulation of the E-minor triad over a sustained pedal E, while the viola announces the theme, itself built entirely on the same triad. Suddenly, without preparation, the harmony changes to C minor, maintaining the same texture and play of sound until measure 31. Sound quality and harmonic color join here to create a pervasive mood of melancholy.

Elisabet von Herzogenberg, in an 1883 letter to Brahms, made particular mention of a chromatic third relationship in Grieg's music, noting that Grieg

has determination of character too, which is so rare that one can condone this sort of thing

more easily than in some others.[7]

Grieg's progression is even more striking than those cited previously, there is no common tone in his example, while Examples 6-8 and 6-9 connect the tangential harmonies by means of a common tone.

***Chromatic Bass Lines.*** "Dido's Lament" from *Dido and Aeneas* (1689), by Henry Purcell, the Crucifixus from the Mass in B Minor by Bach, and the opening section of the Fantasia in C Minor, K. 475 (1785), by Mozart are familiar examples of the use of descending chromatic bass lines to express a pathetic affect. Kurth says, concerning the Fantasia in C Minor, K. 475, of Mozart:

its opening yields nothing to Romantic sound-fantasy (*Klangphantastik*) in the boldness and brilliance of color with which it immediately moves the harmony into the distant dominant and subdominant regions.[8]

These bass lines descend; in doing so, they exemplify a traditional way of deploying chromaticism in Baroque and Classic music. Less often chromatic bass lines ascend. One powerful use of a rising chromatic bass takes place in the first movement of the Sonata in A Major, Op. 2, No. 2 (1794–95), by Beethoven, measures 61–74, underpinning a broad harmonic digression in the second key area of the exposition. Another instance is the opening of the second movement of Berlioz's *Symphonie fantastique* (see Ex. 4-17).

Chromatic bass lines generate a kaleidoscopic play of chord color; the harmonies move along a spectrum of implied tonal centers. When they shift slowly, with luminous scoring, as in the opening measures of the coda of

Smetana's overture to *The Bartered Bride* (1863–66), they draw attention to the color effect of each chord as well as to the juxtaposition of different chord sounds (Ex. 6-10). The bass rises chromatically from D flat to E over a space of twenty-six measures. Texture and rhythm combine in this passage to focus attention upon the color of the scoring and harmony. The furious eighth-note motion that precedes this passage suddenly comes to a halt, creating a moment of stillness on the open fifth, D flat–A flat. This provides a curtain for the winds to take up a grateful songlike melody in the remote key of D-flat major, floating over sustained harmonies that shift slowly upward by chromatic half-steps through D major, E-flat minor, E-flat major, and E minor, finally to arrive at E major. In the course of this progression the exotic sound of the augmented triad is heard twice. The entire progression is a huge parenthesis, an "eye of the hurricane" that interrupts the hectic action of the final moments of the overture.

*Interchange of Mode.* In tonal harmony, the sharing of cadential functions —tonic, subdominant, and dominant—by parallel major and minor modes opens the way to interchange of mode. For instance, a subdominant-function harmony from the minor mode may replace its major-mode counterpart; likewise, a minor-mode tonic-function harmony may replace its major-mode counterpart. Interchange of mode occurs frequently in eighteenth-century music and is especially striking when a minor tonic is involved, as in the finale to Mozart's "Prague" Symphony (1786), measure 31, or the first movement of Haydn's "Oxford" Symphony (1789), measure 61.

While such progressions have a heightened effect of harmonic color, thanks to their touches of chromaticism, their principal value in Classic music is to escalate the harmonic thrust, either by initiating a broadly scaled tonal digression or by leading to an important new harmonic station. In such situations, a kind of "whiplash" or "recoil" effect is created, as the harmony shifts to the minor mode in order to make a run toward the eventual major mode.

Romantic harmony employs interchange in this traditional manner and at times exploits its color as special value apart from cadential action. A notable passage occurs in Brahms's *Tragic* Overture, Op. 81 (1880) (Ex. 6-11). The B-major harmony darkens to B minor, the major and minor triads are juxtaposed. Then, in an unorthodox interchange that hinges on the note D, B minor gives way to B-flat major as F sharp and B drop to F and B flat respectively. These two interchanges initiate a broad digression to the minor mode of D that prepares the return of the lyric theme of the overture in D

EXAMPLE 6-10.    Rising chromatic bass. Smetana, Overture to *The Bartered Bride*, 1866.

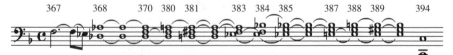

EXAMPLE 6-11.  Interchange of mode. Brahms, *Tragic* Overture, Op. 81, 1880.

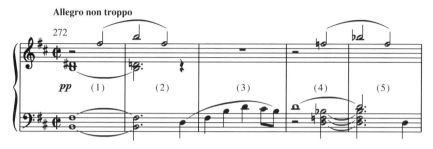

major. Trombones and muted strings lend an understated yet impressive color.

A reversal of Brahms's B minor–B-flat major interchange, still hinging on the third, takes place in the second movement of Schubert's Quintet in C Major (Ex. 6-12). The first section of this movement closes with a quiet pause on the tonic chord of E major. The third, G sharp, shifts enharmonically to A flat, while E and B rise to F and C respectively. This strange cadential link, with the tonic note, E, serving as a leading tone to F minor, binds a luminous E major to a turbulent F minor, serenity and quietness followed by wild agitation.

The interchange of parallel major and minor becomes a motive in the first movement of Schubert's Quartet in G Major, Op. 161 (1826). Throughout this movement major and minor continually alternate, often in a short span of action, at other times to delineate broad sections of the form. In Example 6-13 Schubert emphasizes the major-minor opposition with texture, dynamics, and tessitura. The bright, sustained G-major sound is abruptly cut off by the peremptory, slashing upbeat figure of the G-minor chord; the three quiet, close-position tones are overwhelmed by a fortissimo chord of eleven tones spread over three octaves.

*Composite Tangential Progressions.* A series of juxtaposed harmonies may mix root movements of a tritone, third, or half step with interchange-of-mode progressions. Through their abrupt changes of harmonic color and meaning, such progressions represent a compact embodiment of harmony as color in Romantic music. They also tend to build stronger cadential drives than other manifestations of harmonic color.

The progression in Example 6-14 links root movements of a tritone and of chromatic and diatonic thirds. The root movements in Example 6-15 are, respectively, chromatic third, chromatic half-step, then diminished-seventh cadence to A, then chromatic third once more. Erwin Stein comments on this progression, "It is the suggestive power of the harmony that imposes itself upon a melodic line which in itself is not strongly characterized."[9] In both examples, the harmonies are assigned to winds and brass, creating an organlike richness that imbues the shifting harmonic hues with fullness and vibrancy.

EXAMPLE 6-12.   Interchange of mode. Schubert, Quintet in C Major, Op. 163, 1828, second movement.

Used by permission of Dover Publications, Inc. Reproduced from *Franz Schubert's Werke*, Series 4, ed. Eusebius Mandyczewski. Breitkopf & Härtel (1890).

Another example, from the Prelude to Act III of Wagner's *Siegfried* (1869), is a remarkable string of triads that shift in a kaleidoscopic play. Three kinds of progressions are involved: (1) third-related chords, (2) tritone-related chords, which in this context make a sharply defined Neapolitan sixth–dominant progression, and (3) authentic cadences. Each chord in the progression is a triad, and all but the first of each cadential pair are in first

EXAMPLE 6-13.  Interchange of mode. Schubert, Quartet in G Major, Op. 161, 1826, first movement.

Used by permission of Dover Publications, Inc. Reproduced from *Franz Schubert's Werke,* Series 4, ed. Eusebius Mandyczewski. Breitkopf & Härtel (1890).

EXAMPLE 6-14.  Tangential progressions. Dvořák, Symphony in E Minor, Op. 95, 1892–93, *From the New World,* second movement.

inversion. The harmonic colors are clear, unmixed with dissonance, and the shifts are bold and simple. The frame for this action is the two-measure phrase; the regularity and symmetry of the melodic-rhythmic layout enables the harmony to "turn the corner" with clocklike precision at two- and one-measure intervals as illustrated in Example 6-16, which gives the parts assigned to the trombones. These instruments, together with other winds, provide a core of sound against which the hectic dotted rhythms of the melodic figures, doubled lavishly, provide an elaboration and a brilliant fullness of sound.

A remarkable color montage occurs in one section of the "Danse arabe" from the *Nutcracker* Suite, Op. 71a (1892–93), by Tchaikovsky. Over a pedal point that anchors the harmony on G, the upper voices, moving in parallel major and minor thirds chromatically, form a kaleidoscopic series of momentary glints of color (Ex. 6-17).

EXAMPLE 6-15.   Tangential progressions. Wagner, *Siegfried,* 1869, Act III.

EXAMPLE 6-16.   String of triads. Wagner, *Siegfried,* 1869, Act III, Prelude.

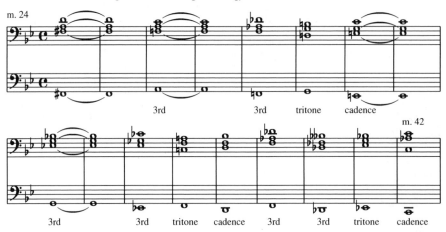

# Tritone Harmonies

Chords in use during the eighteenth and nineteenth centuries that incorporate the tritone include dominant seventh, diminished seventh, dominant ninth, half-diminished seventh (the seventh chord built from the leading tone in major and the second degree in minor), and the augmented sixth types (French, German, and Italian). These are illustrated in their simple forms in Example 6-18.

The so-called German and Italian augmented sixth chords, i.e. ${}^{\sharp6}_{\flat5}{}_3$ and ${}^{\sharp6}_3$ have the sound of a dominant seventh chord, with the Italian version lacking the fifth. Whatever the spelling of these chords may be in the context of the passage in which they occur, and whatever their disposition may be as far as inversions are concerned, they can project themselves as striking moments of harmonic color that have an inner validity, apart from their roles in the key schemes which incorporate them.

EXAMPLE 6-17. Pedal point. Tchaikovsky, *Nutcracker* Suite, Op. 71a, 1892–93, "Danse arabe."

Reproduced with the kind permission of Boosey & Hawkes, Inc.

EXAMPLE 6-18. Tritone harmonies.

| dominant seventh | diminished seventh | dominant ninth | half-diminished seventh | French sixth |

The half-diminished seventh chord plays a special role in Romantic harmony. It projects a distinctive harmonic color, restless and dark. Elisabet von Herzogenberg noted the "strangely affecting horn-blasts" in Brahms's song "Meerfahrt," Op. 96, No. 4 (1884):

the F sharp over the A minor harmony [m. 3] the C sharp over the E minor farther on [m. 29] and last of all the B natural [m. 58] [over the D minor].[10]

Example 6-19 isolates the chain of tritone harmonies from the opening of the Prelude to Wagner's *Tristan und Isolde* (1856), beginning with the so-called *Tristan* chord, a half-diminished seventh. By half-step movement and by common-tone connection, these tritone chords merge one into another. While each tritone subtly implies a new tonal direction, each chord, scored with the rich instrumental colors of Romantic orchestration, creates a self-validating effect of sound.

EXAMPLE 6-19.   Tritone harmonies. Wagner, Prelude to *Tristan und Isolde*, 1856–59. Tritone chords in mm. 1–17 marked with an asterisk.

# *Modal Harmony*

Effects of color taken from modal harmony appear occasionally in Romantic music. These may consist of a momentary inclusion of a characteristic tone or a passage of some length set in an archaic mode.

For Romantic music modal color provides nuances or shadings within the governing major-minor functional harmony. Specifically, modal effects are incorporated into tonal harmony by tones that characterize the modes and that, for our ears, distinguish them from the major and minor scales of key-centered harmony. Thus we speak of the Lydian fourth (raised) and the Mixolydian seventh (lowered) in the scales with a major tonic triad; the Phrygian second (lowered), the Dorian sixth (raised), and the Aeolian sixth and seventh (each lowered) in the scales with a minor tonic triad.

Of the modes, the Aeolian appears most often in Romantic music. It is used in Example 4-10, the opening to Tchaikovsky's *Romeo and Juliet* Overture-

Fantasia, to give the color of an ecclesiastical procession. In Example 9-7, the opening of Mendelssohn's *Hebrides* Overture, Op. 26, the play of chords and figures without the leading tone, A sharp, for the key of B minor, is a representation of the bleak seascape of the North. Example 11-3, from Mahler's *Das Lied von der Erde*, is a song set in the Aeolian mode to convey an Eastern folkloric mood.

The Phrygian second produces an effect of tightness and contraction when it is bound by melodic half step to its tonic. One of the most surprising uses of this degree is in the final cadence of Schubert's Quintet in C Major, where the dominant $^6_4$ harmony occurs over a D flat (Ex. 6-20). This chord is a French sixth type,[3] but built on the lowered second instead of the lowered sixth degree, and it resolves to the tonic instead of a dominant. For his final gesture Schubert extracts the D flat–C melodic progression, assigning it in a three-octave spread to the entire ensemble. The Phrygian second—a startling, strange, and disquieting ornament to the final tonic, C—may be sensed as consistent with the sudden half-step shifts at the beginning and end of the movement, measures 13–19 and 389–95, as the harmony suddenly moves from B-flat minor to B minor to C major.

In a similar way, the cadence of the theme in the fourth movement of Brahms' Symphony No. 4 in E minor uses F natural–E in the bass, a hint of the Phrygian mode.

EXAMPLE 6-20.    Phrygian mode. Schubert, Quintet in C Major, Op. 163, 1828, finale.

425

Liszt introduces the Phrygian second in the third measure of his Sonata in B minor (see Ex. 3-12); this "depressed" tone reinforces the effect of introspection, of troubled questioning with which the sonata begins; the effect is especially telling since the Phrygian second, A flat, enters almost as a misstep, a stumble near the end of what the listener can expect to be a descending natural G minor scale. The A flat hints at a three-flat key signature. Once more the scale attempts a descent, beginning in the harmonic minor of G, with F sharp and E flat, but once more stumbles, this time on C sharp, creating an augmented second with the following B flat. The B flat, reinterpreted as A sharp, together with C sharp, provides a link to the most important and characteristic chord of the first key area of this piece, the diminished seventh of B minor, on which the opening theme is built. Thus, the Phrygian second is used both as a point of harmonic color and the beginning of a process of harmonic alteration that will arrive at the main harmonic business of the piece. The scale on B at the end of the sonata (see Ex. 3-11) combines elements of the two opening scales; the raised third, D sharp, forms an augmented second with the Phrygian C natural. As the bass pauses on C natural this tone provides a link to the high A minor harmonies that interrupt the downward scale. Eventually, the bass will reach its destination, the final B.

The best-known appearance of the Phrygian mode in nineteenth-century music takes place at the beginning of the second movement of Brahms's Symphony No. 4, Op. 98 (1884–86) (Ex. 6-21). While the F natural defines the Phrygian scale, it is the note E and the perfect fifth C–G, that create the color of the passage, so much so that we can hear the figure as being in C major, a horn call given out in unisons and octaves, as though it were a solemn incantation. The oppressive effect of the minor second that characterizes the Phrygian color in the two examples previously cited, is entirely lacking here. Indeed, in terms of scoring and chord color, the passage in measures 1–4, is a beautifully-subtle expression of Romantic exploitation of contrasting sound qualities. The bold horn figure, in C major, hinging on E, slides smoothly into a full harmony on E major in 6-4 position, with a shift of scoring to suave clarinets and bassoon and a sudden drop from forte to pianissimo. In each case, C major and E major, the harmony lacks the footing of a root position, and therefore, takes on a glint of unstable color.

Brahms' usage here leans more to the ancient ecclesiastical view of modes, in which the final E, the ambitus, the species of fourth and fifth, C–G, and the constellation of related degrees, C, G, determine the mode, rather than do characteristic tones.

Chopin introduces a plaintive Phrygian touch to the melody of his Mazurka in C-Sharp Minor, Op. 41, No. 1 (1839) by incorporating D naturals in the figures of measure 2, 4, and 6 (Ex. 6-22). The simplicity and repetitious character of the melody strongly suggests a folk song. Chopin absorbs and softens the Phrygian effect by alternating C-sharp minor with F-sharp minor, a scale to which D natural belongs.

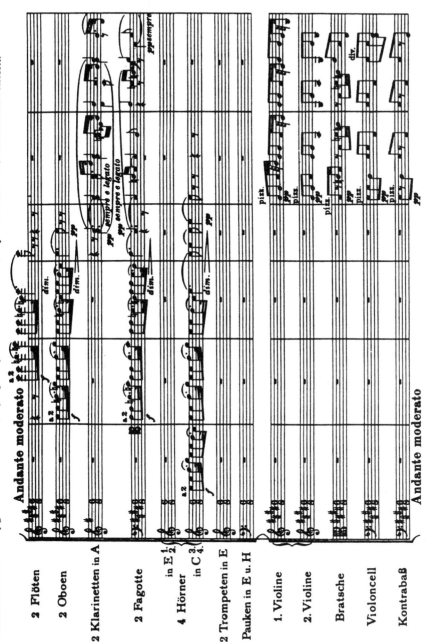

EXAMPLE 6-21.    Phrygian mode. Brahms, Symphony No. 4 in E Minor, Op. 98, 1884–86, second movement.

EXAMPLE 6-22.    Phrygian mode. Chopin, Mazurka in C-Sharp Minor, Op. 41, No. 1, 1839.

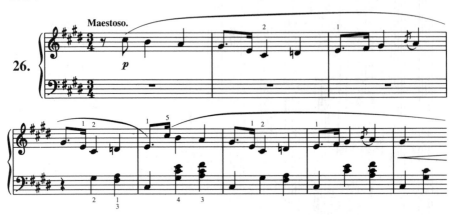

Chopin, *Mazurkas.* Copyright © G. Schirmer, Inc. Used by permission.

Tchaikovsky makes arresting use of the Lydian fourth in the opening of his Serenade in C Major, Op. 48 (1880) (Ex. 6-23). A bold C major chord in first inversion alternates with a root-position dominant seventh on D, setting the F sharp at a tangent against the C-major sound. Repeated, the effect is like a summons, twice uttered. Had Tchaikovsky inserted a subdominant harmony or even a VII⁷ chord instead of the D dominant seventh, the effect would have been far less arresting.

In a far different mood, Sibelius inflects a songlike melody in the second movement of his Symphony No. 2 in D major (1901–1902) with the Lydian fourth, B sharp in F-sharp major (Ex. 6-24). An effect of nostalgia, perhaps pathos, arises from the fleeting sharp fourth, which vanishes as a traditional tonal cadence is approached. While the modal touch hints at a folk-song style, the full scoring with divided strings, *ppp*, is typically late Romantic.

The final cadential section of Liszt's cantata *Die Glocken des Strassburger Münsters* (The bells of the Strassburg Cathedral, 1875) boldly juxtaposes the triads of C major and B-flat major to create a Mixolydian effect, providing we recognize C major as the ruling key of the work; the B-flat triads anchor the lowered seventh degree as a momentary suspension of functional tonality (Ex. 6-25). Two features contribute to the effect: (1) the seventeen measures preceding the first B-flat major triad project a vivid impression of C major, so that the B-flat major triad enters as a surprising shift of harmonic color, unlike any preceding progression in the work; and (2) the scoring of this section exploits harmonic, instrumental, and vocal color to the fullest by means of a grand fortissimo tutti, including harps, organ, and bells. The sustained harmonies in the chorus and organ are activated by triplet quarternote rhythms in the winds, brass, and strings. A stunning effect of reverberation is achieved to amplify the sense of the text, "the true God."

EXAMPLE 6-23.   Lydian Mode. Tchaikovsky, Serenade for Strings in C Major, Op. 48, 1880.

Kalmus.

The Dorian sixth, F sharp, at measure 2 of the Lion's March in Saint-Saëns *The Carnival of the Animals* introduces an odd, parodistic twist to the unison melody of the strings (Ex. 6-26). Conventionally, the apex of the figure would be an F natural, and the effect of the passage would have a pathetic color. The F sharp forms a prominent tritone with C in the following measure, a bit of grotesquerie that throws the key out of focus.

The pentatonic scale, which appears from time to time in Romantic music, is a component of a great deal of folk music throughout the world. Because the scale lacks the specific agent for key definition in functional tonal harmony—the tritone between the fourth and seventh scale degrees—its use in Romantic music tends to be coloristic than harmonically purposeful.

Composers have often set melodies in the pentatonic scale when the topic alludes to folk elements. Thus the second movement of Mendelssohn's Symphony No. 3 in A Minor, Op. 56, the *Scottish* (1842), emulates a lively Scottish dance with a quick duple theme set in F major, using the pentatonic degrees. The familiar "Going Home" theme from the second movement of Dvořák's Symphony in E minor, Op. 95, "From the New World" (1892–93), also uses the pentatonic degrees. Both themes are set as short symmetrical periods; their final cadences revert to tritone harmony to make a dominant-tonic close. The pentatonic scale here thus creates a miniclimate, a moment of exotic harmonic color.

The most extensive use of pentatonic color is to be found in the overture *La grande pâque russe*, Op. 36 (1888), by Nicolai Rimsky-Korsakov. As an evocation of the ringing of the church bells on this festival day of Easter, Rimsky-Korsakov weaves pentatonic sound, with or without the second

EXAMPLE 6-24. Lydian mode. Sibelius, Symphony No. 2 in D Major, Op. 43, 1901–1902, second movement.

EXAMPLE 6-25.   Mixolydian mode. Liszt, *Die Glocken des Strassburger Münsters*, 1875.

degree of the scale, but always with the sixth, into the very fabric of the piece. We hear cadenzas, brilliant passages in strings and winds, fanfares in the brass—all based on the pentatonic scale. In addition to being an essential melodic ingredient in this work, the pentatonic scale is here a factor in a brilliant play of Romantic instrumental and harmonic color. At various times, the pentatonic scale is heard in solo violin, solo flute, solo cello, in trumpets,

EXAMPLE 6-26.   Dorian mode. Saint-Saëns, *The Carnival of the Animals*, 1886 (1922), Introduction.

Reproduced with the kind permission of Boosey & Hawkes, Inc.

bassoons, horns, strings, the full orchestra. Moreover, key or scale color adds another grand dimension to the use of this resource. The pentatonic grouping is heard at different times on G, D, A, C, F, E, and B flat. The composition, with its varied scoring and range of triad colors, is a tour de force in the management of musical sound, in which the pentatonic scale plays a vital role.[11]

The harmonic values examined in this chapter are distinctly nonfunctional; that is, while all the progressions illustrated above move in and around tonal centers and eventually arrive at cadences, their special appeal lies in the immediate impressions they create as points of color. Harmonic movement here achieves coherence principally through conjunct part writing rather than cadential impulse. In relation to key, these harmonies are centrifugal, loosening the tight bonds of cadential logic. This compromising of key by harmonic color constituted a phase in the history of harmony that eventually arrived at musical impressionism.

PART TWO

# *TRADITIONAL SYNTAX*

# CHAPTER SEVEN

# *Period Structure*

The internal evidence from scores cited in Chapters 2–6 testifies persuasively for the new and colorful climate of sound that pervades Romantic music. Equally persuasive is evidence that points to a retrospective view of musical syntax in nineteenth-century musical theory and practice. Since the interaction between new sounds and traditional syntax is the focal point of this book, it is essential to look at the nineteenth century's conception of musical syntax, a view that remained consistent throughout the century. This view was based on procedures evolved during past centuries and embodied in a comprehensive codification of syntactical processes, which theorists described in great detail in the monumental nineteenth-century treatises on musical composition.[1]

Traditional syntax includes:

1. *Harmony*—chord structure and progression, cadences, key definition, key distribution, thoroughbass
2. *Rhythm*—meter, topical patterns, groupings by two or three on various levels
3. *Melody*—linear contours, familiar topical content, paired alignment of melodic figures
4. *Texture*—mutual action of the component parts or voices
5. *Form*—phrase and period structure, traditional layouts such as dance, rondo, two-reprise, sonata, concerto, etc.

The most critical aspect of traditional syntax for the present approach is *period structure*. If sound tends to sustain itself, to spin out, to extend our impression of the passage of time in music, then the period, with its articulations, acts against this motion by locating instants of arrival on various levels of clarity and firmness. The remaining chapters in this book explore the interplay between these two processes on various levels of structure.

This chapter describes the history of the period in order to show its relevance in the theory and practice of nineteenth-century music. The term *period* has had two meanings since it came to be applied to musical syntax. In one sense, it was borrowed from the rhetoric of language—oratory and written exposition—where a period was described as a complete statement, a fully presented train of thought, whose message was finished only with a formal close, a period. The length and inner construction of such a statement could vary according to the intention of the speaker, writer, or composer. Such a period may be designated as a *rhetorical period,* since its shape and extent depends on the meaning of the statement. In another view—possibly reflecting poetry and dance—the period, while retaining its sense of completeness, has been defined as a grouping of phrases, most often two that are joined by symmetries, parallel constructions, or statement-counterstatement relationships. This sense of the period may be designated as *symmetrical,* since it presupposes a framework of structural balances that rest on parts of equal or comparable length. Technically, the prototypical symmetrical period fixes conditions for harmony and phrase length: to be eight measures long, to start on the tonic, to pause on the dominant at measure 4, and to close on the tonic at measure 8.

In practice and in theory, these two kinds of period interpenetrate each other. The rhetorical sense can expand the framework of the symmetrical period, while the symmetrical framework offers perimeters for the rhetorical flow of meaning. Of these two views of the period as a musical process, the rhetorical is the older and the more speculative; it can be traced as far back as the sixteenth century. The symmetrical view begins to emerge in the eighteenth century; it becomes firmly set and codified by the beginning of the nineteenth century.[2] For this study, that codification is of critical importance. In the nineteenth century, the symmetrical period pervaded musical thought and practice on pedagogical and compositional levels, was a fundament of music theory, and was embodied in most types of composition, from simple dances and songs to symphonies and operas.

The emergence of the symmetrical view is linked to historical changes in the harmonic processes that defined tonal harmony: cadential action; classification of chords and chord types; key definition through indication, establishment, and confirmation; and the crystallization of key relationships along hierarchical lines. Among these processes, cadential action is the most critical in shaping period structure. The kinds of cadences employed and their frequency play important roles in determining the lengths of periods and their internal configurations. The following synopsis reviews concepts of period structure and the harmonic processes associated with them. These concepts reflect a view of musical rhetoric that had remained consistent for more than the two previous centuries; they served as a basis for musical education in the nineteenth century, and they constitute the underpinnings of much Romantic music.

## The Rhetorical Period

The period as a musico-rhetorical process was described as early as 1558 by Gioseffo Zarlino, who associated the cadence in music to the end of a sentence in language:

> Wherefore the cadence is of equal value in music as the period in oration; thus, it may truly be called a period of cantilena.[3]

Zarlino demonstrated how the musical sense can be sustained or suspended by avoiding cadences until the final formal cadence is reached. His example, comprising 140 tacti, includes more than a dozen points at which cadences are bypassed. These points imply stepwise cadences on the tones F, G, C, a, d, e. Leading tones for G, d, e, and a are not indicated by *musica ficta* because of the voice leading. The tritone, the generating force in tonal harmony, plays an insignificant part. Zarlino's period unfolds in a continuous flow, without palpable symmetries, a model of a rhetorical period in late Renaissance style.

Johann Walther implied that the cadence was a factor in period structure; his 1732 definition of the *periodus harmonica* states that "every paragraph [*Absatz*] in a piece of music can be so named.[4]

The rhetorical view of period structure likewise is the controlling idea in Jean-Jacques Rousseau's definition of the term *prima intenzione,* which compares strokes of musical genius to

> those long but eloquent Ciceronian periods in which the sense, suspended throughout their entire duration, is determined only at the last word.[5]

Heinrich Koch, in 1802, retained the same rhetorical sense of the period in his definition:

> *Periode:* A technical term [*Kunstwort*] that is borrowed from oratory and signifies the connection of various phrases to form a complete sense. . . . In this work the term *period* is always used to signify a section of a musical composition that ends with a cadence.[6]

The rhetorical period has no prescribed length. It might consist of a few words or tones, as "I go," or it may encompass a simple tonic-subdominant-dominant-tonic progression in root-position chords. It might, on the other hand, comprise a sentence or paragraph, a section of many phrases, all of which converge on the final close to round off the sense of the statement. Further, an entire work or major segment thereof could be considered a period, since only at the end of such sections does a final dénouement take place to complete the grand sense of the work. Anton Reicha's *Traité de mélodie* (1814) quotes a period from Haydn's Symphony No. 44 in E Minor, Hob. I:44 (circa 1771) that encompasses forty-two measures, the entire second part of the Adagio.[7] Koch, in 1793, characterized the first reprise of a sonata or symphony movement (the exposition of a sonata form as we know it) as a single *Hauptperiode*.[8]

Kollmann, in 1796, referred to a period of Haydn as

> one of those fancy periods of some extended length in which the composer seems to lose himself in the modulation for the purpose of making the ear attentive to the resolution.[9]

As the comments cited above imply, the defining act in shaping a rhetorical period is its cadence. Cadences also play decisive roles in articulating the inner structure of the period. In eighteenth-century music, most progressions are geared to key definition by means of cadential action, using the tritone as the essential control. Cadences promote inner segmentations within the period; these segmentations in turn tend to be balanced among themselves in length and melodic content as well as in harmonic directions. The absorption of dance topics and layouts into theater, church, and chamber music in the eighteenth century is linked with cadential segmentation. In practice, this linkage promotes symmetries in phrase arrangements.

## *The Symmetrical Period*

During the eighteenth century the emergence of symmetry as a principal aspect of periodic layout is reflected by the increasing attention given by music theorists to punctuation and the arrangement of melodic-rhythmic materials. The first volume of Joseph Riepel's important *Anfangsgründe zur musikalischen Setzkunst* (1752) is *Rhythmopoeia*, a consideration of the rhythmic organization of music, providing an exhaustive set of examples in which short melodic figures are grouped according to their content and their punctuation. In Riepel's view,

> since 4, 8, 16, and indeed 32 measures are those which are thus planted into our nature, it appears difficult to hear another order with pleasure.[10]

The *Rhythmopoeia* does not use the term *period*. Indeed, there was some confusion in nomenclature at this time concerning the inner structure and the punctuations of musical "sentences." In Johann Georg Sulzer's *Allgemeine Theorie der schönen Künste* (1771–74), the following comment appears:

> The names used to designate the smaller and larger sections of a melody are still somewhat indefinite. One speaks of *Perioden, Abschnitten, Einschnitten, Rhythmen, Caesuren,* etc., in such a way that one word will have two meanings and two words will have the same meaning.[11]

While avoiding all such terms, Riepel's treatise clearly marks the units within the examples, referring often to measures grouped by fours, sometimes by threes, fives, sixes, and sevens, and spelling out melodic content and effects of closure in great detail.

Other theorists followed Riepel's lead. The treatises of Koch, Momigny, Daube, and Reicha represent the trend toward clarification and classification of events within the musical period.[12] Inevitably, this trend, both in music and theory, led to the idea that symmetry was a basic value in music. François Chastellux in 1765 credited the Italians with fostering musical symmetry:

> They [the Italians] saw very well that they could not invent a melody unless they held to a simple and unique idea and gave this idea proper expression in form and proportion. This observation led them to discover the musical period. A minuet, a gigue have their definite measures; melodies form phrases, and these phrases have their regular and proportional elements. . . . Although our small French pieces, minuets, gigues, etc. appear to be like those of the Italians, one must not assume that they are periodic. It is not enough for a melody to have a certain number of measures. . . . When the expression of the melody is to be periodic, a certain unity must be present, a balance in the members out of which the melody grows, a rounding-off of the melody, which hold the attention to the very end. Most older French melodies are almost nothing but rows of tones, which have neither rule nor aim.[13]

Daube in 1773 compared symmetry in music with the quality in other arts:

> Wherein arises the symmetry of architecture? In the beautiful relationship of the various masses of the component parts. . . . beautiful symmetry is found today in painting, sculpture, dance, poetry, and literature, and all others that represent beauty and creativity. We also know this in music, but our forefathers had little knowledge thereof.[14]

Reicha, in his *Traité de mélodie* (1814), also considered symmetry to be one of the attributes of beauty in music:

> Paisello, Martin . . . Cimarosa, Haydn, Mozart, et al. have accustomed us to melodies that are rhythmically well defined and, because of this, are incomparably more felicitous than those of Hasse and his generation which lose their effect after three or four measures.[15]

In the nineteenth century, the scales tip toward symmetry as a principal process in period structure. Definitions of the period began to limit the form to its simplest embodiment—an eight-measure passage, built of two four-measure phrases, complete in itself as a musical statement. In Reicha's words:

> The periods composed of two phrases [*membres*] belong already to regular periods. The first phrase should have a half cadence, the second a perfect cadence.[16]

Reicha's statement precedes the two-phrase period from Gluck's *Armide* shown in Ex. 7-1.

Lobe described a simple period as consisting of two connected phrases comprising eight measures (Ex. 7-2). Marx explained the period as a tone structure in two phrases (phrase and counterphrase) joined in a greater whole. (Ex. 7-3). Although Simon Sechter did not use the term *period* in his drastic simplification of its harmonic plan (Ex. 7-4), his "sentences" (*Sätze*) are clearly identical with periods. He says that "sentences of eight measures are the simplest and most useful." Arrey von Dommer's 1865 revision of Koch's *Lexikon* says that all period forms stem from a basic form (*Grundform*), the simple eight-measure period (Ex. 7-5). Finally, at the end of the nineteenth century, Riemann succinctly presented in his *Musik-Lexikon* (1905) his notion of the period as the largest section of music that can be

EXAMPLE 7-1.   Two-phrase period. Gluck, *Armide*, 1777, Act IV.

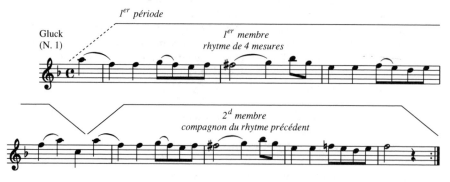

EXAMPLE 7-2.   Simple period. Lobe, *Lehrbuch*, vol. 1, 1858, p. 21.

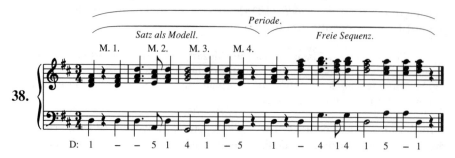

EXAMPLE 7-3.   Phrase and counterphrase. Marx, *Lehre*, vol. 1, 1841, p. 28.

EXAMPLE 7-4.   Eight-measure sentences. Sechter, *Grundsätze*, part 3, 1854, p. 39.

produced by metric definition; it has an extent of eight actual measures that embody its completely regular structure.[17]

Technically, the symmetrical period fixes a priori conditions for harmony and melody. Sechter's period outlines in Example 7-4 all begin with tonic harmony, pause on the dominant in the fourth measure, and close with tonic harmony. While many options are available within the pattern, the fixed conditions comprise a half cadence in the fourth measure and a full close in the eighth. The "regular" period, as a general concept that arises from all the theorists cited, also begins with tonic harmony, but the cadences at measures 4 and 8 have more options for their points of harmonic arrival than Sechter allows. For the "regular" period, melody also fits to simple, clear patterns. Most often, the fifth measure restates the first measure's figure (see Examples 7-1, 7-2, 7-3 [inverted], 7-5). For utmost regularity only the final measure or measures are altered to accommodate the full close (see Ex. 7-1).

This brief historical sketch points to the great shift that took place over three centuries in the idea of the musical period. Zarlino's view, taken from oratory and based on the message contained in the period, regardless of its length, is a broad rhetorical concept linked to intellectual perception. Riemann's much narrower view, governed by the arithmetic of meter and rhythm, addresses itself to kinesthetic experience, the regularity and symmetry of motion.

EXAMPLE 7-5.   Beethoven, Sonata in D Major, Op. 28, 1801, second movement.

The differences between the rhetorical and the symmetrical period reflect other aspects of music—social, stylistic, and technical. The period as a parallel to the rhetorical sentence was linked to an elite group of practitioners in the sixteenth and seventeenth centuries—composers, performers, and a limited number of listeners. The period as a circumscribed, symmetrical, eight-measure formula was linked to the broader range of participants in the nineteenth century. It embodied bedrock simplicity and total intelligibility for a vast listenership. It could frame the efforts of the rank amateur as well as those of the accomplished composer.

Stylistically, the symmetrical eight-measure period represents the popular music of the nineteenth century—marches, songs, dances, easy tunes of all kinds—produced in huge quantities, thanks to the ease with which the formula could be used. Instruction books of every kind, from comprehensive treatises to simple do-it-yourself manuals, all begin the process of teaching composition with the symmetrical period.

Indeed, by the 1830s symmetry had become so much a part of musical syntax that Gottfried Weber had to warn,

> The further the symmetry of the rhythm is carried, the more plain, even, and obvious the music will be . . . therefore, this rounding-off should not be overdone.[18]

Weber's admonition, like many other criticisms, points to what was actually taking place; certainly in the popular, social, and so-called trivial music of the nineteenth century, long chains of symmetrical periods were linked together with pleasant, easily assimilated melodic content. Weber's comment indicates a shift of attitude from that of the later eighteenth century, where symmetry was considered one of the chief values in music. Still, overuse by mediocre composers did not lessen the symmetrical period of its archetypal power.

The very simplicity of the symmetrical period constitutes its usefulness. For Romantic composers, the period was a structural common denominator, a kind of genetic code. Their musical perceptions were saturated with this pattern; the music they heard, the instructions they received, their early studies and youthful beginners' compositions—these all were shaped to the symmetrical period as a control, a kind of structural cantus firmus. From the most banal *Trivialmusik* to the grandest flights of invention in the great Romantic symphonies, the configurations of the symmetrical period, open or veiled, are present. Much of the music—and especially the waltzes, makurkas, and other dances—of Schubert, Schumann, Mendelssohn, Chopin, Brahms, and Verdi, to cite some of the most celebrated composers of the Romantic era, is based largely on the symmetries of the eight-measure period.

Schumann's comments on Berlioz's irregular phrase structure, as Alfred Einstein notes, imply that balanced periods were norms at that time: "Again in his discussion of the *Symphonie fantastique*, Schumann expressed very sharply what it was that seemed strange to German taste in Berlioz's kind of melody, in the 'structure of the individual phrase':"

> The modern period has perhaps produced no other work in which equal and unequal mensural and rhythmic relationships have been combined and employed so freely as in this one. Consequent almost never corresponds to antecedent; answer almost never corresponds to question. This is so peculiar to Berlioz, so much in keeping with his Southern character and so strange to us Northerners, that the uneasy feeling of the first moment and the complaint about the obscurity are perhaps pardonable and understandable. But with what a bold hand all this is carried out, so that nothing at all may be added or effaced without taking from the thought its sharp penetration and its power—thereof one can judge only for oneself by seeing and hearing it. It seems as if the music wished to tend again towards its very beginnings, where as yet the rule of the downbeat in the measure did not weigh heavily upon it, and to raise itself to unrestrained speech, to a higher poetical kind of punctuation (as in the Greek choruses, in the language of the Bible, in the prose of Jean Paul).[19]

Even more telling is the evidence of symmetrical arrangements in the early works of Romantic composers. Together with their lessons in harmony and counterpoint, they learned to lay out their music in symmetrical phrases and periods. Chopin, according to Jan Kleczyński, a Polish pianist, drew the attention of his students to clear phraseology, using the eight-measure group as an example.[20] Even Wagner, the master of "endless melody" deployed phrase structure in his early works along symmetrical lines. For example, in an early Sonata in B-flat Major (1831–32), the first movement opens with groupings of four plus eight plus eight measures. Other early and minor works of Wagner exhibit similar articulations.[21]

What the Germans call *Vierhebigkeit* is not simply the "tyranny of the bar line." Rather, for Romantic composers symmetry was an element of leverage that controlled and supported the flow of the musical action, to be exploited for its own values and to provide touching points in extended trajectories.

Both rhetorical and symmetrical periods are shaped and articulated by middle and final cadences and by complementary layouts of figures and phrases. In simple symmetrical periods these elements balance neatly. In periods that spin out to greater length and in which symmetries are disturbed, cadences and complementary arrangements become points of reference, locations that act as controls against the centrifugal force of the disturbances and extensions. By locating cadences and complementary layouts in modified and extended period forms, we can assess the effects that generate greater periodic length. In particular, we can pinpoint the role of sound in expanding the trajectories of periods in Romantic music.

Other parameters—harmony, melody, rhythm, and their particular application or embodiment in Romantic music—are important points of entry into the analysis of Romantic music. Though they are incorporated into the present approach, it is nonetheless the interaction of sound and syntax, especially the influence of the coloristic effects described in Part 1 on period structure, that is the principal concern of ensuing chapters.

# CHAPTER EIGHT

# *Rhetorical Reduction*

The symmetrical period, in view of its importance as the model upon which so much Romantic music is based, can be used as an instrument in analysis. The following chapters of this book employ a process designated here as *rhetorical reduction* to show the relationship between the archetype and the fully composed musical examples illustrated hereinafter. Rhetorical reduction, in the following examples, works in two ways:

1. *Melodic reduction* isolates the commonplaces of melody, harmony, and rhythm contained within the excerpts, placing them into a hypothetical symmetrical period; it retains the essential structural and rhetorical features of the original music, reducing most of the sound values to melody and accompaniment, or to melody alone.
2. *Textural reduction* exposes a simple two-part framework modeled on traditional harmonic counterpoint of the eighteenth century; it becomes an exercise in the *stile legato,* governed harmonically by the principles of thoroughbass. Melodic ornamentation is removed.

The topical content of melodic reduction reflects the popular taste of nineteenth-century listeners—an easy, singsong manner that balances all parameters. Textural reduction emphasizes smooth voice leading in the bound or strict style.

These reductions should be taken as *probes,* not *proofs.* In no way are they to be taken as composer's sketches for the works analyzed. Still, it can be reasonably assumed that these reductions do represent a valid stylistic point of departure for a composer beginning to invent the passages being discussed. This assumption is especially persuasive in light of the total absorption by Romantic composers of periodic symmetries and conjunct voice leading on every level of their experience—learning, listening, performing, composing small and large works, and even in critical comments and in the codifications of treatises.

The processes of reduction described above have been adapted from traditional methods of teaching musical composition. They are the exact reverse of the techniques of "elaboration" that constituted the most important melodic process in eighteenth-century music and that continued to direct melodic action in the Romantic era. Melodic reduction reverses the process of extension described by Johann Friedrich Daube in *Anleitung* (1797–98), which shows how a short melody can be extended to a length of a hundred or more measures through repetitions and transpositions of its figures.[1] Koch provided a full-scale example of this procedure in his *Versuch* (1782–93).[2] In the same vein, Logier showed how to extend a short, eight-measure melody to a larger one, sixteen measures in length, as in Example 8-1.

Elaborations from simpler models were explained in great detail by theorists throughout the eighteenth and nineteenth centuries. The simplest models of all were alla breve melodies and their equally simple basses, both in first- or second-species counterpoint, motion in whole or half notes. An example of the ornamentation possible against such a "structural" passage occurs in Ernst Wilhelm Wolf's *Musikalischer Unterricht* (1788) (Ex. 8-2).

Similarly, Logier provided the two-part alla breve counterpoint in Example 8-3a, with figured-bass designations, then illustrated its ornamental elaboration with several full-voiced examples, one of which, in a songlike manner, is given in Example 8-3b.

These examples illustrate ornamentation as a process in musical composition. Dozens of instruction books from the eighteenth and nineteenth centuries describe this process in many ways, precisely, and in detail. The reverse process, analytic reduction, appears rarely in composition treatises, since reductive analysis as a branch of music theory became important only in the later nineteenth and early twentieth centuries. Still, here and there, some theorists did use simplification to explain the construction of a melodic-harmonic phrase or period. De Momigny reduced the sixteenth notes of a melody by Handel to eighths (Ex. 8-4). Logier similarly reduced the opening theme of the third movement of Mozart's Quintet in C Major, K. 515 (Ex. 8-5).

Rhetorical reduction offers two specific values for analysis: (1) Because it requires discrimination to select those features of the original that indicate its essential character, it represents a kind of inverse of the compositional process, providing insights into the composer's linkages; (2) Because it draws attention to the special gestures that must be restored in order to reconstruct the original, it highlights the central role of sound in Romantic music.

Both methods of reduction, melodic and textural, differ from other reductive techniques of analysis—Schenker, Reti, Hindemith, Roman-num-

EXAMPLE 8-1. Period extended. Logier, *System*, 1827, p. 310.

EXAMPLE 8-2.   Wolf, *Unterricht*, 1788, examples, p. 17.
a. Structural line.

b. Ornamentation.

EXAMPLE 8-3.   Logier, *System*, 1827 pp. 299–300.
a. Two-voice framework.

b. Elaboration.

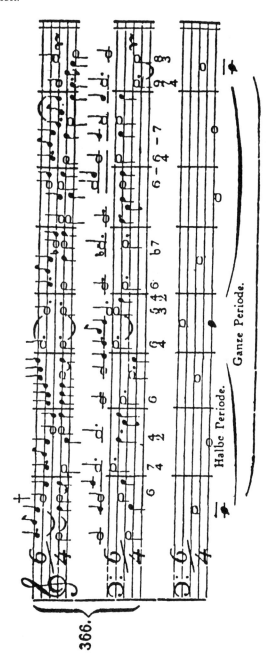

366.

EXAMPLE 8-4. Momigny, *Cours complet,* vol. 3, 1806, p. 96.
a. Florid melody.

b. Reduction.

EXAMPLE 8-5. Simplification of melodic line. Logier, *System,* 1827, p. 284.

eral harmonic analysis—in that they retain the core of the expressive, stylistic, or structural content of the original. In melodic reduction, which will be the principal method used in chapters to follow, the topical content may be rendered even more clear, more palpable than in the original; such reductions might qualify, in some instances, as typical nineteenth-century tunes. They may also be thought of as variations of the original, or conversely, as themes of which the actual originals might themselves be variations.

Both methods, melodic and textural, travel among various parameters, rather than hold to any single line of reduction. Thus harmonic, melodic, rhythmic, and textural elements can be coordinated in the process of simplification. Their usefulness in this study is to serve as expedients, as laboratory exercises that have an idiomatic affinity with their originals.

# PART THREE

# SOUND AND PERIOD STRUCTURE

# CHAPTER NINE

# Symmetrical Arrangements

Symmetrical period structure and sound act on each other reciprocally in Romantic music in several ways. The fullness or intensity of sound gives a colorful presence, a sense of consequence, to symmetrically arranged melody. The glow given to straightforward tunes by scoring and texture is particularly evident in the thousands of dances composed and arranged during the Romantic era. Schubert's German Dances, Dvořák's Slavonic Dances, Brahms's Hungarian Dances, Grieg's Norwegian Dances, the waltzes from Richard Strauss's *Der Rosenkavalier*—these as well as dance melodies incorporated in larger works give evidence for the "upgrading" that scoring created for symmetrical, popular-style melodies in Romantic music.

Conversely, symmetry can shape, balance, and control the flow of sound, especially in relation to melody. It can establish boundaries, limits against the centrifugal effects that sound can generate through flow or by means of its unstable harmonies.[1] The examples in this chapter illustrate both kinds of sound-syntax interplay in turn.

## Symmetry Enhanced by Sound

The inventive, sparkling orchestration of Johann Strauss, Jr., creates an elegant setting for the simple yet captivating third strain of *Tales from the*

*Vienna Woods,* Op. 325 (1868) (Ex. 9-1). Strauss's large wind and brass sections demand for balance a sizable string group of symphonic proportions. The tune itself is a fetching melody. It can be hummed by a single person, strummed on a mandolin or piano, played by a small combination of instruments, as no doubt was done countless times after the publication of the waltz.

EXAMPLE 9-1.    Full scoring. Johann Strauss, Jr., *Tales from the Vienna Woods,* Op. 325, 1868, third strain.

Reproduced with the kind permission of Boosey & Hawkes, Inc.

In the reduction in Example 9-2, a simple Alberti bass condenses the original bass and afterbeat accompaniment, while the melody glides over this figure without the rhythmic snap of the original waltz tune. The reduction, which retains essential rhetorical features of the original yet lowers the affective level of the tune to a simple naïveté, lets us observe, point by point, the features that give the original its air of sparkling sophistication. The

EXAMPLE 9-2.   Rhetorical melodic reduction. Strauss, *Tales from the Vienna Woods*, Op. 325, 1868, third strain.

composer clothes the tune with a fresh and alluring play of sound from the orchestra. Doublings of all figures, sweeping countermelodies that enrich the texture of sound, reinforcements of the brass as the tune reaches for its apex, the sparkle of the harp figure that binds the massive bass-afterbeat accompaniment, the fullness of the string sound and the sudden ceasing of the afterbeats in the twelfth measure as the melody poises for an instant on C—all these effects glorify a symmetrical tune typical of nineteenth-century popular music. The scoring *enhances* the tune, but the tune could well stand by itself or with the accompaniment furnished in Example 9-2.

The *più lento* section of Brahms's Intermezzo, Op. 10, No. 4 (1854), opens with a symmetrical eight-measure period (Ex. 9-3). Its melody, in a typical Romantic song manner and in a broadly swinging $\frac{6}{4}$ meter, maintains a perfect balance between the antecedent and consequent phrases. Its bass line moves principally in parallel thirds and sixths with the tune. Example 9-4 shows the passage reduced to its simple songlike elements; the triplets are removed, parallel thirds and sixths are extracted from the texture, while the entire reduction is raised an octave into a lighter range of sound. In the work itself, the melody is imbedded in a subtle flow of sound—low-pitched, resonant, covering the tune from below and above with broken-chord figures. The pedal sustains the sound while the cross-rhythms of triplets against eighth notes create a constant stirring of the sound, activating it restlessly within each quarter-note beat.

Brahms' performance instructions give a rare clue to the importance of sound as a value in this piece. He calls for "intimate sentiment without marking the melody too much." The pianissimo dynamics, the sustained pedal, the low register, and the vibrant figuration create a play of sound in which the melody's contour articulates and helps to direct the flow. Sound here validates the rather simple, singsong melody; sound enriches symmetry while it is governed by the precise periodic order. The result is a profoundly moving statement that joins the simple and the subtle.

EXAMPLE 9-3.   Melody in middle of texture. Brahms, Intermezzo, Op. 10, No. 4, 1854, più lento.

While the Strauss and Brahms examples both present perfectly symmetrical periods, their inner sound-syntax relationships are different. Strauss's tune stands by itself; it benefits by its scoring but can please even by a single-line hearing, picked out on piano or mandolin. Brahms's period needs its sound; its melody is but one strand in a rich texture, and the melody itself has far less lilt and grace than does Strauss's tune.

## Sound Controlled by Symmetry

The opening measures of the Prelude to Verdi's *Aida* (1853) form a precise symmetrical period, as in the Strauss and Brahms excerpts. But Verdi's

EXAMPLE 9-4.   Rhetorical melodic reduction. Brahms, Intermezzo, Op. 10, No. 4, 1854, più lento.

OR

melody (Ex. 9-5) inhabits a totally different world of sound than that of Brahms. Brahms's tenor melody is surrounded by rich sonority, while Verdi's melody floats through the upper reaches, joined by a thin wisp of accompaniments. Each melody uses sound in its own way to enhance its expressive quality—the Intermezzo of Brahms a sentimental song hinting at a touch of melancholy, the Prelude of Verdi a poignant arioso.

Verdi's minimal texture, first one, then two lines, opens space for the lines to undulate with frequent changes of direction. The slow tempo fixes the attention on each tone or tone combination, both with respect to sound itself and to the shifts in harmonic direction; these shifts pivot on single tones rather than full chords, yet they introduce striking changes of harmonic color as well as intensely focused cadential drives.

Verdi's harmony runs counter to the usual diatonic balances that are part of the symmetrical period. Chromatic passing tones, a wide range of distantly related harmonies from D minor to F-sharp major, a tight fabric of momentary tonics woven with the two strands of the texture—these centrifugally directed sounds are held firmly in check by the absolute symmetries within this period: one plus one, two, one plus one, two. Example 9-6 exposes the underlying harmony in a two-part reduction, which paradoxically adds a bass to the first two full measures.

The three excerpts above all illustrate a precise periodic symmetry colored and enhanced by special values of sound. Sound, in these examples, serves symmetry, giving it a characteristically Romantic glow; still, sound is held firmly in check by the perimeters of the symmetrical period, its equal phrases,

EXAMPLE 9-5.  Verdi, Prelude to *Aida*, 1853.

EXAMPLE 9-6.  Rhetorical textural reduction of mm. 1-8. Verdi, Prelude to *Aida*, 1853.

its counterstatement of material, its cadences arriving on schedule. In the next two examples, sound exerts its centrifugal energies: it threatens to disrupt symmetry, yet it is still controlled by the exponential layouts of pairs of two, four, eight, and sixteen measures.

Mendelssohn's *Hebrides* Overture, Op. 26 (1832), evokes the image of a bleak northern seascape chiefly through the imaginative play of sound (Ex. 9-7). The composer's characteristic syntax provides an ideal channel for the flow of sound in this piece. He has often been criticized, even denigrated, for the regularity of his phrase structure, where figures and phrases are grouped consistently in complementary arrangements. For the *Hebrides* Overture, this kind of syntax is an ideal modus operandi. Here the regularity suggests to the listener the constant undulation of waves, the to-and-fro rocking of the boat, the rise and fall of the wind.

Harmonic color is the chief agent of sound. The central key, B minor, has a pervasive presence throughout much of the work, imparting to it a shadowy color and a melancholy mood. The tone F-sharp plays a significant role in shading the sound of B minor. Throughout the first seven measures, F-sharp is sustained in octaves against shifting harmonies. By sustaining the fifth of the key instead of the tonic, Mendelssohn has created a floating, suspended effect, a backdrop, and thus he touches off the impression of continued monotony within which an aimless yet restless motion can stir.

Another element in the play of sound in this piece is the upward sideslip by thirds. Traditionally, bass movement by thirds proceeds downward, often in preparation for a powerful cadence. The decisive effect of such a traditional progression as that in Example 9-8 affirms the key as though it were concluding an argument. The tone that binds the progression is B. By reversing the series, moving the bass *upward* by thirds Mendelssohn creates a progression that pivots on F-sharp (Ex. 9-9). The progression has an open-endedness proper to the impression of the sea suggested by the pictorial indication of the title. This open effect is especially persuasive in view of the presence of the minor dominant in the movement upward by thirds.[2]

F sharp is also a fulcrum for harmonic "teetering" in the second key area of this overture. Although the key is now D major, Mendelssohn, seemingly reluctant to turn completely away from his home key of B minor, uses F sharp as a pivot to swing back and forth between the two keys in measures 48, 52–53, 61–62, 72–73, and 85. At the end of the exposition, F sharp again becomes the switching point, together with D, when the fifth of the D-major harmony, A, disappears to allow the key to slip once more to B minor at the beginning of the development.

While harmony establishes the basic color of the piece, scoring is critical in bringing the color to its telling effect. Mendelssohn's orchestra has exactly the same disposition as that of the last Haydn symphonies—strings, winds in pairs, horns and trumpets, timpani. Yet the sound that the orchestra of the 1830's could produce far outreaches the orchestral effects of Haydn's time in color and mass. Improvements in wind instruments enabled performers to sustain tones with rich color and intensity so that a sustained tone could produce a striking, arresting musical effect. Haydn's orchestra in London had 12 violins, 4 violas, 3–4 violoncelli, 1–2 contrabasses. Orchestras in Mendelssohn's time often doubled these numbers. A band of 24–28 violins can touch a magic note in sustaining F-sharp softly, almost hypnotically. Such an effect belonged to the orchestra of the Romantic period; it is a choice example of "composing" the first sound in a piece. Example 9-7 quotes the first sixteen measures, the opening period of the piece.

The opening period is neatly segmented into four four-measure groups. Thus it embodies absolute symmetry in its phrase structure. But Mendels-

EXAMPLE 9-7. Sixteen-measure period. Mendelssohn, *Hebrides* Overture, Op. 26, 1832.

Example 9-7.   (continued)

Mendelssohn, *Hebrides,* Eulenburg Edition. Used by kind permission of European American Music Distributors Corporation, agent for Eulenburg Editions.

sohn makes some subtle adaptations of the structure, giving special values to both the small- and large-scale layouts.

His principal idea is an arabesque contained within a single measure; it embodies a single harmony but it is striking in its melodic contour as well as in its play of rhythm, where it works a rather complex upbeat-downbeat pattern within the measure. This arabesque figure has the power to renew itself constantly, which it does throughout the piece. It is introduced quietly, almost as an afterthought, as a patterned opening-out of the harmony, but as the music progresses this figure takes on the character of a leading theme, compact and driving.

Since the figure embodies a single harmony within a single measure, it lends itself to exponential treatment, specifically in pairs of paired statements. Perhaps Mendelssohn's most critical decision regarding syntax was to take the option to repeat the figure, thus doubling the scale of the first period from eight measures to sixteen. Without the repetition, the first period might have come out as a typical eight-measure segment, Example 9-10.

The breadth of the double statements establishes long trajectories that support the deliberate unfolding of the overture's harmonic plan, in sonata form. But within the opening period the double statements create a crisis of rhythm. Were they to maintain their doubling automatically, the period

EXAMPLE 9-8. Downward motion by thirds.

EXAMPLE 9-9. Harmonic reduction of mm. 1–9. Mendelssohn, *Hebrides* Overture, Op. 26, 1832.

would not close at the sixteenth measure but reach its cadence one measure later. Mendelssohn peremptorily compresses action in measures 14-16 in order to reach the tonic on the third beat of measure 16. The two-measure momentum is arbitrarily "tripped up"; the cadence, although authentic, is light, even a bit inconsequential. In this situation, symmetry momentarily overrides sound and movement, forcing a regular closure upon action that has an open-ended tendency. While the compression embodies traditional period structure at cadences, the momentum of the innovative sound carries the action forward. Symmetry, here, does not arrest the flow of sound. However, symmetry opens its own path to a much stronger confirmation of the home key. This will take place solidly on the downbeats at measures 26 and 30. The doubling of the *micro* figure generates the growth of the *macro* action.

One detail of harmony remains to be noted; this is the subdominant harmony at measures 7–8. Traditionally, measure 8 would close provisionally upon dominant harmony, to be answered by tonic harmony closure in measure 16. Mendelssohn maintains the fluid harmony of his opening measures by sliding through IV at measure 8; this constitutes a much less clear harmonic articulation than we would hear with V, and the period has *no* half-cadence. Thus, the light authentic cadence in measure 16 is prefigured by the non-cadential articulation in measures 8–9. Seventeen measures later, the first key area closes with a powerfully rhythmic authentic cadence and a series of harmonic reinforcements through measures 17–30. In details of harmony and scoring, Mendelssohn in his music shows an inventiveness that has a typical Romantic individuality. In the larger units of syntax—periods and key areas—he has a strong grip on traditional procedures, especially in the *Hebrides* Overture.

The ninth number from Schumann's *Davidsbündlertänze*, Op. 6 (1837) (Ex. 9-11) incorporates symmetry in a very different manner than the excerpt

EXAMPLE 9-10. Rhetorical melodic reduction of mm. 1–16. Mendelssohn, *Hebrides* Overture, Op. 26, 1832.

EXAMPLE 9-11. Symmetry controlling shifting harmony. Schumann, *Davidsbündlertänze*, Op. 6, No. 9, 1837.

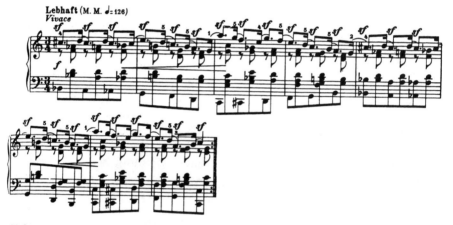

Kalmus.

from Mendelssohn's *Hebrides* overture (Ex. 9-7). Whereas Mendelssohn arranged simple triads in pseudomodal progressions, avoiding strong dominant-tonic cadential action, but retaining a crystal-clear symmetrical layout, Schumann saturated his period with restless cadential progressions incorporating many harmonic and melodic dissonances. Rigorous symmetry and volatile, shifting harmony are at odds with each other. The precise two- and four-measure templates compress a restless harmonic thrust that will barely reach its cadence upon the last beat of measure 8. Further complexity arises from the hint of hemiolia in the melody in measures 3–4 and 7–8.

The piece begins off-center, with a dominant-seventh chord on B flat. A long C-sharp appoggiatura in the soprano makes the chord unlikely to be heard as the dominant of E flat. If the alto's A flat were respelled enharmonically as G sharp, the chord could be construed as a German sixth in D minor, and that indeed is how the chord resolves. But the bass continues its downward chromatic motion through A flat to G, where a full measure of dominant-seventh harmony on G establishes C as the tonic. Still, the long appoggiaturas on every beat but the last spur the action forward and add intense color to the restless harmony. The full texture, the rather low center of tonal gravity, and the relentless sforzandos all contribute to the declamatory style.

Example 9-12 reduces the melody and texture to a two-part counterpoint, while Example 9-13 demonstrates what the two-part reduction could be, had the piece begun on the tonic. Example 9-13 retains salient features of Example 9-12, notably the melodic apexes in measures 3 and 7 and portions of the descending chromatic bass, measures 1 and 5, as well as the C sharp–D progressions in measures 3 and 7. The beginning on C, of course, changes the character so that Example 9-13 becomes a minuet.

This excerpt from the *Davidsbündlertänze* typifies Schumann's most characteristic piano texture. He marshals the sound resources of the nineteenth-century piano to create an intense declamatory style, with full harmonies and a rather low center of textural gravity. While he often breaks up the chord, dispersing his harmonies in arpeggio figures, the heavier textures better support his serious and eloquent manner of expression.

EXAMPLE 9-12. Rhetorical melodic reduction of mm. 1–8. Schumann, *Davidsbündlertänze*, Op. 6, No. 9, 1837.

EXAMPLE 9-13. Rhetorical melodic reduction altered to begin on tonic harmony of measures 1–8. Schumann, *Davidsbündlertänze*, Op. 6, No. 9, 1837.

In its simplest manifestation, symmetry in period structure can be rigid, exerting total control over musical time within its balanced layout of phrases. But its very firmness, the clarity of its processes, invites manipulations; within the *impression* of symmetry there can be the play of stretching, compressing, distorting, reinforcing, digressing. The pairings and the cadences of the symmetrical period become points of departure and of reference in an expanded rhetorical trajectory.

The next chapters investigate ways that sound can modify periodic symmetries and extend periodic trajectories. By these means the interaction of sound and syntax reaches beyond the boundaries of the symmetrical period to affect the shapes of larger structures.

# CHAPTER TEN

# Modifications of Symmetry

Disturbances of periodic balance in eighteenth-century music—digressions, repetitions, insertions, elongations of melodic or harmonic components—could extend periods to enormous lengths. For example, the first period in the opening movement of Mozart's Quintet in C major, K. 515, covers fifty-seven measures, yet its perimeters match those of the model eight-measure period form. It comprises two huge phrase groups, measures 1–20 and measures 21–57. Both groups begin with the same melodic material. The first group comes to a pause on the dominant in measures 19–20; the second group closes with a powerful authentic cadence.

Harmony and melody were the principal agents in modifying periodic symmetries in the eighteenth century; sound became another agent in the Romantic era.[1] Sound, by focusing the attention of composer, performer, and listener, can affect the flow of musical time, slowing it to a virtual standstill, as does the long, drawn-out A of the trumpet at the beginning of Wagner's *Rienzi* (1842). Bold effects introduced unpredictably, can manipulate time in eccentric ways, as in the opening section of the finale of Berlioz's *Symphonie fantastique*. When sound, even for a moment, draws attention to itself as an expressive value in music, it gives that moment a greater autonomy and can thus affect the unfolding of musical forms in ways not available with traditional topical and affective stances.

The analyses to follow here and in Chapter 11 take as guidelines the features of the symmetrical period: intermediate and final cadences; complementary arrangements of figures and phrases. In the modified and extended periods of Romantic music we can still trace underlying elements of the symmetrical period. These enable us to locate critical points of articulation; they also shed light on the ways in which modification and extension take place.

The examples in this chapter retain relatively clear profiles of the symmetrical period. They present complementary pairings of opening phrases; they have well-articulated middle cadences and decisive final cadences, regardless of their length or inner expansions. Chapter 11 examines periods that have significant extensions, often caused by interpolations within the period, so that periodic balance is markedly disturbed. While the two categories of expansion—modification and extension—overlap, here they are presented as two different processes. In brief, modified periods make overt allusions to the conventional symmetrical period; that is, they behave as though they were symmetrical even when they are not. Extended periods, in contrast, place rhetorical emphasis on the expansive forces that obscure but do not efface their links to the symmetrical period. The present chapter looks at two means of modifying symmetrical periods, by sustained sounds and by harmonic progressions.

## Symmetry Modified by Sustained Sounds

Subtle and elegant distortions of periodic symmetry, along with delicate, highly contrasted figures, evoke an elfin mood at the beginning of Weber's Overture to *Oberon;* the passage is quoted in full in Example 4-16. By extrapolating from the two reductions in Examples 10-1 and 10-2, we can pinpoint Weber's modifications of symmetry.

Example 10-1 gathers the tones of Weber's melody into a symmetrical period whose affect is that of a sentimental song. Measures 3–4, the *a'* figure of the reduction, match measures 1–2, the *a* figure, while measures 5, the *b* figure, and 7, the *b'* figure, match each other. Balance is maintained in every parameter—melody, harmony, rhythm, texture. At a moderato or andantino tempo instead of adagio, this melody would have a length of about twenty seconds. The original, when the adagio tempo and five fermatas are observed, takes at least one minute in actual performance. The adagio tempo, of course, is critical to this longer duration. It serves principally as a control that allows the play of sound to emerge and to reverberate, the horn and winds suggesting the magic sounds of Oberon's enchanted forest. Weber highlights each effect by isolating it and by setting striking colors in juxtaposition against each other. The fermatas isolate the contrasting colors, modify the period, and enhance the effect of reverberation and fading out, a hint of the faraway.

EXAMPLE 10-1.  Rhetorical melodic reduction of mm. 1–10, matching figures. Weber, Overture to *Oberon*, 1825–26.

EXAMPLE 10-2.  Harmonic reduction of mm. 1–10. Weber, Overture to *Oberon*, 1825–26.

Harmonic touches contribute to the elusive quality of this excerpt. Example 10-2 shows, in measures 4–5, a chromatic shading that touches on III and VI (F sharp) where we might expect the customary dominant, A. Moreover, the delay and digression in measure 4 shifts the C sharp to measure 5 instead of the second half of measure 4, where it would match the A of measure 2. Two measures of interpolation, mm. 6–7, add to the stretching of symmetry and provide room for the delightful contrast of staccato woodwind sound, elegantly placed in contrast to the suave legato of the opening melody. They constitute a harmonic parenthesis between two positions of the supertonic.

Large-scale periodic balance is maintained in the opening measures of Schubert's Quintet in C Major (Ex. 10-3a), but the special sound qualities discussed in Chapter 5 (Ex. 5-7) affect the inner structure and the length of each member of the period.

The composed *messa di voce* that begins the quintet sets no clear rhythmic frame of reference for the first four measures and only tentatively so in measures 5–6. As a counterstatement to these first six measures, Schubert

EXAMPLE 10-3.    Modifications by means of sustained chords.
a. Schubert, Quintet in C Major, Op. 163, 1828, first movement.

Used by permission of Dover Publications, Inc. Reproduced from *Franz Schubert's Werke*, Series 4, ed. Eusebius Mandyczewski. Breitkopf & Härtel (1890).

introduces an elegant melody, measures 6–9, touched with memories of eighteenth-century galanterie, short-breathed, colored with appoggiaturas.

The antecedent member of this period reaches a length of ten measures as a result of the prolonged chords in measures 1–6. All the melodic material of this member, however, can easily be gathered into a four-measure phrase, as shown in the reduction (Ex. 10-3b). Moreover, the scansion of this phrase breaks down irregularly, as six plus three plus one; the final measure is added to complete a four-measure group. Sound has stretched syntax.

The consequent member, measures 11–20, is a complement to the first member. It follows a comparable melodic path but moves in a different band of the pitch spectrum. The sound is low, heavy, suggesting the pathetic rather than the sweetly poignant. While the galanterie with its appoggiaturas answers the sustained sounds, the figure has little of the buoyancy of measures 7–9. In this low range the setting of the melody has a richness rarely heard in earlier music. Topically, the entire first period shows the declamatory style of the arioso, charged with intensity, full texture, and irregular motion.

b. Rhetorical melodic reduction of first period.

Schubert's harmonic trajectory adds something to the striking effect of sound. It is outlined by the following degrees: I–V; II–V–I. This is a rather uncommon arrangement of complementary harmony in a period, and it gives the change in register, measure 11, a striking effect, rather unexpected following the traditional dominant of measures 9–10. However, this harmonic arrangement was now and then used in Classic music. The opening of Mozart's Sonata in D Major, K. 576 moves through the same sequence of harmonies. This is quoted in Example 10-4. But where Mozart's harmony is geared entirely to action, expedited by the lightness of a minimal two-voice texture, Schubert's harmony, set in close position with full textures and a slow, irregular rate of chord change, directs the listener's attention to the change of register in measure 11, the midpoint of the period.

# Symmetry Modified by Harmonic Progressions

Periodic symmetry is supported by complementary harmonic arrangements, such as I–V, V–I; I–IV, V–I; and so on. Such arrangements bind the music tightly to its central key. Other arrangements can disturb the sharp tonal focus, leading to digressions that modify symmetry. The examples to follow illustrate such modifications.

The broad opening measure in the second movement of Schubert's Quintet in C Major is the first gesture in what will become a period of tremendous length, twenty-four measures of adagio time. Notwithstanding its length, this period has the contours of the prototypical symmetrical period: an antecedent member that closes on a half cadence, and a consequent member

EXAMPLE 10-4. I–II–V–I plan. Mozart, Sonata in D Major, K. 576, 1789, first movement.

© 1956 Theodore Presser Company. Used by permission of the publisher.

that echoes the melodic contour of the opening and closes on an authentic cadence (Ex. 10-5).

Schubert sustains the sound of E major for the first full $\frac{12}{8}$ adagio measure, within which we hear a magical play of sound, dispersed, with gentle glints surrounding a flowing core. Only on the last two eighth notes of the measure does the second violin give any impression of a melody. Schubert activates the ambience of E major by lining up rhythmic fragments in countertime alternating high and low registers. The first violin is assigned anapest meter, the cello answers with iambs, while the three inner voices respond with elongated dactyls. This play of meters provides a model for the succeeding measures of the E-major section. This is a simple serial arrangement of tones of the type that Chopin often lays out in his piano music. The accompaniment suggests the plucking of a mandolin, of the sort that supported the singer of popular songs in the Viennese wine houses. What might have been a popular song, perhaps a berceuse or possibly a slow barcarolle, is stretched to enormous lengths. The song moves deliberately, with a gently swinging flow. Example 10-6 extracts the song from the long, drawn-out flow of sound. The reduction makes some changes in the harmonic progression to conform to standard usage in Schubert's time. The eight-measure period reaches a cadence on the dominant, and its accompaniment has been reduced to an Alberti bass. The meter has been halved, to a typical $\frac{6}{8}$ barcarolle time.

At the beginning, something odd happens to the song. Its harmony goes askew! Were it to traverse a traditional cadential path its harmony would proceed as follows: I–II–V–I or I–V–V–I, and the cadential cycle would have been completed in the fourth measure. Instead, it begins immediately to ascend a circle of fifths to arrive at the distant degree, C-sharp major, in the fourth measure, from which high point it slowly settles down to the

EXAMPLE 10-5. Extended period. Schubert, Quintet in C Major, 1828, second movement.

EXAMPLE 10-5.  (*continued*)

Used by permission of Dover Publications, Inc. Reproduced from *Franz Schubert's Werke*, Series 4, ed. Eusebius Mandyczewski. Breitkopf & Härtel (1890).

EXAMPLE 10-6.  Rhetorical melodic reduction of theme. Schubert, Quintet in C Major, 1828, second movement.

dominant, B major. If this harmony were to underlay a simple barcarolle in $\frac{6}{8}$ meter, the effect would be somewhat awry, even grotesque. Schubert holds each chord for a full measure, allowing the listener to savor the effect of the unexpected turn of harmony along with the play of sound and figure within each measure. The effect is strange, somewhat elusive, but compelling.

An example from Beethoven, a slow movement in the same key as Schubert's adagio, begins with much the same harmonic itinerary, I–V–II–VI (Ex. 10-7). The movement begins in motet style, adding a voice with each chord of the reverse progression, quite unlike Schubert's full-voiced texture. Beethoven complicates the harmony in measures 4–6 but quickly restores clear harmonic direction by moving toward an authentic cadence in measure 8; Schubert does not reach the comparable cadence until measure 24. Beethoven follows the reverse progression, after a bit of wandering, with a powerful drive to the cadence; Schubert embraces the reverse progression on its own terms because it fits to his idea of sound as a primary value. In the Schubert and the Beethoven examples the same unusual progression supports two very different affects—a solemn, archaic mood and a barcarolle.

When Schubert does reach the cadence of the period, he reinforces the effect of closure by following it with two additional cadential gestures, measures 24-28, each of which traverses the familiar path I–Ib⁷–IV–V⁷–I. Harmonic rhythm quickens; interchange of mode, secondary dominants, appoggiaturas, and neighbor tones add color. After the long, drawn-out centrifugal harmonies of the period itself (the tonic appears only in measures 1, 15, and 24 of the period), these cadential gestures have a deeply poignant effect as they move momentarily away from the tonic and return.

Chopin's Prelude in E Minor, Op. 28, No. 4, has some features in common with the preceding two examples from the Schubert Quintet. The entire piece reproduced in Example 10-8, consists of a single period whose contours, like the Schubert excerpts, reflect the conventions of the symmetrical period—

EXAMPLE 10-7.  I–V–II–VI plan. Beethoven, Quartet in E Minor, Op. 59, No. 2, 1805–6, second movement.

Used by permission of Dover Publications, Inc. From *Beethoven's Werke*, Serie 6, published by Brietkopf & Härtel (n.d.).

well-defined antecedent and consequent members, parallel melodic begin-nings for the two members, half and authentic cadences to articulate the form. Also, like the Schubert examples, the prelude uses sound values to modify symmetry.

Chopin's decision to begin the prelude on a close-position first inversion of E minor was critical both for the form and the sound of the piece. A first inversion of a triad lacks the stability, the firmness of a root position chord. Because such inversions usually appear in the course of a phrase, the left hand's first sound conveys a subtle effect of movement already under way.

Parallel sixth chords amplify a conjunct melodic line. Their harmonies need not crystallize into complementary tonic-dominant alternations. There-fore, a phrase built on or incorporating parallel sixth chords is not as closely bound to symmetry as a phrase alternating basic harmonies. The prelude's

EXAMPLE 10-8. Period modified by descending bass. Chopin, Prelude in E Minor, Op. 28, No. 4, 1838.

EXAMPLE 10-8.   (*continued*)

initial sixth chord sets in motion a line of descent that comes to rest eventually at measure 12, a much longer trajectory than would be the case in a "regular" period. The second part of the piece carries out much the same procedure. In both parts the harmony is eventually anchored by powerful arrivals at the dominant (mm. 10, 17), which is extended, (mm. 10–12, 17–24) by neighbor harmonies that enhance its drive.

The chromatically descending bass eventually obscures the symmetry of the upper line; it allows the melody to spin out in slow iambic meter. The steady repetitions of this slowly moving figure mask its potentially songlike character.

The reduction in Example 10-9 isolates some familiar syntactical components. It puts the latent symmetries of the period—figure and phrase—into sharp focus. It stands on solid harmonic and rhythmic ground, beginning on root-position harmony and aligning the figures clearly in two-plus-two and four-plus-four groups. The harmony retains some of the chromatic shading of the original, but it alters and simplifies the chord-to-chord connection so

EXAMPLE 10-9.   Rhetorical melodic reduction. Chopin, Prelude in E Minor, Op. 28, No. 4, 1838.

that cadential action is brought into high relief, especially in measures 1–2, 7–8. Measures 3–6 pick up the descending sixth-chord action of the original. The accompaniment, with its simple broken-chord figure, eliminates the element of color that characterizes the original. As a result, the elusive, introspective mood is turned into a plaintive, songlike one.

Schumann creates a remarkable rapprochement between some simple structural features and a number of elegant and unique inventions in the opening period of his Fantasia in C Major. Example 10-10a quotes the period, measures 1–19. Example 10-10b gives the measure-to-measure harmonic progression. Example 10-10c compresses the progression into its basic cadential elements. Example 10-10d extracts a simple tune from the opening period.

Unbroken figuration is the principal agent that creates a climate of sound at the beginning of the piece. The steady, driving pattern establishes a pervasive presence for C major. The key of C major is clearly indicated by a series of its diatonic harmonies, but at no point does the music achieve a cadential establishment or confirmation in that key. Moreover, the harmonies that embody C major in measures 1–7 create an uncertain harmonic climate within that key. For its time, the 1830s, this climate was unique, unlike that of any earlier work in the Western repertoire. Specifically, the sound gives an impression of two harmonies intertwined, supertonic seventh and dominant seventh.[2] This impression is created partly by the left hand's action; the tones G and D are the prominent bass notes, outlining the dominant harmony, while D and A on every third beat give the color of supertonic harmony. In the right hand the tones A and C, as suspensions, contribute to the uncertain harmonic color. The leading tone, B, is absent in the first six measures, yet the prominent Gs in the bass emphasize the dominant as a harmonic factor in this passage. Eventually, at measure 19, the period closes with a solid authentic cadence in G major, only to return immediately to the less stable harmony of measures 9–12.

Example 10-10.    Schumann, Fantasia in C Major, Op. 17, 1836–38, opening period.
a. Opening pedal on dominant.

Kalmus.

b. Harmonic reduction of mm. 1–19.

c. Compression of basic cadential formulas.

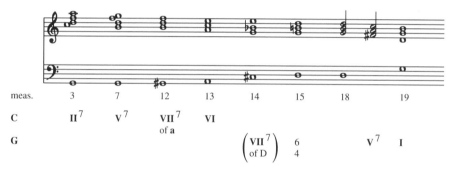

| meas. | 3 | 7 | 12 | 13 | 14 | 15 | 18 | 19 |
|---|---|---|---|---|---|---|---|---|
| C | II$^7$ | V$^7$ | VII$^7$ of a | VI | | | | |
| G | | | | | $\left(\begin{array}{c}\text{VII}^7\\\text{of D}\end{array}\right)$ | $\begin{array}{c}6\\4\end{array}$ | V$^7$ | I |

d. Rhetorical melodic reduction of mm. 2–19.

m.  2  3  4   5  6  7  8   9  10 11 12   13 14  15  16  17 18  19

The traditional structural features exposed by the reductions in Example 10-10b–d include:

1. The pedal point on the dominant that anchors the harmony
2. The powerful cadential drive that develops through the nineteen measures
3. The formal modulation to G, complete with cadential six-fours and dominant sevenths
4. The internal balanced period structure, built of two complementary phrases
5. The simple descending melodic line, songlike and conjunct, that helps to bind the action, promoting both direction and coherence

Upon the sturdy armature established by these components, a fluid declamation emerges. While the music begins in C major, this key is indicated at first by its dominant, not its tonic. The piece seems to begin in medias res, the two-measure curtain setting the textural and harmonic climate for the first principal section of the piece. The figuration sustains a rare mood, tentative and floating, with somewhat astringent harmonies that touch on diatonic dissonances–sevenths, ninths, elevenths, thirteenths—while avoiding the tritone until measure 7.

The period form serves as the underlying frame to direct the effect of sound, to control the extent and goal of its flow. Symmetry is slightly modified—one and one-half measures precede the complementary pattern, and the cadence in G major is broadened by one measure by the hint of a deceptive cadence in measure 17. Of these modifications, the first is much more important; it sets the climate of sound, generates the flow on which the harmonies of the right hand will float.

Keyboard texture plays a supporting role in the sound of this passage. Neither the compass (less than three and a half octaves) nor the figuration contribute striking values that immediately command the listener's attention, as they do in the Liszt and Chopin examples discussed in Chapter 3. The close-position sonorities in the right hand are placed in a middle register; they do not have the brilliant, tense effect of higher octaves nor the rich fullness of lower octaves. The active figuration in the bass generally moves in a middle to high register, clear but not colorful. On a rather lightly strung piano of Schumann's time pedalling would sustain the low G's while adding resonance to the involutions of the figuration; the heavier pedalling of the modern piano would require some modification in order not to blur the action.

Schumann's texture is retrospective, an adaptation of continuo practice. The uppermost line is a simple treble melody; the chords immediately below represent the filling-out of the harmony by the right hand of the continuo player; and the active bass represents the thoroughbass line itself, ornamented in a manner available to expert continuo players in the eighteenth century.

Still, Schumann's adaptations of traditional harmonic and period procedures reach far into the world of fantasy. Conventional procedures, except for range, are blurred. By stretching out the action, pausing on unusual harmonic mixes and passing tones, compromising the pedal point, and reversing the melodic roles of treble and bass (active versus static), Schumann shapes a period that holds the listener in suspense until the cadence at measure 19.

The final example of modified symmetry is taken from Isolde's aria, the so-called *Liebestod*, that closes the third act of Wagner's *Tristan und Isolde*. After the turmoil and anguish centered on the dying Tristan, Isolde begins her final expression of love in a relatively calm manner (Ex. 10-11). Wagner turns to the style of the Romantic *Lied;* the music opens as if it were to be a love song. Its first six measures embody symmetries in melody, rhythm, and

EXAMPLE 10-11.   Wagner, *Tristan und Isolde*, 1859, Act III, "Liebestod."

EXAMPLE 10-11.   (*continued*)

harmony, especially in the orchestral background to Isolda's declamation. Measures 1 and 2 pair with measures 3 and 4; measure 5 pairs with measure 6. The concentration of major triads lends the harmonies a sweeter, more transparent quality than does the concentration of tritone harmonies that precede this aria throughout the opera.

Still, harmony is the modifier of symmetry in this passage. Harmonic stability is compromised by Wagner's assigning $\frac{6}{4}$ and $\frac{6}{3}$ inversions to most of the harmonies. The chromatic shifts create an open-ended flow of sound with no firm sense of a ruling tonal center, no clear projection of periodic arrival. Juxtapositions of strikingly different harmonic colors, assigned to the warm lower registers of strings and clarinets, draw the listener's attention to sound as a chief expressive value. The harmonic reduction in Example 10-11 places all harmonies in root position; the effect is considerably more "square," the color shifts are bolder, but the sense of open-ended flow is lost. Thus, Wagner's choice of chord position is critical for the expressive quality of this passage.

Had this passage returned to its opening key, A-flat major, it would have constituted a symmetrical period. But Wagner's unstable inversions and quick chromatic shifts open the way to harmonic digressions, and he makes a new beginning in B major at the twelfth measure. Example 10-12 reduces the passage to eight measures and completes the circle of minor thirds that

EXAMPLE 10-12. Rhetorical melodic and textural reduction and adjustment to symmetrical period structure. Wagner, *Tristan und Isolde*, 1859, Act III, "Liebestod."

would have led the excerpt back to A-flat major—A flat, C flat, D, F, A flat. The result is the first period of a *Lied* in a later Romantic style. Paradoxically, the circle of thirds itself is an embodiment of symmetry, although it needs the rhetorical gesture of an authentic cadence to become integrated into traditional period structure. The harmonies in the reduction in root positions, create bolder contrasts between pairs of chords and emphasize the essential squareness of the first six measures. Some minor melodic adjustments in measures 2 and 4 insure proper voice leading, avoiding Isolde's irregular declamation, which nonetheless fits to the scansion of the orchestral background measure for measure. Most important is the close in the opening key with a strong authentic cadence to fulfill the requirements of traditional periodicity. The original version, on the contrary, hints momentarily at A flat in measure 11, placing it in a $^6_4$ inversion and reading it as a subdominant to the preceding dominant of E flat major—an equivocal, shadowy recollection of the opening key before the music shifts quickly to what will be the closing key, B major.

In their sound-syntax relationship, the eleven measures cited in Example 10-11 constitute a veritable paradigm for Wagner's rhetoric: paired opening statements set on different degrees with a shift of tonal direction, leading to a narrowing, a dissolution, followed by a new start along the same lines. This action is held together and kept moving by Wagner's rich harmonic language, itself a modification of traditional cadential processes.

As in the other periods examined in this chapter, Wagner's colorist harmonies act as special qualities of sound that generate local irregularities in period structure—tentative beginnings or internal expansions. These, in turn, compromise absolute symmetry. Yet the excerpt from *Tristan und Isolde* is the only one of the periods discussed here that escapes the bonds of its structural paradigm and avoids closing with a clearly marked cadence.

# CHAPTER ELEVEN

# Extensions

The periods discussed in this chapter, though they are still linked to the symmetrical paradigm, incorporate significant disturbances in the way of extensions: interpolations, parentheses, harmonic digressions, cadential expansions by means of pedal points, repetitions, or reinforcements. These extensions distort periodic symmetry more radically than did the periodic modifications examined in Chapter 10. The music selected here for analysis represents two kinds of declamation: *songlike,* in which the regularity of phrase order is interrupted, and *discursive,* in which development procedures —spinning-out of action, sequences—is part of the essential syntax.

The excerpts from the *Symphonie fantastique* of Berlioz and *Das Lied von der Erde* by Mahler represent the songlike arrangement. The examples from the Symphony No. 1 by Brahms, the Sonata in B minor by Liszt, and the Prelude to *Tristan und Isolde* by Wagner represent discursive layouts.

## Songlike Declamation

Berlioz announces the *idée fixe,* the opening theme of the allegro in the first movement of his *Symphonie fantastique* with a vibrant, intense, unaccompanied unison on G. This tone is assigned to the first violins (see Berlioz's prescription, p. 55) subtly shaded by the flute on the same tone (Ex. 11-1).

EXAMPLE 11-1.   Berlioz, *Symphonie fantastique*, Op. 14, 1830, first movement. (See Ex. 11-8a, m. 71, for the upbeat to the theme in m. 72.)

Used by permission of Dover Publications, Inc. Reproduced from: *Werke von Hector Berlioz*, Vol. 1, ed. Charles Malherbe and Felix Weingartner. Breitkopf & Härtel (1900–1910).

Throughout the length of the theme this tone quality is maintained, shaded with swells and fadings upon longer notes. The massive unison setting gives the theme a striking presence, as though it were declaiming an impassioned arioso.

Once the lyric mood of the theme is set, Berlioz interjects, after six measures, a series of sporadic percussive trochees in the lower strings (thirty-five to forty). Sound becomes polarized as the high, smooth melodic line and the low, brusque unpredictable accompaniment confront each other both in time and at distant pitch levels.

Such extreme contrasts in sound quality highlight a startling effect of rhythmic counterpoint, as if we were hearing two very different tempi engaging in a tug of war, resolved only by the fermata that absorbs both lines (m. 109) just before the cadence of the theme.

Despite the frequent and irregular changes of motion within the theme— long notes against short, stops, starts, changes of tempo—the theme retains a sense of symmetrical groupings. Two long complementary phrases (mm. 72–86) precede series of four-measure phrases that build a chromatic rising sequence (mm. 87–102). The theme closes at measure 111, with an elegant periodic cadence reminiscent of Classic declamation which offers an instant of relaxation in the turbulent flow of the music. This familiar traditional gesture is set off by the most colorful harmonic-textural moment in the theme, a series of chromatically descending sixth chords. The entire theme encompasses a period of forty measures, in which length is generated by a play of sound on different rhythmic and pitch levels.

From this extended statement a symmetrical sixteen-measure period can be pieced out. Example 11-2 reduces the notes of the theme to equal quarter notes, laid out in four-measure phrases that expose the pairings of melodic figures, and bypasses the broad chromatic sequence of measures 87–100 to move directly to the cadence. With the flavor of a popular song or dance of Berlioz's time, the reduction retains the shape of the theme, its inner balances, and something of the stretto effect toward the end, but cuts away everything that sound promotes in the way of irregularity and extension. Setting the reduction against the original, we can point to some specific tactics used by Berlioz to modify and extend traditional symmetry with effects of sound:

1. The initial downbeat, G, a quarter note in the reduction, is sustained for five beats in the original. This immediately sets a trajectory that will require considerable time to reach its point of arrival. Other melodic tones match this irregularity.
2. A stretto develops in the melody as punctuations appear at increasingly shorter intervals, until finally the melody runs without a break in sound to its cadence.

EXAMPLE 11-2. Rhetorical melodic reduction of mm. 72–112. Berlioz, *Symphonie fantastique*, Op. 14, 1830, first movement.

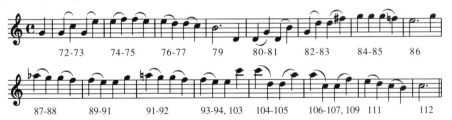

3. The percussive interjections of the lower strings chop the time values in the first part of the period into irregular pieces. This process gives a powerful sense of consequence to the figures themselves, putting them into sharp relief against the interpolated silences. The very weight of the figures, performed by a massive string corps, is critical for the striking sound and the irregular syntax.

Texturally, the theme is an eccentric version of a simple melody and accompaniment layout, a tune supported by drumbeats.

The *idée fixe* undergoes a number of transformations during the course of the symphony, reflecting the changing moods or pictorial implications of the five movements. The middle movements isolate the theme from the main action of the movement, lending it a faraway, pastoral quality. In the finale the theme is twisted into a grotesque dance. Already in its first appearance, though, thanks to Berlioz's scorings and his disturbance of symmetry, the *idée fixe* has something of the character of a parody, distorted, a part of the fantasy indicated by the subtitle of the movement "Dreams and Passions."

In Gustav Mahler's music, as in that of Berlioz, song, dance, or march are often impinged upon by strikingly contrasted sounds and figures. This we hear at the beginning of his song cycle *Das Lied von der Erde* (1908). Measures 1–33 of "Das Trinklied vom Jammer der Erde" (Ex. 11-3) make up a harmonic period that begins and closes in A. Imbedded in this period is a two-phrase song, reducible to eight measures, complementary in its harmonic, rhythmic, and melodic relationships (Ex. 11-4). The reduction's setting is syllabic, the melodic movement conjunct, the range limited to a sixth, and the rhythm steady and regular, in quarter notes interspersed with longer notes.[1]

Mahler creates a bleak environment for this section of the song. As a key and as a color A minor's presence is felt in fourteen of the thirty-three measures, embodied in various ways:

1. A melodic outline in the horns, mm. 1–9
2. Full tonic harmonies, mm. 2–8, 25
3. Movement through diatonically related harmonies: E minor, mm. 10–11; G major, m. 12; F major, m. 13; C major, mm. 14–16
4. Authentic cadence, mm. 32–33

Example 11-5 shows the essentially diatonic harmonies, the slow harmonic rhythm, and the traditional descending bass, followed by tonic-dominant progressions.

A remarkable feature of the procedures thus far described—song, syntax, and harmony—is their limited scope. In these thirty-three measures we hear just eleven changes of harmony, while the phrase structure has a comparable footing, solid and simple.

Mahler introduced extraordinary means to elaborate and extend the declamation. He juxtaposed ornamental figures against one another and against the leading melodic lines in bold, short range contrasts. In these

EXAMPLE 11-3.  Mahler, *Das Lied von der Erde,* No. 1, 1908, "Das Trinklied," mm. 1–33.

EXAMPLE 11-3.  (*continued*)

EXAMPLE 11-3. *(continued)*

EXAMPLE 11-4. Rhetorical melodic reduction of mm. 16–33. Mahler, "Das Trinklied."

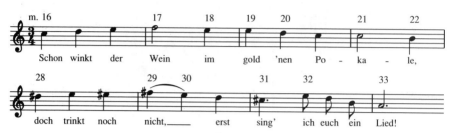

thirty-three measures we hear dozens of short, incisive figures enter and
disappear. Arpeggios, tiratas, appoggiaturas, dissonant neighbor and passing
tones, concitato figures, and acciaccaturas momentarily flash and disappear,
lending poignancy to the prevailing A-minor sound. Silence plays an
important role here as it puts each figure into relief. Through this collage of
mixed figures, exquisitely timed, Mahler developed a tension that sustains
the action and expands the period from a hypothetical eight measures to
thirty three.

Timbre and harmonic color sharpen the relief that isolates each figure.
Mahler treats the orchestra as a huge chamber ensemble in which individual
lines and gestures are set in upper registers, punctuated by incisive interpolations in bass voices, in contrast to the lavish doublings of his contemporary,
Richard Strauss. When lines are played together, they sometimes have the
effect of heterophony, as in measures 3–4, where four different versions of
the neighbor-tone figure move simultaneously. Each timbre makes a brief
and striking point, an accent of color, often edgy, rarely suave, separated
from others rather than blended.

Harmony contributes its ornaments to color the basic A-minor sound. At
the beginning we hear a complex changing-tone figure, D sharp, D, F, E, D
sharp, that impinges with an edge upon the basic A-minor sound and sets the
mood of sharp poignancy.

Then a decisive move: in measure 6 we hear G natural, which, by ignoring
the leading tone, introduces a pentatonic flavor to the harmony, negating its
cadential possibilities. Later, two broad strokes of harmonic color shade the
basic A minor: the extended Neapolitan harmony, with its depressing B flat
and E flat (mm. 17–24), and the momentary turn to A major, with F sharp
and C sharp (mm. 29–32). The first of these introduces the solo voice; the
second highlights the pathetic contrast of A major and A minor at the close of
the period.

While the entire period is set generally at a fortissimo dynamic, many
shadings add their color to the ornamentation—diminuendos, crescendos,
sforzandos, dynamic accents, momentary pianos. These often apply to one
part or section, rather than to the entire ensemble. The most telling dynamic
effect is the piano at measure 29 when the song reaches its melodic apex on

EXAMPLE 11-5.    Harmonic reduction of mm. 1–33. Mahler, "Das Trinklied."

the note F sharp; at this point the astringent harmonies relax and arrive at a major six-four chord on A, a glowing touch of bright harmonic color that stands in striking contrast to what has gone before.

Mahler's dispersal of sound through timbre, pitch, and dynamics, along with his isolation of melodic figures and his tactical use of silence, imparts a substantive content to each gesture that reaches beyond the traditional role of ornamentation. Paradoxically, his ornaments, as well as his harmony and his phrase structure, have a common, popular flavor and shape, taken item by item. Yet their juxtapositions engender a dreamlike continuity, with a strong suggestion of expressionist declamation against the simple harmonic, melodic, and rhythmic leading lines. Framed by the elaborate ornamentation, Mahler's song emerges between its interpolations in a clear, straightforward manner, directly presented by the singer.

Mahler's ornamentation differs markedly from both of his predecessors, Mozart and Chopin, and of his contemporary, the younger Arnold Schoenberg. For example, Mozart's ornamentation heightens the expressive effect of a melodic line through a rich variety of closely linked compatible figures, elegant and persuasive (Ex. 11-6)[2]. Chopin's ornamentation flows forward to animate a sturdy harmonic-rhythmic motion in repeated patterns and to create an expanded, pervasive climate of sound. Schoenberg's ornamentation tends to become entirely substantive and independent. His convoluted figures lack a matrix of support in sound. For example, the first group of piano figures in Schoenberg's *Pierrot lunaire* Op. 21 (1912), remote in pitch and texture, become clearly ornamental when they are supported by close-position harmonies in the bass (Ex. 11-7).

Song also plays a vital role in the introduction to Berlioz's *Symphonie fantastique,* but its presence is shadowed by Berlioz' eccentric handling of sound and figure (Ex. 11-8a). Imbedded in the irregular action that covers the surface of the music is a melody in the French manner, declamatory, conjunct, and free of ornamentation. The song has a deliberate pace; its motion is arrested by frequent caesuras and by long notes. Were it to have a text, the setting would be syllabic as in the arias of Berlioz' operas, and its affect would likely be pathetic or poignant.[3] In its "natural" course, it would come to a close at its sixteenth measure, gathering four phrases of four measures each into a symmetrical period (Ex. 11-8b).[4] The song, as a hypothetical cantus firmus or cantus prius factus, is a thread of continuity

EXAMPLE 11-6.   Ornamentation. Mozart, Sonata in D Major, K. 576, 1789, second movement.

EXAMPLE 11-7.   Ornamentation. Schoenberg, *Pierrot lunaire*, Op. 21, 1912, "Mondes-trunken."

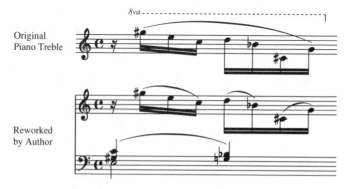

that moves through the introduction's fantastic musical landscape. At times it is lost among the tangents that suddenly appear, but both the song and the introduction itself come to a final, formal close together with the arrival at C major in measures 63–64.

Three processes typical of Berlioz's style work together to create the "hostile" environment of the song. These are:

1.  Berlioz's management of orchestral timbres. Every measure has something striking in the way of color or texture.
2.  Berlioz's use of conventional melodic figures drawn from preceding styles. Free imitations, descending conjunct basses, traditional cadences, appoggiaturas, Alberti-bass accompaniment—these are among the figures Berlioz has drawn from material generally available at that time, and which he colors with his scoring.

EXAMPLE 11-8.   Extended period.

a. Berlioz, *Symphonie fantastique*, Op. 14, 1830, first movement, introduction

3. Berlioz's tendency to isolate these figures and timbres in time and space. Often he puts figures into high relief by surrounding them with silences and gaps in pitch, imbuing them with a greater sense of substance than if they were part of a continuous or blended declamation. Moreover, their appearances are often brief, creating effects of high contrast—a collage rather than a continuity. When set against the song, such figures take on an eccentric life of their own—a counterpoint rather than a supporting accompaniment.

Example 11-8a.  *(continued)*

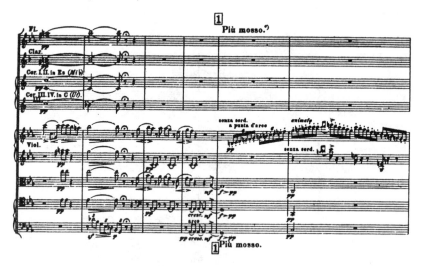

EXAMPLE 11-8a.  (*continued*)

EXAMPLE 11-8a.   (*continued*)

Used by permission of Dover Publications, Inc. Reproduced from: *Werke von Hector Berlioz*, Vol. 1, ed. Charles Malherbe and Felix Weingartner. Breitkopf & Härtel (1900–1910).

EXAMPLE 11-8b.    Rhetorical melodic reduction of "song" melody.

The reciprocal action of song, sound, and figure builds the considerable extent of this harmonic period, sixty-four measures long. While long-range harmony and the song itself keep the action on track, the detours arise from orchestral effects, tangential figures, and harmonic nuances that expand the form from within.

Extensions and interpolations in this introduction are scaled to two levels, the long-range and the local. Long-range interpolations interrupt the progress of the song at measures 17 and 46. At measure 17 an interchange of mode, C major instead of C minor, introduces a startling change of affective stance—brilliant, hectic figures in triplet sixteenths, detaché in contrast to the dark, legato, somewhat tentative declamation up to this point. The scoring for strings and winds has a high-pitched glitter. Berlioz dovetails the two expressive stances (pathetic and brilliant) by the cadence in C major, which closes at the second measure of the brilliant passage (m. 18) while all the other action is in train. The C major that enters so positively, quasischerzando, in measure 17 is quickly and peremptorily undermined by a rapid descent through the circle of fifths, a kaleidoscopic glint of harmonic color (mm. 20–21). Structurally, this descent makes a return to the region of the home key, C minor, at measure 24, but too soon. The melody is not ready to return. It does so at measure 28, but is reread in E-flat major—itself a striking harmonic transformation of the song and a contribution to the color value of the introduction. In this passage (mm. 17–28), the melodic material and the scoring gradually shift from scherzando to the song. Action slows, texture becomes fuller, dynamics introduce nuances that color individual tones, figures, and chords. The entire passage validates its melodic, harmonic, and rhythmic details through a shifting play of orchestral tone color, deferring, at the same time, the recall of the song.

The extension starting at measure 46, initiated by a deceptive cadence, is a parenthesis that delays the harmonic arrival until measure 63. This section is a tour de force of harmonic and orchestral color. A flat, the agent for the deceptive cadence, is held for fourteen measures. Above this tone appear harmonies that involve striking changes of color: D-flat major, A-flat major, E major, C sharp minor, G sharp minor, E major once more, a diminished seventh in which the A flat is taken enharmonically as G sharp. Although disguised, the melodic control above the A flat is a chromatic rise and fall. Here Berlioz opens out his canvas, making a pointillistic play of color, strictly ordered, according to sonority, register, time, and figure as in a prelude. Each unit of this passage is two measures in length, in contrast to the irregularities, the imbalances, the pauses, the interruptions that have gone before. Here Berlioz recalls a trade-off common in eighteenth-century music: when the harmony shifts quickly, the syntax tends to be symmetrical and even; when the harmony stays close to the home key, phrase structure can tolerate greater irregularities. Each figure in the pattern from measure 46 has its own character; each alternates with the others. The listener, charmed by the exquisite sound—the mellow song of the horn, the subdued tracery of the accompanying instruments cutting across the melody, suggestive of the fairy world of Queen Mab and Oberon—is nonetheless "on hold" harmonically; the pedal A flat retains its obligation to account for the deceptive cadence that it produced. When A flat is reread as G sharp resolving to A minor (mm. 59–60), the entire parenthesis falls into place as a delay of the close of the song. Remarkably, at this point, Berlioz turns to one of the most formal cadences in the traditional grammar, a VI–II–V–I progression that had for more than a century the rhetorical effect of a formal close.

In addition to the two long-range parentheses, Berlioz uses local gestures as well to stretch the time scale of the introduction. The opening lead-in; the fermatas in measures 4, 6, 12, 13; the repeated phrase in measures 11–14 and 36–39; the spun-out dissolution of the song melody in measures 41–45— these all increase substantially the duration of the song, and they represent Berlioz's grand strategy along the dimension of musical time. He also works strategies in musical space. Most significantly, he deprives the song of a conventional accompaniment, of the sort ordinarily found in Romantic songs—sustained chords or modest arpeggio figures, as in Example 11-9. By isolating the song and by inserting short figures against it, Berlioz gives the texture the character of a cantus firmus with counterpoint. Each stroke is a tactic based on vivid timbres—the pithy, exotic wind sounds in measures 1–2, the intense unisons of the large first violin section on the song itself, the sudden appearance and disappearance of pregnant figures in the lower strings, all highlighted by silence.

When the song returns in measure 28, it enters a more friendly environment, prepared by the preceding four measures. Instead of the disembodied, broken figures set against the song in its first appearance, we hear a continuous flow of sound. Yet this is no simple melody-accompaniment texture. Berlioz lays out four lines of action: the song itself, a brilliant figuration in the flute and clarinet in sextuplets, a countermelody in the low strings, and held chords in the oboes, horns, and bassoons. Each of these lines has its own track and its distinctive tone color. The texture is layered, not blended, with different pitch levels maintained for each line; thus the entire range of musical space frames the texture, without the doublings and blendings that Brahms, Wagner, and Richard Strauss favor. Moreover, the eccentricity of this texture is highlighted by the reversal of pitch levels—the

EXAMPLE 11-9.   Hypothetical accompaniments for melody. Berlioz, *Symphonie fantastique*, Op. 14, 1839, first movement, introduction.

tessitura of the song lies below its accompanying figuration. Rich and striking as this texture may be, it is sustained only for a brief four measures; simply another facet in the kaleidoscope of tone color that validates the elusive rhetoric of the introduction.

The melody, with its open, sentimental address, is drawn into the fantastic world of the symphony by the distortions, impingements, and interruptions it undergoes in the course of its unfolding. Yet none of this would have been possible had not Berlioz a firm grounding in traditional syntax—cadential, key-centered harmony, the formulas of thoroughbass and free counterpoint, the clarity of complementary phrase structure, and the traditional eighteenth-century textural polarization of soprano and bass.

## *Discursive Declamation*

In songlike declamation, development procedures—sequences, harmonic shifts, interpolations and dissolutions—disrupt the internal structure of the period. In discursive declamation, the same procedures are intrinsic parts of the structure. As might be expected, discursive periods tend to be rhapsodic, and the styles in the periods to be discussed have much in common with the fantasia.[5]

Notable instances of discursive periods occur in the opening and closing sections of Liszt's Sonata in B Minor. The distinctive textures and harmonies of those sections were discussed in Chapter 3; the effect of those elements on syntax is examined here.

The sound of diminished-seventh harmonies—restless, compact, highly colored, uncertain in harmonic direction—pervades the opening section (mm. 1–32). Traditionally, these harmonies have been associated with the darker affects—pathos, tragedy, a sense of menace; they inhabit the world of the fantasia, the arioso, the recitative obligé; they lend themselves to improvisations, to abrupt and drastic changes of feeling. They also constitute a threat to the integrity of phrase and period structure when they obscure points of harmonic punctuation.

In these first thirty-two measures, Liszt works out a unique rapprochement between such unstable harmonies and traditional syntax. At the core of this passage lies disguised a symmetrical period (Ex. 11-10). This period makes several bows to tradition—antecedent and consequent phrases, a half cadence answered by an authentic cadence, parallel layout of melodic figures. But the traditional gestures are disguised. The half cadence at measure 15 is no "comma," but an "exclamation point" and a "question mark," since it is represented by a diminished-seventh chord rather than a stable triad on the dominant. At the end of the period (mm. 31–32) we barely hear the touch of an authentic cadence, the mere shadow of a harmonic close, as F sharp descends stepwise to B without the harmonies that usually support dominant and tonic chords. Still, these points serve their syntactical purpose, to delineate the perimeters of a symmetrical period—attentuated, to be sure, in the context of Liszt's fantastic, flamboyant style.

Harmony also compromises the balance between parallel melodic figures. The figure that announces both phrases (mm. 9, 25) is set each time with an unstable, off-center harmony. In measure 9 it is the diminished seventh of B minor; in measure 25, it is a powerful and surprising E-flat major chord in $\frac{6}{3}$ position. Unexpected as this sound may be, it is held on track in the harmonic flow by its emphasis on the note G—fourfold scoring in extreme high and low registers—and its retention of something of the harmonic color of the diminished-seventh harmony by the two tones it shares with that chord, G and A sharp/B flat.

The location of the two phrases of the period within these 32 measures exposes another aspect of Liszt's strategies in design. The segments are, respectively: improvisatory introduction, 8 measures; firm thematic statement, 7 measures; discursive sequence, 9 measures; firm thematic statement, 8 measures. These proportions exhibit an approximate balance between "free" and "fixed" sections.

Applying another traditional parameter, the two-reprise form, (see Chapter 12, p. 241) we can make out a I–V, x–I plan, as follows:

| Introduction | mm. 1–8 | |
|---|---|---|
| Reprise I | mm. 9–13 | close on dominant harmony (I?–V) |
| Reprise II | mm. 14–24 | rising sequences *monte* |
| | mm. 25–32 | close in tonic (x–I) |

Still another control over the centrifugal tendencies of the harmonies and the textures of this section is the pairing of figures. Example 11-11 shows Liszt's consistent grouping of measures and figures by twos on several levels. These pairings have the effect of rationalizing what otherwise might sound like random tangents or, at best, patchwork. Such pairings give solid footing

EXAMPLE 11-10.   Complementary period in first key area. Liszt, Sonata in B Minor, 1854, mm. 1–32.

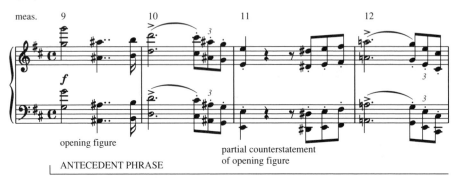

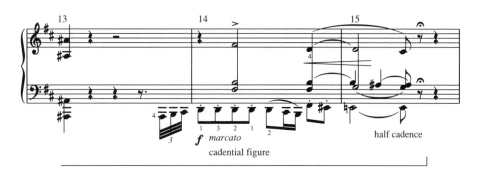

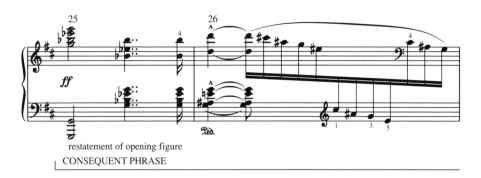

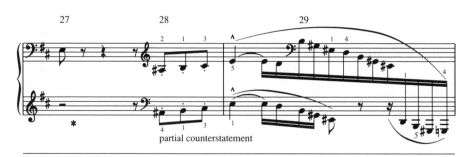

EXAMPLE 11-10.   (*continued*)

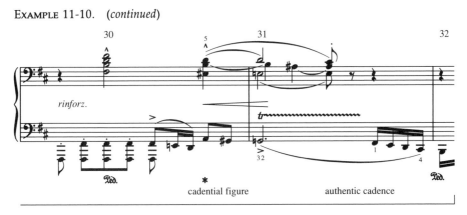

cadential figure          authentic cadence

to musical statements, creating their own internal stability and projecting a strong sense of articulate intention. They are especially useful throughout this sonata, with its saturation of improvisatory elements. Taking a cue from Liszt himself, a transformation of the period in Example 11-10 into the rhythm of the second half of the fugue subject, measure 466, that is, steady eighth notes, reveals a rhetorical reduction that fits neatly into an eight-measure period, as shown in Example 11-11. Stylistically, the form and the topic of this reduction is compatible with much of Liszt's music, especially in view of his Hungarian dance sources.

Finally, a most remarkable element in Liszt's strategy for this section is his handling of the note G. At first, it stands as a point of tonal reference for two exotic scales, respectively, a Phrygian scale and a scale incorporating two augmented seconds, with a strong Eastern European color. No clear key orientation is present; G can move in any direction. Its uncertainty, coupled with its low register and the sideslipping dissonances, projects a powerfully portentous mood. By measure 9, G is eventually defined as a member of a diminished seventh chord, with strong orientation to B minor. From this point on, G appears frequently, as part of a number of harmonies: E–G–B–D, A–C–E flat–G, C–E flat–G, G–B flat–D, E–G–B, C–E–G–B, and E flat–G–B–flat, as well as the original diminished-seventh chord. Implicitly or explicitly, G is heard as a harmonic element in twenty-seven of the thirty-two measures of this passage. Finally, G becomes a powerful functional element: the minor sixth of B as an appoggiatura that leans on the dominant F sharp, and contributes forcefully to the cadential effect of measures 31–32. From complete equivocality, through a number of adventurous harmonic detours, G is led to its specific time-honored role—to participate in the cadence as a component of subdominant harmony.

The last measures of the same sonata (mm. 729–60, reproduced in Ex. 3-11) constitute a harmonic period that represents a final area of arrival for the home key, B. This section—a coda that follows the end rhyme of the recapitulation, in which measures 712–28 answer, in abbreviated fashion, measures 398–415 and 335–47—is a surprisingly brief peroration for the

Example 11-11.    Rhetorical melodic reduction; pairings of phrases. Liszt, Sonata in B Minor, 1854, mm. 1–32.

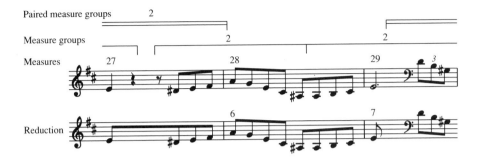

tremendous expressive and structural scope of the sonata. Yet this section is the most refined and beautifully shaped part of the entire work. Its traditional purpose as a coda is cadential, but unlike the codas of Beethoven, where harmonic digressions precede a powerful return to the home key for the final cadence, Liszt's coda is simply a series of cadences. These cadences have a quality of transfiguration, of apotheosis. Liszt's magic play of texture and tone color draws them into the expressive orbit of the sonata; they act as a reflective counterstatement to the furious motions and grandiose declamations that characterize the principal sections of the sonata. Yet despite its impression of elusiveness, of improvisation, this coda is carefully and precisely put together.

The cadences move by gradations from definition to dispersal, from the common to the unique. They proceed in the following sequence:

Definition
1. *Deceptive cadence*, mm. 728–29. The proper dominant seventh of B is followed by a diminished-seventh chord leading toward subdominant harmony.
2. *Plagal cadence*, mm. 732–33. The subdominant here is represented by Neapolitan harmony, whose bright, close-position color lends a glitter to the plagal effect, especially poignant over the insistent tonic pedal point.

Partial definition;     3. *Authentic cadence substitute*, mm. 743–44.
partial dispersal          Liszt here substitutes exotic harmonies with
                           dominant functions

for the syntactically firm dominant seventh
to accomplish the final dominant-tonic effect
of closure for his sonata. The tritone sound,
maintained over seven measures (mm. 737–
43), enables Liszt to disperse his texture
while he maintains the cadential tension
necessary to direct the harmony toward its
point of arrival.

4. *Nuances with some cadential function*, mm. 745
–48. Here the B-major harmony takes part in
a quasi-cadential effect generated by the action of the natural and lowered sixth degrees. This effect has a plagal coloring, although it has no standing in traditional
cadential syntax. It is a special detail in this
sonata.

Total dispersal      5. *"Trace" of Phrygian cadence*, mm. 751–52. The
final note of the descending scale, C natural,
in measure 751, connects, albeit obscurely,
with the B of measure 752. Here the cadential connection is tenuous, owing partly to
the extremely low register, partly to the instant of silence between the two tones.
Nevertheless, the settling action of the descending half step accomplishes its purpose
of arrival.

Total dispersal      6. *"Tritone" cadence*, m. 756. The final and most
exotic of the cadences moves from an F-
major chord in $^6_3$ position to a B-major chord
in $^6_4$ position; the progression is set *ppp* sustained, with full, close-position harmonies,
in a high register—all of which creates an
elusive, fading effect.

While half steps play an essential role in all the cadences in the coda, from
measure 750 onward they take on a special aspect: they are isolated from the
functional harmonies in which they traditionally operate. The connection in
measures 751–52, C to B, is purely melodic; in measure 756 F moves to F
sharp while C moves to B. Ordinarily, F and C, F sharp and B are members of

stable harmonies—triads. Liszt thrusts these tones into contrary-motion half-step progressions, as though they were leading tones seeking resolution.

The final subcontra B, barely distinguishable in dynamics and register, is a minimal validation of historic harmonic form—the close with the tonic of the home key in the bass. It, like the leading tones, is separated from any substantial context of sound; yet it resolves the C of measure 753 that was cut off by the high register chords, measures 754–59.

Despite the blurring of cadential action in the coda, the harmony remains true to its essential purpose—to settle the home key. Two processes, acting as "background" controls, secure this objective. The more basic process is the focus of all cadential gestures on B; there are eight of these, measures 732, 737, 744, 746, 748, 752, 756, and the final arrival on B in measure 760. The second process is an adaptation of a centuries-old formula, the progression I–Ib$^7$–IV–V$^7$–I over a tonic pedal. This progression, occasionally heard in opening and closing phrases of Classic and Baroque works,[6] here covers a broad trajectory, from measure 733 to measure 744 (Ex. 11-12). Moreover, the final progression carries the dip into the subdominant area even further as it uses the subdominant of the Neapolitan in B major as the penultimate chord; thus the use of the F major $^6_3$ can be regarded as a further step in a historical procedure.

Rhythm works with harmony and texture to build Liszt's grand strategy of closure. The rhythmic scenario matches cadential definition precisely. As cadential definition becomes attenuated, so does rhythmic-metric demarcation. A process of rhythmic dissolution takes place extending from the well-defined four-measure groupings at the beginning of the coda to the total disorientation of time at the end. The process by which this dissolution takes place is orderly in its own right. Liszt fashions a stretto, a narrowing of scope among the figures, as follows:

A. Figures fitted to the measure
  4 plus 4            mm. 729–32 plus 733–36
  2 plus 2            mm. 737–38 plus 739–40
  2 plus 2            mm. 740–41 plus 742–43
  (overlap)
  2 plus 2            mm. 744–45 plus 746–47
  ½ plus ½            m. 748
B. Figures working counter to the downbeat
  1                  m. 749 (counterstatement to m. 748)
  2 plus 3            mm. 750–51 plus 752–54
  1 plus 1            mm. 755 plus 756
  1 plus 1 plus 1    mm. 757–59
  1                  m. 760

Each of the groups in the outline is built from literal or varied repetition. The period thus achieves most of its extension by the simplest of means, that is, double statements of figures and phrases. These, of course, are linked and carried forward by the cadential action described above.

EXAMPLE 11-12.   Harmonic progression. Liszt, Sonata in B Minor, 1854, coda, mm. 728–60.

Measures 729–36 constitute two four-measure phrases, of which the second is a transposed restatement of the first. This phrase group is the most palpably regular rhythmic structure in the entire sonata; it first frames a clearly projected plagal cadence (m. 733), then in the second phrase prepares for the dominant harmony of measures 737–44. The rhythmic action begins to spin out (mm. 740–43), introducing an element of dispersal.

As the cadences become dispersed, so does the rhythm. First, a displacement of one-half measure (m. 749) throws the listener off with respect to strong-beat perception. Then, in measures 750–54, downbeats are suppressed. From this point to the end, every gesture begins on a weak beat, creating a sense of measure shift, and an impression of faltering. At the very last the subcontra B, like a distant stroke on the timpani, provides a trace of downbeat, underpinning the sustained luminous sweetness of the tonic $^6_4$ with the merest token of a root position. This is perhaps the most affecting moment in the entire sonata. Long after the music has ceased, the listener can sense the sustained echo of the six-four harmony and the memory of the low B, which, by its isolation, leaves us with a question as much as with an answer.

Example 11-13 gives a rhetorical textural reduction of the coda suggesting a hypothetical symmetry of two four-measure phrases with contrasted melodic material. The antecedent corresponds exactly with the proportions of measures 729–37; the consequent departs considerably from the following measures, reflecting Liszt's process of rhythmic dissolution.

By means of broad time values (compared to the reduction), full harmonies, separation of chord segments by distant registers, strategic use of silence, and restatements, Liszt exploits sound in this coda to give a sense of open space, both in pitch and time. Extending over the broadest space is the relationship between the first and last harmonies of the entire work. Both harmonies stand as surrogates for standard cadential chords; the diminished seventh at the beginning, which replaces the more usual $V^7$, and its eventual answer, the tonic $^6_4$ at the end, instead of $I^5_3$ create an immense harmonic arch that for the composer and for his listener might have had a binding, rationalizing value.

A comparison of the roles played by sound and syntax in the Berlioz and Liszt excerpts reveals some fundamental, even polarized, contrasts. Berlioz's point of departure is the song, laid out in syntactically clear phrases, well-defined key relationships, and traditional cadential arrangements. Around this firm base of syntax, Berlioz's orchestra plays with sound to loosen some of the edges, to digress, to displace momentarily, to isolate

EXAMPLE 11-13.  Rhetorical textural reduction of mm. 729–44. Liszt, Sonata in B Minor, 1854, coda.

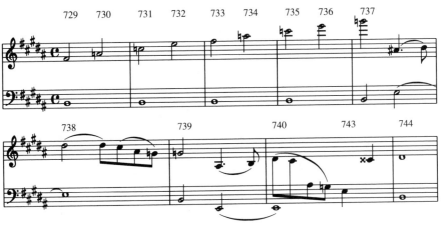

figures. The direction is centrifugal, working against a solid foundation. Liszt's starting position seems to be the fantastic, the flamboyant gesture, the arresting sound, cascading, exploding, searching in remote registers—all directed to immediate effect. Instead of clear tonics and dominants, we hear shadow harmonies saturated with tritones that skulk around the key. Neither the figures nor the harmonies lend themselves to the crystallized formations of traditional period structure. On this potentially chaotic material Liszt superimposes an order, indicating cadences in accordance with periodic usage, counterstating figures in pairs, setting up an elusive yet basically conventional antecedent-consequent phrase structure, with a token yet profoundly important point of closure in his home key at measure 32. For Berlioz, the point of reference is syntax, colored by sound; for Liszt it is sound, put into order by syntax.

In Chapter 4 we observed how Brahms scored the opening of his First Symphony to create a towering, organlike edifice of sound. Here we see how that opening initiates an immense period that spans the entire introduction to the first movement (Ex. 11-14). With its surely led chromaticisms and its sharp contrasts of topic, this symphony's introduction has strong echoes of the eighteenth-century fantasia, whose style often appeared in symphonic introductions (Haydn's Symphony No. 104 in D major, Mozart's Symphony No. 38 in D major, and Beethoven's Symphony No. 4 in B-Flat major, for example).

The broad outline of the period is:

| Antecedent member | mm. 1–9 | opening motive | I–V |
| Consequent member | mm. 25–38 | opening motive | V–I |

The action between measures 9 and 25 constitutes a huge parenthesis in the period, while the final measures of the period, 30–38, make up a cadential

EXAMPLE 11-14.   Brahms, Symphony No. 1 in C Minor, Op. 68, 1876, first movement, introduction.

(*continued*)

EXAMPLE 11-14.   (*continued*)

Reproduced from Johannes Brahms, *Säintliche Werke*, vol. 1, ed. Hans Gal. Breitkopf & Hartel (n.d.). Copyright © 1974 Dover Publications. Used by permission.

extension anchored on the dominant. Example 11-15 reduces these thirty-eight measures to sixteen, simplifying the elaborate rhythmic shifts in the $\frac{6}{8}$ meter to a straightforward $\frac{2}{4}$. The reduction exposes the essential balance within the period. Both members begin alike melodically; tonic-dominant harmony is answered by dominant-tonic.

The reduction highlights another feature of the opening melodic material, its conjunct movement. Brahms alternates this movement with other melodic figures, using scoring to emphasize the melodic contrast. Example 11-16 outlines these shapes and the orchestration that supports them.

All the action in the introduction takes place deliberately and spaciously, with a sense of substantial weight, thanks to the fullness and color of sound established in the first measures. The sustained forte and the layered doublings of the first nine measures create a favorable climate for a multiple tug-of-war among rhythm, melody, and harmony. The upper lines pull against each other rhythmically and melodically as the middle line moves steadily downward in dotted quarters while the upper line thrusts upward in an eccentric action that cuts across the dotted quarters. The steady eighth

EXAMPLE 11-15.  Rhetorical melodic reduction of mm.1–38. Brahms, Symphony No. 1 in C Minor, Op. 68, 1876, first movement, introduction.

notes of the pedal act as a catalyst that reconciles the counteractions of the upper lines and hold them firmly in rhythmic focus. Harmony contributes to the eccentricity of this passage as it touches momentarily on altered tones—B flat, C sharp, A natural, F sharp, E natural—and takes advantage of the rhythmic displacement of the top line to create an oblique action that introduces pungent dissonances. Still with its firm pedal point on C, harmony anchors this passage, while it generates a conflict with the dissonances in the upper voices.

While C minor maintains a strong presence throughout the introduction, it is principally by indication and inference that it does so. We must wait until the onset of the allegro for a confirmation of the key; here, finally, the dominant harmony of the introduction resolves to the tonic harmony that opens the allegro. Indeed, it is only at the fifth measure of the allegro, measure 42, that we first hear, in this symphony, a complete C-minor triad. To this point, the harmonic focus has been principally on the dominant, starting at measure 9. Brahms emphasizes arrivals at the dominant in measures 9, 13, 25, and 29 with standard orchestral tutti scoring, forte; on the other hand, movement between these points partakes of less common harmonic and orchestral color. We hear the piquant sound of unison winds and plucked strings on the diminished-seventh intervals in measures 9–10 and 13–14, answered by the suave color of strings, placed low in close position, touching on the remote harmony of G-flat major in measure 11. This sequence is transposed a fifth to the flat side; when C-flat major appears momentarily it becomes a starting point for a rising line of sixth chords that will reach the Neapolitan in measure 19, to prepare the dominant in measure 21. Now, when the dominant is reached, it takes on a color often heard in Brahms's music; it is shaded by a third below, E flat. This sound makes its point as a color, a resonance, rather than as a function in cadential harmony. The color is validated and intensified by its scoring—the entire mass of strings in octaves and unisons on the upward undulating figure. These four measures, while they hold the dominant in view, use harmonic and instrumental color to delay the arrival of the functional dominant.

EXAMPLE 11-16. Outline of melodic and scoring features. Brahms, Symphony No. 1 in C Minor, Op. 68, 1876, first movement, introduction.

| Measure | Harmony | Figure | Contour | Texture/Sound |
|---------|---------|--------|---------|---------------|
| 1–9 | I–V | a. | conjunct, gradual rise | Tutti, multiple doublings full range, trio-sonata texture (bass and two converting upper parts) |
| 9–10 | | b. | disjunct, steep fall | three-octave unisons, winds supported by strings |
| 11–12 | | c. | conjunct, gradual rise | close-position chorale (four-part, note-against-note texture), strings reinforced by winds, middle to low register |
| 13–14 | | b. | disjunct, steep fall | three-octave unisons, winds supported by strings |
| 15–18 | | c. | conjunct, gradual rise | close-position chorale, strings reinforced by winds, middle to low register |

| 19–21 |  | d.  | conjunct, gradual descent | three-octave unison, winds and strings |
| 21–24 |  | e.  | disjunct, undulating rise | two-octave unison strings, prelude style |
| 25–29 | V | a. | conjunct, gradual rise | Tutti, multiple doublings, full range, trio-sonata texture |
| 29–37 |  | f.  | conjunct/ disjunct, undulating | solo winds and strings, two- and three-part writing in three-against-one counterpoint |
| 38 | I | a. |  | Tutti |

While the harmonic fabric of the introduction is rich in color, each nuance is absorbed into traditional cadential formulas. Even the highly colored passage, mm. 21–24, eventually anchors the harmony upon a firm dominant, measure 25. The cadential implications of measures 1–29 are both subtle and persuasive; they hint, they indicate, but they do not confirm. On the contrary, from measure 29 the effect is that of a harmonic clarification of the preceding action, as Brahms begins his unequivocal cadential approach to the C minor of the allegro.

The layout of melodic figures, rhythms, harmonies, and phrase groupings reflects a balance among centrifugal and centripetal forces. The figures that form the core of the period (mm. 1–9, 25–29) have conjunct rising lines cast in irregular rhythms, with some color of chromaticism. This centrifugal motion is held on course by the pedal point and the drive to the dominant. Within these two phrases melodic motives lack clear-cut complementary arrangements, except for measures 5–7, where an internal stretto intensifies the cadential drive. On the other hand, the parenthesis in measures 9–24, where the harmony pivots around the dominant with incidental tangents that move far afield, is clearly laid out in four complementary groups of four measures each, as can be seen in the reduction in Example 11-17.

The cadential extension (mm. 29–37) carries out the most traditional textural and harmonic procedures in the introduction. It works essentially with species counterpoint, three against one, in a clear-cut play of free imitation, with light, well-balanced textures that have a soloistic flavor. The harmony straightens out, pivoting steadily on the dominant. The scansion is irregular, three plus six; the final six-measure group stretches the reach for the cadence to the allegro. Still, the entire cadential extension represents rhythmically a clearing-out of the syncopations and hemiolias that have troubled the preceding action. In this sense, the larger rhythmic plan is a huge iambic process, from upbeat instability to downbeat stability.

In the opening of the Prelude to *Tristan und Isolde,* Wagner adapts the two basic configurations of traditional period structure—pairings and closure—to a statement that obscures the familiar balances and articulations of the period. Measures 1–24 constitute a harmonic period that closes on an

EXAMPLE 11-17.    Rhetorical melodic reduction of mm. 9–24. Brahms, Symphony No. 1 in C Minor, Op. 68, 1876, first movement, introduction.

authentic cadence in A major (Ex. 11-18). Within these twenty-four measures we hear pairings of figures, repetitions, intermediate cadences—elements taken from the symmetrical period form.

The obscurity that masks the various periodic processes in this prelude emanates from harmonies that are unstable in their functional implications and rich in color value. (See Ex. 6-19 for a précis of the harmonic progression in mm. 1–17.) The opening chord of the prelude, the so-called *Tristan* chord, is the talisman that opens this world of harmonic color. It has a profound effect upon the way the period unfolds. The chord itself and Wagner's use of it epitomize the coordination of the traditional and the innovative. Traditionally, the half-diminished seventh chord had a place in the vocabulary of functional harmony for more than a century before Wagner's use of it in *Tristan*. As a seventh chord on the seventh degree of the major scale, it had occasionally been used as a dominant-function chord in the major mode

EXAMPLE 11-18.  Wagner, Prelude to *Tristan und Isolde*, 1859.

thanks to its tritone; on the second degree of the minor scale, it served a subdominant function, in the minor mode, progressing to the dominant. Then again, the chord could take its place in a circle-of-fifths progression that would eventually reach a tonic or dominant harmony. Wagner's use of the chord draws not so much on its role in cadential harmony and key definition as on its restless, strangely evocative color. Its diminished fifth provides the unsettling effect of the tritone while its minor seventh, on the sixth degree in major or the tonic in minor, has something of the quality of an appoggiatura that indicates a resolution downward by half or whole step.

EXAMPLE 11-18. *(continued)*

Used by kind permission of European American Music Distributors Corporation, Sole U.S. and Canadian agent for Universal Edition.

Each syntactical process—harmony, texture, rhythm, and melody—is profoundly affected by the climate of sound created by the opening chord. Wagner enriches its sound by length and texture, sustaining it for what seems to be an indefinite length (five eighths, actually, in a slow $\frac{6}{8}$ meter). We cannot make out a pulse, a meter, a rhythm, but the sound itself is compelling, holding time in check. Its scoring—high cellos, compact winds in a low register—intensifies its color value.

Wagner's leading of the chord is harmonically equivocal. Traditionally, its resolution would have the effect of a contraction, as the minor seventh closes to a perfect fifth or major sixth and the diminished fifth closes to a major third or perfect fourth (Ex. 11-19). Wagner instead leads the voices outward to the next chord, creating an effect of expansion. The chord seems to dissolve as it sideslips into another seventh chord, rather than resolve to a triad, or as a II$^7$ in minor, to a V$^7$.

Half steps in the melody slide across the bar line, momentarily changing the color of the harmony, yet fitting themselves to the rich, unstable, tritone-saturated sound. These harmonies do not resolve; they merge into each other by the smoothest of paths—common tones, conjunct motions, minimal leaps. They shift at irregular instants, disguising completely the notated $\frac{6}{8}$ meter. While the half-diminished seventh and other tritone chords have a prominent presence in eighteenth- and nineteenth-century harmony, Wagner's concentration of tritone harmonies and the tangential shifts by which he links them through manipulation of half-step motion is innovative especially in the degree to which he applies this technique.

Wagner's texture, on the other hand, is firmly grounded in traditional four-part harmony. Indeed, to project and sustain the climate of intense harmonic color, he must maintain a dense chordal texture. While it might be difficult to assign functional labels to all of Wagner's harmonies (witness the long-standing controversy regarding the identity of the *Tristan* chord), it would raise no special problems to signal each chord by a figured-bass designation and by chord type, such as diminished-seventh type, dominant-seventh type, major triad, and so on. Also, Wagner's bass lines support his harmonic progressions with all the continuity and direction of an eighteenth-century continuo bass. Wagner's harmonic technique is thus a kind of latter-day *stile legato*, deliberate, conjunct, forceful, and concentrated.

The orchestra contributes to the harmonic color and action of the prelude by its size and makeup. The large cello section enters in unison in the instrument's best singing register, pianissimo, to create an intense hypnotic effect with its restrained *messa di voce*. The cellos are joined in the first full chord by a group of seven wind instruments, clustered low. Within a few seconds, Wagner transfixes the attention of the listener and establishes both the color and the time values that he will use throughout the opera.

The region in which this climate of sound develops is marked out by Wagner's manipulation of musical time. Here the most critical factor is duration itself. At the beginning of the prelude, Wagner loosens the constraints of time—meter and rhythm—to allow each sound to have a pervasive effect, a sense of uncertain reaching that has intense emotional

EXAMPLE 11-19.   Traditional resolutions of half-diminished seventh chords.

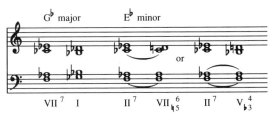

implications. While the meter is $\frac{6}{8}$ and the tempo is slow, a listener cannot grasp a clear meter until the music has reached the midway point of the seventeenth measure. Sustained tones, irregular groupings of long and short notes, silences, as well as the idiosyncratic modifications imposed by conductors, draw attention to the poignant effect of each sound.

Wagner's harmonic language provides the basis for this metric-rhythmic fluidity. Generally, we tend to hear a tritone chord in a rhythmically active position, as an arsis, an upbeat, proceeding to a stable harmony, a triad in a downbeat or thetic position. With the constant flow of tritone harmonies, upbeat values become prominent, while downbeat values are shadowed, rendered less firm. In the Prelude the flow of action is made even more continuous by the volatility, the flexibility of the $\frac{6}{8}$ meter, with its play of duple and triple groupings, hemiolias, and shifted agogic accents.

To keep the harmonic-rhythmic flow under control, Wagner controls every beat, and indeed, fractions of beats. A play of poetic meters emerges from the fluid, irregular declamation. These meters separate, mix, run together, and overlap. The meters most suited to Wagner's declamation are those with their long components in the middle or the end of the foot: iambic, anapest, amphibrach. We hear the declamation of these poetic meters in accents of length, that is, in agogic accents, rather than in accents of stress by dynamic or harmonic emphasis. Example 11-20 shows the overlay of meters in measures 1–14.

To control the fluid play of poetic meters, Wagner develops a broad strategy. The period, measures 1–24, becomes a huge iambic foot. From measures 1–17, the listener cannot be certain about the $\frac{6}{8}$ meter, owing to the sustained chords, fermatas, silences, and bar-straddling melodic-rhythmic action. At measure 17, the meter clearly appears, proceeding in a slow, swinging manner, like the oscillation of a long pendulum. Thus we have a long-range rhythmic progression from light to strong, from arsis to thesis. Such management of rhythmic definition supports Wagner's expressive idea—to disorient at first and then to take the listener into his, the composer's, mysterious realm. The polarization of rhythmic values and procedures—extreme fluidity versus total control—parallels the similar treatment of harmony.

Within the broad iambic foot the fluid progression of shifting meters is held on course by simple groupings in which melodic figures complement one another. These figures line up as follows:

Half
measures   2+6   2+5   3+4      4    2  2   3  2+2+2   2  2+2  3

Measures   1 2 3 4|5 6 7 8 9 10 11|12 13|14|15|16 1|7 18 19 2|0 2|1 22 2|3 24

(Brackets indicate groupings of similar figures; slashes through measure numbers locate the demarcations of groups.)

Melody performs its traditional role, to shape and articulate the surface of the musical action. In doing so, it exhibits a tightness of connection and a

EXAMPLE 11-20.  Scansion and distribution of meters. Wagner, Prelude to *Tristan und Isolde*, 1859.

smooth flow between figures comparable to the progression of chords and the interlocking of poetic meters. The tightness of melodic action arises from a number of traits:

1. Short figures or motives, distinctive patterns consisting of three to ten or more notes, are the building blocks of Wagner's melody. (These motives have acquired the name *leitmotif;* each of these signifies a situation, mood, person in the music drama.)
2. Virtually the entire melodic continuity of the prelude is built as a chain of motives. There are very few "neutral" melodic tones, very little passagework (a few sixteenth notes passing through measures 23 and 24), no ornamental figures for the sake of "grace," as in most eighteenth- and nineteenth-century music.
3. With the exception of widely spaced expressive leaps, the melodic action remains conjunct, promoting a smooth melodic flow.
4. The motives themselves have a mutual compatibility. They all have upbeats, trailing tones (i.e. feminine endings), or both, so that they can merge smoothly, one into another, without marked caesuras or contrasts. Example 11-21 illustrates these similarities and compabilities.

EXAMPLE 11-21.  Similarity of motives. Wagner, Prelude to *Tristan und Isolde,* 1859.

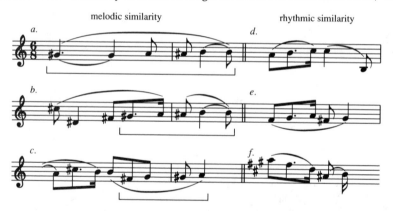

5. Large-scale melodic contours organize the action in rises to apexes in wavelike motions. As motives or motive groups succeed one another, the pitch level tends to rise until maximum tension is created, after which there is a drop, often to the beginning of a new rise. These apexes thus are turning points in the form of the piece. The first rise begins with the A in the violoncello and reaches its apex at measure 17, with the B more than two octaves above the starting point. The second rise begins also with A, measure 17, and a gentler ascent reaches to C sharp a tenth above, measure 24. These two apexes coincide with the two cadences of this period. Later, the

ultimate climax, on a high A flat, is buttressed by a return of the *Tristan* chord, respelled according to the scale of six flats (E-flat minor or G-flat major), measure 83.

6. Wagner uses melodic phrases as modules, that is, segments that are relocated during the course of the piece. The opening material is recalled to bring the prelude to a close. The phrase beginning at measure 17 with the motive

returns at measures 32, 55, 74, 80, and 95, either verbatim, developed, or varied. This motive is the most pervasive melodic figure in the piece, although the pair of figures at the beginning are the most salient because of their position in the form. The relocation of phrases is a manifestation on a broad scale of Wagner's tendency to restate and develop a motive within a phrase, rather than to introduce bold contrasts of figure.

Wagner's control over the fluid harmonic, rhythmic, and melodic action works from both ends of the structural spectrum, small and large. We have seen how individual figures are deployed. On the scale of the period itself there is an overarching continuity based on the embodiment of the tonic, A, around which this segment circles deliberately. A is first indicated by the opening note and by its dominant seventh. Then C and E are implied. E becomes the dominant of A, leading to a strong implication of A by means of a deceptive cadence to F, V–VI. From this point, measure 17, we hear two broad cadential swings, from F to G to C, a IV–V–I implication to measure 20, and an even broader swing from D to B to E to A, a IV–II–V–I cadence in A major, the only authentic cadence in the entire prelude. Even here chord color adds its exotic value; the resolution to A major involves a prominent use of the raised second degree in both the dominant and tonic harmonies, while the third is doubled in the resolution. As an expression of the key of A, this period carries out the traditional procedure to anchor the uncertain flow: *indication* of the tonic at the beginning, *establishment* of the tonic as the ruling key in measure 17, and *confirmation* of the tonic in measure 24. Each of these processes, though strongly affected by Wagner's declamation, is essentially traditional.

If we factor out the harmonic richness and fullness of the period, we remove the ambience within which the rhythmic, melodic, and textural elements move so slowly and irregularly. Retaining the essential melodic, rhythmic, and harmonic configurations, we can fit these shapes into a regular $^6_8$ meter without pauses, extensions, and repetitions to expose the period's basic symmetries. The rhetorical reduction in Example 11-22 retains some flavor of the original and by contrast enables us to pinpoint those decisions of

Example 11-22.    Rhetorical melodic reduction. Wagner, Prelude to *Tristan und Isolde*, 1859.

Wagner's that give the original its unique aspect. As it stands, the reduction could be taken as a sketch for a theme of which the original could be a variation. The reduction might also qualify as a thematic transformation of the original, parodistic in the manner of Richard Strauss. In any case, considering the features retained and extrapolating the original from this hypothetical reduction can give us a vivid idea of the ways in which Wagner used intensive, compressive harmonic-rhythmic action and texture to build an extended period.

The Prelude to *Tristan* stands a world apart from the introduction to Brahms's First Symphony in expressive implications. Yet the two segments discussed here have some striking points of similarity in syntax. Both segments constitute harmonic periods. Each is articulated harmonically at both ends by an indication or establishment of its tonic, and each circles around the tonic within the period without settling on it at any point (actually, Brahms travels farther afield than Wagner, touching on G-flat major for an instant in m. 11; Wagner circles among keys closely related to A). Both deal flexibly with compound triple groupings within a $^6_8$ meter in slow time. Shifts of accent, hemiolias, irregular lengths of tones abound in each (Brahms immediately establishes a firm, powerful eighth-note pulse; Wagner's music has no discernable pulse until the seventh measure). Perhaps the most notable point of similarity is the shape of the opening treble figures in the two works. Each rises chromatically in a somewhat uncertain rhythm (Brahms spins out the melodic line in a powerful, yet irregular rise; Wagner assigns the treble figure a specific role in the phrase structure—to complement itself in a set of pairings).

These similarities not only reflect some general aspects of mid-Romantic declamation and layout but also throw the contrasts between the two works into sharp relief, allowing us to pinpoint important features of style in each work. On one hand, the symphony's powerful drive, its sharp contrasts, formally opposed, are supported by solid, well-balanced sonorities, in tutti-solo textures. On the other hand, the tentative flow of the prelude is edged forward by rich, pervasive sounds that ease in and out of our perceptions.

PART FOUR

# *SOUND AND FORM*

# CHAPTER TWELVE

# *Small Forms*

Form in nineteenth-century music is based principally on eighteenth-century models, adapted to incorporate elements of sound and syntax evolved during the Romantic era. Evidence for this retrospective orientation appears in the instructions for composition and in the descriptions and outlines of forms, small and large in the textbooks of the time, such as those of Reicha, Weber, Czerny, Marx, Lobe, Jadassohn, Prout, and Riemann.[1] Of these studies, the most detailed is that of A. B. Marx. The first two volumes of his *Lehre von der musikalischen Komposition* are largely concerned with musical form, from the alpha of small two- and three-part forms to the omega of sonata form. While Marx carefully covers the intervening ground between the small and large forms, classifying various types of rondo and sonatina, other writers present a polarity of formal configurations, dealing principally with the small two- and three-part layouts and then with sonata form.

Whatever the degree of detail in these descriptions, from the cursory overview of Czerny to the treatment in depth by Marx, the parameters explained are those of key, harmony, rhythm, and melody. Texture and quality of sound do not enter into the formal descriptions. Instead, concern with sound values is a separate matter, to be dealt with in instrumental tutors and in orchestration treatises in the details of texture and scoring. Still, as in phrase and period structure, large-scale Romantic syntax is profoundly conditioned by sound as well. The way a piece begins, how it continues, tracing shapes and trajectories, reaching stations of the form—these are all conditioned by the ways in which sound is produced and sustained, and by how it clothes the action of rhythm and melody. Each work discussed in the

239

following chapters has an individual way of incorporating sound values into the complex of processes that shape its form.

The method applied heretofore in the analysis of period structures—to characterize the sound values and to determine their effect on the symmetries, extensions, and connections of syntax—is now put to work in examining full-scale forms. As in the analysis of period structures, the aim here is to throw light from one point of perspective upon an individual work of art. Following the organizational lead of nineteenth-century theorists, this chapter and the next investigate the role of sound qualities in shaping small forms and the sonata form, respectively.

A significant trend in Romantic music was the emergence of the short piece as an important genre. Etudes, preludes, impromptus, and songs without words were composed in great numbers for the piano, while the song became a leading vehicle for many composers. These works were imbued with much deeper strains of feeling than we find in their eighteenth-century counterparts—dances, marches, canzonettas. The climate of sound in the nineteenth century played a vital role in this change of affective content. The richer, more pervasive sounds of Romantic music had the power immediately to envelop the listener within a mood. Many short pieces of this era sound as if the music has been silently moving before the piece begins and will reverberate silently in the imagination of the listener after the piece ends. This is in contrast to the sharply delineated points of departure and arrival that characterize eighteenth-century syntax in small forms.

The briefest of small forms in Romantic music are but a single period in length. These are few in number, yet they epitomize Romantic qualities—inner symmetries; pervasive, colorful sound; a poetic lyricism that has a personal, intimate mood. Chopin was the master of this miniature form. The preludes in C major, A major, E minor, and B minor from Chopin's Preludes, Op. 28, encompass each a single period.

The examples discussed in this chapter represent the patterns most often used in Romantic small forms—the two-part, binary, or two-reprise form, and the three-part or ternary form.[2] Together with the period, these small forms establish the basis for larger forms in nineteenth-century theoretical treatises.[3]

The minimal two-part form consists of two periods.[4] While the cadence in the first part can be made either in the tonic or a related degree, the close of the second part is always in the home key. The most important option for the end of the first part is a cadence in the dominant, after which the harmony returns via one of a number of paths to close the second part in the tonic. The harmonic formula is thus I–V, x–I, a plan that has tremendous possibilities for expansion. Since it involves a harmonic argument—the opposition of dominant to tonic and the eventual victory of the tonic—the two-part form lends itself to discursive treatment. On the other hand, three-part forms involve a contrast in the middle section, an ABA pattern. The tendency in three-part forms thus is to frame content that is essentially lyric, songlike in character.

To be sure, discursive and lyric elements are often commingled in both two-reprise and three-part forms. Two examples in this chapter, the two-reprise song "Wohin" by Schubert and the three-part Etude in C Major, Op. 10, No. 1, by Chopin, illustrate commingling of lyric and discursive elements. Each projects a continuous line of action in which sound is a critical factor. The other examples, Mendelssohn's two-reprise *Song without Words* No. 48, Schumann's three-part "Vogel als Prophet," and Liszt's unique "Nuages gris," incorporate little if any discursiveness.

## *Two-Reprise Form: I – V, x – I*

Mendelssohn's *Song without Words* No. 48, Op. 102, No. 6 (1845) (Ex. 12-1), is cast in two-reprise form with a middle cadence in the dominant key, as follows:

| Reprise I | mm. 1–4 | full cadence on the tonic | I |
| | mm. 5–8 | shift to V; cadence in V | V |
| Reprise II | mm. 9–14 | shifting harmonies; return to I | I (x) |
| | mm. 15–18 | cadence in I | I |

The form is extended at three points:

1. Measures 13–14 extend the *x* section to bring the harmony into position for the return to the home key.
2. Measures 19–29 constitute a varied restatement of the second reprise.
3. Measures 29–33 provide a coda on a tonic pedal point.

Rhythm and harmony establish a clear impression of symmetry. Rhythmic patterns such as those in the first two measures are restated; punctuations are made at two- or four-measure intervals. Harmony reinforces these rhythmic figures through cadential action and key relationships. On the other hand, the melodic line itself overlays the rhythmic-harmonic symmetries with a flowing, principally conjunct line that spins out, lacking the complementary shapes that generally give profile to the underlying balances.

This song is firmly and discreetly supported by a choralelike texture, principally in four voices, at times reinforced. The melody is the articulate upper surface of a rich flow of sound, rather than an active line clearly separated from its support. The full-chord texture indicates a syllabic manner of declamation that projects a more substantial depth of expression than a simple melody and accompaniment could achieve.

The impression of the home key is clear and vibrant in this piece. In turn, the shift from C major to G major, in measures 5–9 is decisive, and the

EXAMPLE 12-1.   Small two-reprise form. Mendelssohn, *Songs without Words*, No. 48, Op. 102, No. 6, 1845.

indications of F major in measures 11–12, 21–22, 29, 30, and 31 assist powerfully in the approaches to cadences in C major.

Still, harmony contributes many nuances that color the traditional chord and key usage. Almost two-thirds of the actual sound consists of unstable harmony—appoggiaturas and chords of the seventh. While most of these dissonances are diatonic, several instances of chromatic harmony illuminate by contrast the general diatonic ambience. These chromatic harmonies introduce critical cadential moments: at measure 7 a diminished seventh intensified by an appoggiatura gives a ceremonial signal for the cadence in the dominant; at measure 14 a dramatic thrust by means of a German sixth chord leads to the cadential tonic $^6_4$ that opens the way to the return of the tonic, measure 15. This is restated in measures 24–25.

Texture and harmony combine to give weight to the irregular rate of chord change, varying from half note to eighth note. Especially in the latter quick rate do we sense an urgency, an increasing tension, as in measures 6, 10, 12, and 29–31.

The rich texture and harmony that supports the deliberate, syllabic style of melodic declamation develops a fullness of content that is barely contained by the feminine cadences in measures 8, 18, and 28. Indeed, the entire piece is articulated by such strong-to-weak trochaic configurations. These textural, harmonic, and rhythmic features, as well as the winding flow of the melody, urge the action forward beyond measure 18, at which point the two-reprise action would be completed according to traditional practice. In this format, 18 measures, the effect would be pleasant, even ingratiating, with a nice sense of balance as the final measure is reached. Mendelssohn, however, creates a poetic, climactic scenario by manipulating repetitions and extensions. The first reprise is not repeated so that it flows smoothly into the following section. The second reprise is repeated; the repetition with its active bass in driving eighth notes builds the piece to a peroration. Afterward, the coda, with its tonic pedal point, creates a more substantial area of arrival, leaving the listener with an impression of a gently reverberating C major. A final rhythmic touch secures the effect of closure; the last measure, measure 33, is thetic (accented) in effect, providing a broad iambic downbeat against the trochaic metric configurations that pervade the piece; this agogic downbeat measure quiets the motion, if not the sound itself.

While the traditional aspects of this piece—two-reprise form, cadential harmony, songlike melody, choralelike texture—clearly show a retrospective stylistic orientation, its nuances and sonorities indicate the nineteenth-century piano's fullness of tone. The simple protocol of this miniature is given a special, important life by the qualities of sound that support it and envelop it.

In Schubert's song "Wohin?," from *Die schöne Müllerin*, Op. 25 (1823) (Ex. 12-2), the accompaniment creates a pervasive climate of sound, a rustling, restless drone that is sustained throughout the song. When the melody enters, it floats on this current of sound, taking on a mellow glow from the resonances of the accompaniment. The melody thus becomes the surface of the sound, merging with the accompaniment to add its own shading to the texture. The modest figuration of the accompaniment has a narrow ambitus set in an unobtrusive lower middle range of the keyboard. By repeating its sixteenth-note triplets incessantly it maintains a gentle stir, a murmur that pervades the entire song. The unbroken flow of the accompaniment works profoundly upon the syntax of the song. Mirroring the flow of the brook upon which the text is based, the accompaniment allows the song to spin out smoothly, to extend itself measurably, and to stop its motion without a conclusive ending.

Within this flow "Wohin?" follows a time-honored harmonic path—the I–V, x–I of eighteenth-century music. Each phase of the harmonic action is clearly delineated. The song presents the home key, G major, firmly and broadly; it makes a decisive move to the dominant and closes the first part with a formal cadence in that key; it then shifts harmonies, touching on A minor and E minor to clear the way for a return to the tonic; and finally, it reaches the tonic and remains there, with a formal close even more decisive than that on the dominant. The shape is that of the traditional two-reprise form, without repetitions of each reprise:

| Reprise I | mm. 1–22 | Tonic (I) G major | I |
|---|---|---|---|
| | mm. 22–34 | Shift to dominant key (V) D major and formal close therein | V |
| Reprise II | mm. 35–53 | Return to tonic through A minor and E minor | x |
| | mm. 53–81 | Arrival at home key and formal close therein | I |

Schubert builds his harmonic trajectory with simple, familiar cadential formulas, smooth modulations, and occasional tonicizations. These are framed by a remarkably regular phrase structure. Of the eighteen phrases in this song, sixteen are precisely trimmed to four-measure length. One phrase (mm. 36–41) comprises six measures, the first two of which encompass the expressive climax of the song and are inserted as a parenthesis that elevates the declamatory effect. The opening introduction adds two measures, while the final phrase covers eight measures; these gently frame the song itself. A single extra bar, measure 34, separates the cadence of the first reprise from the beginning of the second.

The simple four-measure phrases contribute to the melody's singsong, crooning flavor. The tune, repeating and varying itself constantly, is set in a narrow middle range, scarcely more than an octave, except for a high G near the end. Repeated tones and simple chord patterns lend the melody a popular quality typical of songs of the early nineteenth century.

EXAMPLE 12-2. Schubert, *Die schöne Müllerin*, Op. 25, 1823, "Wohin?".

EXAMPLE 12-2. (*continued*)

with re - freshing___ mur - mur. More bright and clear___ did gleam.
im - mer fri - scher rausch - te, und___ im - mer hel - ler der Bach.

Must this then be my path - way? O streamlet, tell me
Ist das denn mei - ne Stra - sse? O Bäch-lein, sprich, wo-

where, My path___ shall I find!___ Thou
hin? wo - hin?___ sprich, wo - hin?___ Du

hast with thy sweet mur - mur, Be - wil - der'd quite my mind. Thou
hast mit dei - nem Rau - schen mir ganz be - rauscht den Sinn. du

hast with thy___ sweet mur - mur Be - wil - der'd quite___ my___ mind. Why
hast mit dei - nem Rau - schen mir ganz be - rauscht den___ Sinn. Was

EXAMPLE 12-2. (continued)

Schubert, *First Vocal Album.* Copyright © G. Schirmer, Inc. Used by permission.

Schubert, in this song, links the alpha and omega of rhythmic definition. The accompaniment has not a single rest as a point of articulation; on the contrary, the melody is regularly punctuated at four-measure intervals and at times by two-measure groups. Both the flow and the singsong symmetry contribute to the remarkable broad sweep of the song, eighty-one measures in length. Phrases are easily repeated, parentheses interwoven, and the final measures spun out, all floating on the stream of unbroken sound.

EXAMPLE 12-3.   Rhetorical melodic reduction. Schubert, *Die schöne Müllerin*, Op. 25, 1823, ''Wohin?''.

The rhetorical reduction (Ex. 12-3) shows, by contrast, how the accompaniment carries the song. The reduction substitutes a conventional on-and-off-beat accompaniment for Schubert's figuration; all repetitions and parentheses are removed so that the melody and accompaniment arrive at their successive stations within the minimum sixteen-measure two-reprise schedule. At the same time the reduction retains the essential songlike quality of the original, perhaps to be sung by a Papageno-like character rather than by a distracted lover. Numbers above the score correspond to the measures that have been retained from the song. In the reduction the melody stands out boldly, in the song the melody floats above its support as though it were the surface of the flow. The song can give the impression of having been in motion before it actually begins, and with the high D poised at the end, in midair as it were, it conveys an impression of not being quite finished. Neither the brook nor the wanderer finds a goal. On the other hand, the reduction establishes decisive perimeters and stations within the minimal two-reprise form.

Within the steady, unbroken flow of the song Schubert introduces subtle shadings of harmonic color that match the sense of the song. The opening in G major sets the mood—the flow of the brook. In measures 11–13 a circle of fifths matches the phrase "Ich weiss nicht" (I know not) with a bit of harmonic instability. Returning to G major, the wanderer says he must follow the rush of the brook, and the music recalls the sense of the opening. The shift to the dominant, D major, brings in a new idea, "freshness," in measures 22–31. A broad harmonic digression that traverses A minor and E minor (mm. 35–49) frames the central question, "wohin?" (whither), as it wanders through related harmonies. The return to the tonic, measures 53–81, is a fanciful play on what the sounds of the brook might mean— nixies in the brook or a miller's wheel. Thus the harmonic orientation parallels the play of feeling between question and acceptance. Only with a clear idea of the harmonic direction and color can the subtle shifts of mood and meaning in the poetry be appreciated.

The special appeal that this song offers thus is generated from its qualities of sound. The means Schubert uses to build trajectories of great length (as in the Great C-Major Symphony) are in operation in this song. With the support that his characteristic sound values provide, he can spin out phrases and periods, repeat them, deploy them on a grand scale.

## *Three-Part Form: ABA*

The exquisite vignette "Vogel als Prophet" from Schumann's *Waldscenen*, Op. 82 (1848–49), touches the extremes of fantasy and regularity. The fantasy element comes to the fore in the texture, the piquant dissonances, the silences, and the steep up-and-down course of the melody. Regularity stands behind this activity with absolutely four-square phrase structure, mainte- nance of figure and affect throughout each of the three sections of the piece, and solid harmonic procedure in respect to key and chord progression.

The form of the piece is clearly laid out in three parts. The third part is a literal restatement of the first in terms of continuity, but since it has some local modifications in texture, it is written out rather than being indicated with a da capo sign. Each part is precisely articulated in two- and four- measure groups, with a hint of a minimal two-reprise trajectory because of the formal shift to a second key in part A, follows as:

| A | Reprise I | mm. 1–4 | G minor to B-flat major | I–III |
|---|---|---|---|---|
| | Reprise II | mm. 5–18 | D minor, F major, C minor | x |
| | | | return to G minor | I |
| B | | mm. 19–22 | G major to D major | I–V |
| | | mm. 23–24 | beginning of consequent | |
| | | | phrase to mm. 19–22, broken | |
| | | | off by shift to E-flat major | |
| | | | in order to effect a return | |
| | | | to A and G minor | |
| A | | meas. 25 | | |

Scoring and scansion contribute to the virtually mechanical regularity that organizes this piece, especially in the first part. Despite the wide range, more than four octaves, the tessitura is high and the scoring light; most of the time, we hear but one, two, or three tones. High tessitura and thin scoring create an impression of lightness and clarity; each tone, each chord, then, projects a sharp presence.

The four-bar grouping of phrases develops as an outcome of the meter. Schumann employs an amphibrachic foot—weak-strong-weak—as the basis of his scansion. At the beginning, each foot precedes a beat of silence, so that the rhythm has the following pattern:

The amphibrachic pattern is restated in measures 5–6, 6–7, 8–9, 9–10, 16–17, 17–18; we hear it eight times in all. Thus, phrase and figure rhythms establish a firm basis of symmetry for the fantasy that imbues the expressive content of this piece.

Piano sonority is the matrix from which the fantasy emerges. Each of the dotted eighth notes, whether a chord tone or an appoggiatura, makes its effect through the crisp "ping" of the piano attack; each then sustains its effect by means of the ability of the nineteenth-century piano to hold its tone without quick decay. The brief resolutions throw the principal effects of tone color onto the long dissonances. The modest action in the left hand, consisting of bass and after-striking middle chord, has the effect of color rather than of rhythmic and textural support in this context of lightness and pianissimo dynamics.

The brief middle section, in sharp contrast, gathers all voices together into a four- to six-part chordal texture, dense, with a quick rate of chord change. The style is songlike, but the song breaks off quickly, as though it were but a parenthesis. While it departs from the elusive fantasy of the first part, this middle section contributes to the general strangeness by the manner in which it returns to the opening. Suddenly, after a clear punctuation in G major (m. 23), there is a removal (*Verschiebung*) of the melody to E-flat major, a slowing of pace, a drop in dynamic level—all deployed to carry the music

EXAMPLE 12-4.    Schumann, *Waldscenen*, Op. 82, No. 6, 1848–49, "Vogel als Prophet."

Kalmus.

back to the fantast of the opening section. Example 12-4 gives the opening measures of each part.

"Vogel als Prophet" exploits two contrasted aspects of nineteenth-century piano sound—the richness of a full, close-position chordal texture and the pointillism of individual tones and thin chords. These textures also recall a traditional role of the piano as a surrogate for ensemble music. The Mendelssohn *Song without Words* and the middle section of the Schumann "Vogel" suggest a choral texture with their full note-against-note harmonies, while the principal section of the Schumann could easily and idiomatically be transferred to a wind ensemble.

The first two measures of Chopin's Etude in C Major, Op. 10, No. 1 (Ex. 12-5) brilliantly exploit the capacities of the Romantic piano. Its bold-arching arpeggio covers more than five octaves in the first two measures alone. When the pedal is brought into play to sustain all the tones of the C-major harmony that have been touched in this trajectory, these two measures create a magnificent explosion of sound.

The figure itself establishes a beautiful balance between its upward, rocketlike thrust and its compensating downward swoop, between upward centrifugal motion and downward centripetal motion. This figure, with its inner symmetry, serves as a two-measure unit, a module that sets a formal control that is firmly maintained throughout the piece. Of the thirty-nine pairs of measures in this piece, only two, those in measures 43–44 and 45–46, break the pattern of steep rise, apex, or peak at the beginning of the

EXAMPLE 12-5.   Chopin, Etude in C Major, 1830, Op. 10, No. 1.

second measure, followed by one measure of steep drop. This interruption has an important formal function to be pointed out below.

The series of brilliant two-measure arpeggios is arranged exponentially into four-measure phrases, then into eight-measure phrase groups, then into periods, respectively sixteen, thirty-two, and thirty-two measures in length (assuming that the fermata at the end of the piece counts for an extra

Example 12-5.   (*continued*)

measure). Thus the scansion by measure groups exhibits a clocklike regularity along powers of two.

As an outgrowth of the square stance set in the first two measures, the form
takes shape in huge, precisely trimmed blocks. There are three of these
blocks, arranged in a modified da capo ABA form. The outer sections are each
solidly anchored to begin and end in C Major. The middle section hinges on

A minor. It opens in that key and closes with a half cadence (mm. 47–48), on its dominant, the chord of E major. In relation to C major, this half cadence pauses on the V of VI. It moves then directly into C major. Such a connection, often described as a third-related progression and considered a typical late Classic or Romantic feature, is actually a carryover from earlier eighteenth-century da capo arias, where a middle section might close on VI or V of VI of

EXAMPLE 12-5.   (*continued*)

the home key.[5] Immediately preceding this point, at measures 43–46, the figuration undergoes a compression into one-measure patterns, a melodic stretto that leads into the return of the opening figure to begin the third part of the form.

This etude is a nineteenth-century version of a centuries-old genre, one that included preludes, introductions, toccatas, and so forth. In these works the principal process was the elaboration of an underlying alla breve, a line of

Chopin, *Etudes*. Copyright © G. Schirmer, Inc. Used by permission.

long notes. While their original function was to set the key or mode for a contrapuntal piece to follow, eventually these introductory pieces became substantial compositions in their own right. Several of the preludes in Bach's *Well-Tempered Clavier* exemplify the genre. Chopin's interest in and knowledge of Bach's music is well documented, and it would appear that the Etude in C Major uses the Prelude in C Major of Book I of the *Well-Tempered Clavier* (Ex. 12-6) as a model.[6] A point-by-point comparison and contrast of the two works can shed light on the sound-syntax relationship within each work.

Bach did not specify an instrument for the *Well-Tempered Clavier*. The Prelude in C Major could have been played on any keyboard instrument available at that time—clavichord, harpsichord, possibly early forte piano, organ. Chopin's instrument was a Pleyel pianoforte. The range of Bach's music is three octaves and a third; that of the etude is six octaves and a third, vastly greater than Bach's. Tone production is very different in these two pieces. Each tone in the prelude is struck or plucked, and will fade more quickly than in a piano rendition. In the etude, each tone can and should be sustained by pedaling within each two-measure unit. Thus we hear a few notes at a time in Bach's prelude; in Chopin's etude we hear the cumulative effect of fourteen notes reverberating at different degrees of presence. The sheer amount of sound in the etude is far greater at any time than in the prelude.

Each piece is based on an alla breve topic, elaborating a cantus firmus–like structural line of whole notes. Bach proceeds deliberately, working out a modest, delicate tracery of figures that draws the attention of the listener entirely to the calm, discursive progress of the harmony. The music itself gives no clue as to expression; we cannot pinpoint its affective content (various performances of this prelude employ brisk tempo, languid rubato, sharp articulation, heavy pedaling, etc.). Even the tempo can vary widely, since Bach does not specify it. On the other hand, the etude signals its expressive stance emphatically. Its allegro tempo and its explosive bursts of sound point to a furioso manner of performance.

The figures in the two pieces have some distinctive points of similarity. Each opening figure traverses the C major triad, beginning on C and rising to E as an apex at the halfway point.

Differences between the figures can be linked to their media of performance. The range of Bach's figure is an octave and a third, placed squarely in the middle range of the eighteenth-century keyboard. Chopin's figure spreads over five octaves and a third, encompassing virtually the entire range of the expanded gamut of the pianoforte. Bach's figure occupies two beats; Chopin's extends over eight. To fill out his one-measure module, Bach repeats the figure on the same harmony, creating a balance and emphasis in the melodic flow. Chopin moves to another chord without repetition of the opening two measures; he allows the figure to play itself out in a "fountain" of sound.

Examples 12-7 and 12-8 reduce these two pieces to their structural lines. The reductions show a remarkable correspondence in their macromelodic contours. Both take E as the opening upper note of the harmony. Both carry out a broad descent from an apex (A in the prelude, G in the etude), down to the final low C (transposing some octaves in the etude). In the course of these trajectories, both Bach and Chopin incorporate circle-of-fifths descents. Bach's circle leads from the dominant to the home key in a short period of

EXAMPLE 12-6.   J. S. Bach, *Well-Tempered Clavier*, Book 1, 1722, Prelude in C Major.

Edwards.

time; Chopin's descent is more complex, drawing in some brilliant flashes of color and working within the orbit of A minor.

Rhythmic processes also reflect the differences in sound values between the two pieces. In Chopin's etude we can make out regular transpositions of the opening four-note figure in the right hand in successively higher octaves; the even-numbered measures invert the figure and the process. The tone E is the highest note in each four-note group of measures 1–2. The regular rhythmic layouts reinforce the sound of the C–E tenths. In contrast, the hint of syncopation in Bach's figure—the sixteenth notes are grouped as five plus three—generates a subtle yet active thrust that gives each restatement of the figure a fresh momentum, quite different from the headlong rush of sound in the etude.

On the macrorhythmic level, Bach's prelude shows some notable irregularities. In contrast to the etude, which maintains a steady four-measure grouping, the prelude groups measures by fours, threes, and twos according to cadential formulas or patterns within the structural melodic line. Individu-

EXAMPLE 12-7.  Rhetorical textural reduction. Chopin, Etude in C Major, Op. 10, No. 1, 1830.

EXAMPLE 12-8. Rhetorical textural reduction. Bach, *Well-Tempered Clavier*, Book 1, Prelude in C Major, 1722.

al impressions of these groupings may well differ; for example, the bass line can be understood in groups of three plus three plus four measures, running counter to the soprano line. This shifting scansion, impossible to put into a simple symmetrical system, imparts a subtle quality of discursiveness to the rhetoric of the prelude.

Chopin's harmonic language is basically the same as that of Bach. Chord formation, the grammar of harmonic progression, voice leading, definition of key, polarity of outer voices, key relationships—all these are common to the music of both composers. One fundamental distinction is the tremendous emphasis given in the etude to each chord through range, dynamics, and time, drawing the listener's attention to the color of each chord as it juxtaposes its sound against those that precede and follow it. Again, it was the capacities of their available instruments that allowed harmony to move buoyantly in Bach's music and to proceed massively in that of Chopin. Tone color, generated from the pianoforte sound, is a central value in Chopin's etude; it is an incidental feature in the prelude, in which a specific instrument was not actually indicated.

While Chopin's cadential formulas are traditional, here and there unusual harmonies add touches of nineteenth-century color, as seen in Example 12-9. Even the frequent use of *stile legato* in this etude, represented by suspensions and chords of the seventh, is made colorful by the expansive texture and the slow rate of chord change.

EXAMPLE 12-9.    Unusual harmonies. Chopin, Etude in C Major, Op. 10, No. 1, 1830.

Examples 12-7 and 12-8 sketch the period structure of the two pieces. Each has three periods, which are marked off by authentic cadences. In Chopin's etude the squareness of the great blocks of sound causes the piece to be built in broad, relatively autonomous sections—a three-part A B A form, i.e., modified *da capo* or simple rondeau. In contrast, Bach's modest figure travels a discursive harmonic path from tonic to dominant, then back to tonic—a I–V, *x*–I plan, laid out harmonically and melodically as a two-reprise form with a huge coda. Chopin's etude is solidly anchored to C major at four points, the beginning and end of each *A* section. Bach, on the other hand, closes the first period of the prelude in the dominant, G, and must rely on his long coda, something like a cadenza, to confirm the home key. The return of the tonic, C, is rather by the back door, as the second unit in a modulating sequence. Thus, the home key is "at risk." It becomes, as the piece progresses, the paramount structural issue, a forensic point to be reestablished and confirmed at length.

As an outcome of the use of sound in these two compositions, Bach's prelude takes shape as a discursive two-reprise form, while the etude is laid out in three "closed" sections, where symmetry holds sound firmly in control and sound fills symmetry with a maximum of inner activity, discursive at times, but essentially balanced.

Franz Liszt's late miniature "Nuages gris" (1881) is a simple two-part piece. It is discussed as the last example in this chapter dealing with small forms because its sound values point to the twentieth century, differing markedly from the typical rich textures illustrated in preceding examples.

This short piece conjoins innovative sound and traditional syntax in the simplest and starkest fashion (Ex. 12-10). Isolated, pointillistic effects, drawn from the color palette of the late nineteenth-century grand piano, are laid out in a series of two- and four-measure symmetries. These symmetries reach an exponential level covering the entire piece in an eight-plus-sixteen-plus-eight-plus-sixteen arrangement. Each gesture is set apart in the texture. At the beginning, individual tones slowly trace a sinuous path around the G minor arpeggio. Later, bass tremolos, disembodied augmented triads, and polyharmonies appear. Thanks to their isolation both in time and register, these sounds have a hypnotic effect on the listener. The pervasive resonance

EXAMPLE 12-10.   Symmetry and exotic sounds. Liszt, "Nuages gris," 1881.

EXAMPLE 12-10. *(continued)*

of the piano supports and joins these sounds in suggesting the drifting motion and fragile texture of wispy gray clouds.

Liszt arranges these sounds simply and conventionally. The opening two-measure figure is repeated verbatim, creating a simple four-measure symmetry. The chords appear later at two-measure intervals, connected by steady stepwise chromatic descent. The entire process (mm. 1–18) is then recalled with variations in texture (mm. 25–42). At the end, Liszt epitomizes the foregoing polychordal mixtures with two seven-note conglomerations. These are carefully arpeggiated, with pedal, so that the individual sounds within these structures will interpenetrate one another without the discordant clash that would result from a simultaneous attack.

This brief work coordinates two extremes in style and structure. Harmonically, it stands at the extreme edge of key-oriented tonality; on the other hand, it maintains a rigid regularity of traditional four-measure phrases. Thus it isolates the features of Romantic music that have been the concern of this book.

Liszt's late piano music has been characterized as pointing to the piano style of the impressionists Claude Debussy and Maurice Ravel. In this work, some specific processes can indicate the connection between the late music of

Liszt and that of the French masters. The preludes of Debussy operate much like "Nuages gris." They fix upon special qualities of sound and present them in paired figures and phrases. On the other hand, the restless, unresolved dissonances of "Nuages gris," the isolated figures, the sense of alienation— these have a clear affinity with the somewhat later expressionism of the Viennese composers Mahler and Schoenberg.

This piece is short and remains obscure in our view of Liszt's music. Yet it epitomizes some important rhetorical directions in its time. It is a musical bellwether that indicates what was happening and what would happen in European music: sound, with the assistance of symmetry, would take over; harmony would be absorbed into color and lose its cadential function.

# CHAPTER THIRTEEN

# Sonata Form

Within the larger forms of Romantic music, the interaction of sound and symmetry still operates principally on a local level, that of phrase and period. But sound has a profound effect on the continuity of the larger forms above the phrase-period level. The present chapter examines some of these continuities to observe the roles that sound can play in shaping Romantic sonata form.

## Descriptions and Definitions

The term *sonata form* belongs to the nineteenth century. Its first systematic use appears to have been by the important nineteenth-century theorist Adolph Bernhard Marx in the second edition of his monumental treatise *Die Lehre von der musikalischen Komposition.* Earlier designations of this form seem casual; they refer to the form of an "allegro," to a "long movement," to a "morceau." Reicha used a more imposing designation, "la grande coupe binaire" (the grand binary division); Czerny designated the form as the "first movement of a Sonata."[1]

The terms used to designate the form of an extended movement indicate some important differences between eighteenth- and nineteenth-century layouts. An appreciation of these differences is critical for a clear idea of what took place in the life history of sonata form from its beginnings in the earlier eighteenth century to its later phases in the music of Brahms, Tchaikovsky, Mahler, and others.

*Harmony.* Two processes conjoined to generate what we today call sonata form: harmonic continuity and melodic articulation. Harmonic continuity was the older and more basic process. It organized all of eighteenth-century music around tonal centers by means of unbroken chains of cadential formulas. By far the greater majority of eighteenth-century compositions showed a harmonic profile that moved from tonic to dominant and then returned to tonic. The presentation of the tonic, its replacement by the dominant, and its eventual reinstatement as the final and ruling key of a piece had the aspect of a harmonic argument, a forensic exercise. We find this trajectory in dances, the da capo aria, suite movements, and concerto movements in the early eighteenth century; in the later part of the century it became virtually a genetic code for most music, regardless of scale.

Although tens of thousands of large-scale movements were written according to this plan, designated here as I–V, x–I, throughout the Classic era, we find no description of their form until very late in the eighteenth century. When theorists began to describe the form of a long movement, they did so in terms of the distribution of keys. Two such descriptions are given below: the first is from *Leichtes Lehrbuch der Harmonie* by J. G. Portmann (1789), the second from *An Essay on Practical Musical Composition* by A. F. C. Kollman (1799).

> The plan or sketch of a musical piece is the proper placement of the principal and secondary keys and the arrangement of these according to what is placed first and how the second, third, and fourth are to follow. For example, I shall give the sketch of an Allegro of a clavier sonata in *D major*. I establish the principal key, D major, in which I begin and "work through" [*modulire*]; then I modulate to the dominant . . . and close therein. This is the sketch of the first part of the allegro. In the second part I begin with various modulations, which lead me again to *D major*, in which I repeat the theme, and permit those melodic figures and passages that were heard in the secondary key to be heard again (in the principal key). I remain there and close.[2]

> In its outline a long movement is generally divided into two sections. The first, when the piece is in major, ends in the fifth of the scale, and the second in the key; but when the piece is in minor, the first section generally ends in the third of the scale and the second in the key. . . . Each section may be divided into two subsections, which in the whole makes four subsections.
>
> The first subsection must contain the setting out from the key to its fifth in major, or third in minor, and it may end with the chord of the key or its fifth, but the latter is better. The second subsection comprehends a first sort of elaboration, consisting of a more natural modulation than that of the third subsection; it may be confined to the third, or fifth, of the key, or also touch upon some related or even non-related keys if only no formal digression is made to any key other than the said fifth in major and third in minor. The third subsection comprehends a second sort of elaboration, consisting of digressions to all those keys and modes which shall be introduced besides that of the fifth (or third);

and being the place for those abrupt modulations or enharmonic changes which the piece admits or requires. The fourth subsection contains the return to the key, with a third sort of elaboration, similar to that of the first section.

The above is the plan of modulation, which is to be found attended to in most sonatas, symphonies, and concertos. . . . But it may be varied almost to the infinite. For the different sections and subsections may be of any reasonable variety of length and the said sorts of modulation and elaboration be diversified without end.[3]

These descriptions spell out the harmonic continuity of Classic large-scale form. They provide information, not instruction. Portmann, however, went further in pointing the way to a student of composition. He paraphrased a movement of a sonata by Mozart, K. 284 in D major (1775), by reducing the harmony to what he called *ground harmony*, then building an entirely new sonata movement that matches Mozart's measure for measure, topic for topic, but with completely different melodic material.[4] This procedure must have been one way in which music was composed in the eighteenth century—far-reaching paraphrases on solid yet flexible harmonic ground plans. For the eighteenth century, paraphrase must have been a practical way to produce a fresh piece of music. The continuity of eighteenth-century key-centered harmony provided the basis for such procedures as well as for fresh invention.

*Melody.* While harmony provided the continuous substructure of form in eighteenth-century music, melody articulated the flow of the music. It delineated topic and expressive content and marked critical harmonic points in the form. At first, its role as formal landmark was modest. Early eighteenth-century forms laid out in a I–V, V–I scheme would generally use the opening and closing measures of the two principal sections to recall and rhyme melodic material. That is, the opening figure, in the tonic key, would be recalled to begin the second section in the dominant or other key; the cadential figure in the dominant would return to provide a final rhyme in the tonic at the end of the movement. Within the movement, the melodic material would be a discourse on figures taken from the principal melodic idea of the movement. Example 13-1 illustrates the typical early eighteenth-century use of melodic articulation to profile the opening and final measures of a two-reprise form.

In the later years of the eighteenth century, melody took on a bolder face in articulating critical harmonic points in the I–V, $x$–I continuity. Melody profiled the principal keys with memorable thematic material; it delineated strong cadential points. In doing so it established continuities of its own in the first reprise that would be paraphrased on the return to the tonic in the second reprise, which we now call the recapitulation. Some recognition of these melodic processes is to be found occasionally in theoretical and critical writings.[5]

The balance and mutual reinforcement that harmonic continuity and melodic articulation established in Classic sonata form provided a model for

EXAMPLE 13-1. Melodic articulations. Bach, Sonata for Violin Alone in C Major, BWV 1005, 1720, fourth movement.

composition that was universal in its use in the later eighteenth century. This model was adopted in nineteenth-century theory and became the final problem in formal composition studies.[6] But the balance shifted in the direction of thematic differentiation, to the long-range contrast of melodic material in the tonic and dominant key areas, respectively. Music theorists of the nineteenth century reflected this emphasis by describing sonata form as being constituted principally of two contrasting themes, which were first presented, then worked over in a development, and finally recapitulated. While the harmonic plan still prevailed as an underpinning, the emphasis shifted decidedly to thematic order.

Descriptions of sonata form abound in nineteenth-century writings on music. The following outline, taken from Arrey von Dommer's 1865 revision of Koch's *Musikalisches Lexikon*, is typical of the general view current during the middle and latter parts of the century:[7]

### First movement

*First part*

| Main theme group | Transition | Second theme | Closing group |
|---|---|---|---|
| Tonic | Modulation to dominant or relative major | Dominant or relative major | |

*Middle part or Development*
Thematic working-over of the motives from the first part
Free modulation; return to tonic

*Repetition*

| Main theme group | Transition | Second theme | Closing group |
|---|---|---|---|
| | Ruled [*Herrschaft*] by the tonic | | |

While the descriptions by Portmann and Kollmann cited earlier are contemporary with the music of Haydn and Mozart, that of Dommer reflects the usage of Mendelssohn, Schumann, and Brahms.

A notable contrast emerges from a comparison of the two types of outline. While they show similar contours in harmony and layout of sections, their priorities are quite different. Dommer and his contemporaries saw sonata form as a disposition of distinctive thematic material, connected by harmonic relationships. In this disposition, the first and second themes take center stage; moreover, formal theory of the time specifies a contrast of character between the two themes, generally bold, masculine, and vigorous against suave, feminine, and singing.[8] Portmann and Kollmann had seen the form as a tour of keys, in which the principal focus is the home key; this tour is articulated by distinctive melodic material, themes, and passages that are identified respectively with the home key and the second or neighboring key. Portmann and Kollmann had made out two sections, based on the departure from and return to the tonic. Dommer made out three distinct sections, based on thematic treatment—statement, working over, and restatement.

These orientations carry distinctive implications for the unfolding of the form. In the thematic plan, the principal activity is to embody themes, to move to and from themes. In the harmonic plan the principal activity is to move through keys. Thus the thematic process tends to develop marked articulations between substantial sections, while the harmonic process connects movement through the major sections in order to arrive at important harmonic goals.

The role of the new climate of sound in this shift of priorities is critical. Sound, by compelling attention through color or mass, can slow down action; individual sections of a form take on stronger, more sharply profiled personalities than they would have in the ongoing harmonic argument of the classic I–V, $x$–I plan. This autonomy promotes marked separations between sections and engenders broadly scaled melodies that dominate within these separate sections. Long-range melodic contrast then becomes essential to articulate the form. In the analyses to follow, a spectrum of procedures in nineteenth-century sonata forms is examined. It shows the range of layout and action between those forms that embody the eighteenth-century harmonic argument and those that use sound and themes as principal elements. The analyses use the following basic premises as criteria:

*Harmonic processes:* embodiment of key by presentation, establishment, and confirmation of key, opposition and reconciliation of key
*Thematic features:* affective stance and distribution of thematic material

Each of the five movements discussed makes distinctive and individual use of sonata-form premises. Sound qualities play an important role in shaping these individual approaches. The first three examples—by Mendelssohn, Schubert, and Brahms—incorporate special features, yet embody quite clearly the nineteenth-century thematic-harmonic plan. The last two—by Mahler and Liszt—on the other hand, while retaining some striking features of sonata form, incorporate elements of fantasia to such an extent that the clarity of the form is obscured and the traditional balance is profoundly disturbed.

# Standard Layouts

The second movement of Mendelssohn's *Scottish* Symphony, Op. 56, which serves as a scherzo, has been modeled closely on the I–V, *x*–I plan. The key scheme is F–C, *x*–F, with properly located recall and rhyme of melodic material. The music moves forward briskly. Its sharply profiled melodic material is clearly and lightly articulated. The harmonic directions are clear, especially in the shift to the dominant, which is accomplished simply via the dominant of C major. The development moves through an orbit of keys related to F. In a manner reminiscent of Haydn, it flirts with the expectation for the return of the home key. It makes a feint toward F several times; each time it turns the harmony aside. Suddenly, with a musical pun worthy of Haydn himself, a sleight-of-hand shift from B flat to B natural brings the harmony back to F by way of a dominant pedal point that underpins the final phrase of the opening theme (m. 183).

Melody and rhythm are packaged neatly into four-measure phrases. At no point is this continuity seriously disturbed, although here and there Mendelssohn drops or adds a measure. The tunes themselves, four to eight measures long (mm. 9–16, 72–75, 93–100) break up easily into figures that are tossed about buoyantly in typical Classic give-and-take.

While harmony, melody, rhythm, and form in this scherzo-like piece echo the style of the late eighteenth century, Mendelssohn's orchestra colors the action with nineteenth-century shadings. The orchestra itself adds just one element beyond the typical Classic ensemble—an extra pair of horns. These, together with what must have been a considerably larger body of strings than in the orchestras of Haydn and Mozart, give body to conventional figures, imparting a sense of immediate, vivid presence. Mendelssohn's use of the four horns is the most prominent aspect of instrumental color in this piece. Of the 270 measures in the movement, more than 100 involve all four horns in a variety of figures—melody, fanfare, repeated and sustained tones. These idiomatic eighteenth-century horn figures add richness of sound to the Highland reel that is the topic of the movement.

The larger orchestra provides Mendelssohn with a typical nineteenth-century orchestral resource—the grand orchestral crescendo. First exploited purely as a device by the Mannheim and Paris orchestras in the middle and late eighteenth century, the crescendo came into its own as an expressive and rhetorical element as the range of dynamics was widened thanks to the expanded size and greater instrumentarium of the early nineteenth century. Mendelssohn exploits the grand crescendo in the broad first key area (mm. 1–56), where the opening theme appears on three dynamic levels, increasing strength each time: solo clarinet, piano, at measure 9; flute and oboe, mezzo forte, at measure 33; and first violins and horns (in part), fortissimo, at measure 49. In contrast, the brief second key area (mm. 72–104) is reached by a decrescendo and remains pianissimo to its closing cadence, with a delightful play of crisp dotted figures.

This order of events, lengths, and dynamics, runs counter to the typical Classic scheme. Characteristically, the first key area in a Classic sonata form is rather brief, especially in relation to the subsequent sections of the exposition, because the harmonic argument demands that the dominant replace the tonic as the ruling key and confirm itself with emphasis at the end of the exposition. Thus the peak of emphasis and confirmation usually takes place at the close of the broad second key area, when the dominant makes its strongest statement. In this movement, however, the peak of emphasis belongs to the first key, at measure 49. The upthrusting, ebullient opening theme has a potential for being carried on a crescendo, especially given the orchestral resources available to Mendelssohn. Using dynamics as his raw material of sound, Mendelssohn has projected a grand dynamic curve that reaches over the entire exposition, from pianissimo to fortissimo and back. The same kind of dynamic curve arches over the recapitulation, beginning with the last measures of the development, but now it reaches its peak at the rhyme of the second key-area material.

Mendelssohn's compact sonata form accommodates these two broad dynamic curves and the change in proportions that the first crescendo causes in the exposition. The next example, the first movement of Schubert's Quintet in C Major, constitutes a broadly scaled sonata form that faithfully retains the Classic proportions. However, in this movement sound plays a different role than it does in Mendelssohn's scherzo.

Chapters 5 and 10 have examined Schubert's deployment of sound at the beginning of the quintet and the effect of this opening sound on the first period of the first movement. Here we look at the ways in which Schubert maintains and develops these special qualities of sound to help set the course of his sonata form.

C major in the first key area (mm. 1–58) projects a strong presence as a key and a vibrant effect as a color. Many glints of chromaticism throw the brightness of C major into high relief; among these are the momentary digressions in measures 3–4, 11–16, and 20–25 and the high coloring of the rising chromatic lines in measures 29–32 and 49–56. Despite a high proportion of altered harmonies, the first key area holds fast and close to its tonic; the alterations have a decorative rather than a purposefully driving effect, and this effect is supported by full, resonant scoring.

C's dominant, G, also figures prominently in this first key area. Having established his tonic, C major, firmly in measures 1–20, Schubert then begins to play games with what will eventually be his second key, G major. He first approaches G in a skewed direction, from a fortissimo unison on B (mm. 24–25). B is itself approached as the resolution of an augmented sixth chord that quickly grows out of a C-major sound. B then drops to G which becomes a powerfully driving pedal that leads to a second confirmation of C major. In turn, this C major plays itself out in an eleven-measure pedal again on G. In all of this action, sound and texture project the harmonic action in a bold, quasi-orchestral fashion, with full scoring and plentiful doublings. By now we have had a strong and sustained presence of G, some eighteen measures all told, closing as a powerful half cadence.

This half cadence itself represents a moment of profound decision. The grand gestures, the maximum sound, and the powerful presence of G that precede this cadence preclude a conventional shift to G as a new key.[9] Something must happen to give G the status of a harmonic objective, to make it a goal in the trajectory of the exposition. Schubert's decision to use E-flat major as a foil to G accomplishes two things: (1) it introduces a wonderful color effect, and (2) it delays the arrival of the dominant so that when it finally appears, it comes as a resolution, beautifully timed, of the harmonic question raised by the shift from G to E flat (Ex. 13-2). Moreover, putting aside for the moment the syntactical and color elements, we can interpret the shift in two traditional ways: (1) as the Gasparini drop of a third, rather than of a fifth, and (2) as an interchange-of-mode parenthesis between the tonic and the dominant (E flat belongs to the minor modes of both C and G).[10]

Schubert's music echoes, at this point, time-honored procedure. The difference lies in Schubert's emphasis; sound highlights the harmonic detour and expands its scope.[11] The appearance of E-flat major itself is given highlights by a subtle play of sound and rhythm. The tune, frankly lyric and mellow as it seems, has trouble finding its true key, and along with this difficulty loses its rhythmic balance. The trouble begins immediately, with the dotted half note that calmly and sweetly announces E-flat major. Were this to be a symmetrically balanced singsong tune, it might go something like the reduction in Example 13-3. The dotted half note—like the whole note in measure 65, a continuation of the suspended G of the preceding measures— holds the listener's attention on the sound itself for a moment, at the same time making room for the accompanying instruments to introduce their delicious little points of sound. These are reminiscent of the *style brisé* plucking of a mandolin, the entire effect redolent of a Vienna coffeehouse tune.

Bold and winning as E-flat major may sound, the key has precarious footing; it reaches no cadence. Quickly, Schubert veers over to C and G, with a formal cadence in G at measure 79. Once again, the harmony is momentarily transfixed on G as an entry to E flat; once again it veers over to C and G, this time to remain in G for the rest of the exposition. The song is spun out at length; eventually it leads to an incisive gesture that acts as a closing theme for the exposition (m. 138).

Each phase of action in this exposition has its own quality of sound and its own topical content. The first key area is like a fantasia, with stops and starts, with changes of texture and figure, highly colored with incidental chromatic inflections. The section that traverses E flat to G is a song, accompanied by a great variety of short figures. The final section is a march, with all five instruments in lockstep. Thus, with respect to topic and texture, this

EXAMPLE 13-2.   Schubert, Quintet in C Major, Op. 163, 1828, first movement.

Used by permission of Dover Publications, Inc. Reproduced from *Franz Schubert's Werke*, Series 4, ed. Eusebius Mandyczewski. Breitkopf & Härtel (1890).

EXAMPLE 13-3.   Rhetorical melodic reduction, beginning m. 60. Schubert, Quintet in C Major, Op. 163, 1828, first movement.

exposition moves from diffusion to coherence to concentration in three phases. In much the same order, the second key, G, is embodied in increasingly solid fashion, from the half cadence at measure 9 through the pedal points (mm. 26–32, 45–58), the tentative approach (m. 79) and clear arrival (m. 100), and the confirmation (m. 138). All these bespeak an increasingly important presence of G major. Beethoven himself could not have done better!

The long-range planning of this exposition shows the same grand strategies that we hear in the great sonata forms of the Classic era. On the other hand, the availability of an ensemble with rich potential for tone color invests local action with compelling effects. Classic sonata action is principally discursive, interspersed with moments of lyric stability. Schubert's rhetoric in this sonata exposition is essentially lyric; it is especially concerned with the play of sound qualities and harmonic color, along with some elements of discursiveness. Therefore, the phases of this exposition come across as episodes, in which bold contrasts of style, texture, and harmony act to articulate the form. The sudden shift from G to E flat is thus consistent with Schubert's sense for sound as an expressive medium; it is also incorporated into Schubert's adaptation of Classic harmonic rhetoric as a way station on the road to the dominant.

The exposition creates a unique rapprochement between local tactics of timbre and harmonic color on the one hand and the grand strategies of the Classic key-area form on the other. Similarly, the development balances these two forces. Schubert's plan is a massive descent stepwise from F sharp to E to D, then by fifths to G and home to C. The plan is articulated as a huge sequence in which the E segment is a literal transposition of the F-sharp segment, while the D segment breaks off after a few measures to set up G.

Example 13-4 gives the critical tones of the bass line in the development. These tones are turning points in the harmonic action; they outline broadly scaled cadential formulas. The white note heads represent tonic-function

EXAMPLE 13-4. Structural bass line of development. Schubert, Quintet in C Major, Op. 163, 1828, first movement.

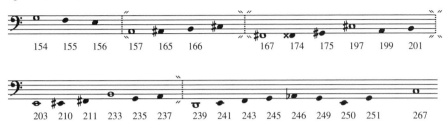

harmonies; the black note heads establish the cadential formulas. Within the segments marked out by dotted lines, the music lingers. It plays out a variety of elaborate textures in slow, regular harmonic rhythm. There are rarely less than five voices sounding at a time, often more. The texture is essentially melody with an elaborate accompaniment, twice coalescing to powerful tutti unisons (mm. 175 and 211). Two topics make up the melodic content; the march that ends the exposition is transformed into a song in the second half of each segment. Thus the march, the unison, and the song display among one another the same bold contrasts of the three sections of the exposition.

Example 13-5 points up another notable feature of Schubert's play with harmony. While the cadential motions are traditional in the deployment of tonic, subdominant, and dominant functions, there is great disparity in the amount of time and attention given to different aspects of key definition. Note the great length of time that Schubert takes to remain in F sharp, exploiting the color of that key; note how quickly the harmony shifts to G sharp/A flat in measure 175, to remain there firmly for twenty-two measures, then quickly turns to E. This is a striking and consistent feature of Schubert's style—to savor each harmonic color at length and to turn quickly from one key or color to another via traditional cadential formulas.

One further point: most *x* sections (developments) in Classic music have a turning point where the harmony shifts from movement away from the dominant to begin a return to the tonic, a place I have termed the point of furthest remove.[12] Schubert's point of furthest remove, as we can see in Example 13-4, appears near the beginning of the development; it is F sharp, a tritone distant from the home key, a point even more remote than the customary V of VI in Classic forms. Still, it serves the same purpose—to set up the tonic as an eventual harmonic target. Example 13-5 shows this basic motion from the point of furthest remove. The lower brackets show the stepwise descent; the upper brackets isolate the critical tones that make up traditional cadential formulas.

Schubert's recapitulation is a literal recall and rhyme of the exposition, with two notable changes. The first involves an activation of the opening harmonies by means of spread-eagled arpeggio figures against the sustained tones. The second involves the transposition from V to I to set up the rhyme. Schubert makes the decisive move early in the recapitulation, using the

EXAMPLE 13-5.    Tonic as target of development section. Schubert, Quintet in C Major, Op. 163, 1828, first movement.

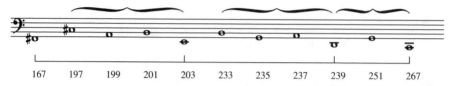

| 167 | 197 | 199 | 201 | 203 | 233 | 235 | 237 | 239 | 251 | 267 |

tangent to B as a turning point. In the exposition, the harmony settles back to G to go on to work extensively in C major. In the recapitulation, a Beethoven-like sleight of hand causes the harmony to slide past B to reach F quickly. From this point, measure 295, everything is rhymed literally to measure 414. Example 13-6 shows the two readings of the half cadence on B.

The coda follows the track of the Beethoven codas: digression, theme in the tonic, and final cadential gestures. Together with these traditional trajectories, this coda echoes intensely the qualities of sound that have saturated this movement and have influenced its form so profoundly. At measure 416 the music moves boldly forward to lead through a series of hectic figures and wild chromaticisms with a strong color of the French sixth. As peremptorily as it began, this digression is cut off, to be followed by the final suave recollection of the opening textures—luminous C-major harmonies. Thus the rich chromaticism, the active figuration, and the glowing sound are all recollected to sum up the movement's remarkable blending of tradition and innovation. Schubert's use of innovative color effects to amplify essentially traditional harmonic progressions contributes profoundly to what Schumann called the "heavenly length" of his music.

Brahms's *Tragic* Overture, Op. 81 (1880), is scored for full orchestra with winds in pairs, supplemented with piccolo and tuba. Constant doublings, often three or four to a single strand, are among the devices that modify the overture's sonata form.

The key scheme is a grandly scaled I–III, $x$–I plan that maintains the Classic proportions:

| | | |
|---|---|---|
| D minor | mm. 1–77 | Key Area I |
| shift to F major | mm. 78–105 | |
| F major | mm. 106–197 | Key Area II |
| $x$ | mm. 198–263 | |
| D major | mm. 264–366 | Partial rhyme of shift and Key Area II material |
| D minor | mm. 367–429 | mm. 423–29: completion of Key Area II rhyme |

The recall of the opening six measures at the end of the second key area (mm. 187–92) is absorbed into the final cadential point of F major. The modal

EXAMPLE 13-6.   Readings of the half cadence on B. Schubert, Quintet in C Major, Op. 163, 1828, first movement.

climate of the theme allows it to be read either in D minor or F major. Following the Classic proportions, the exposition gives almost two times as much weight to the relative major as a counterbalance to the powerful opening tonic impression; consequently, it creates a comparably broader trajectory to return to the home key and provides that key with its final confirmation.

Within this traditional plan, Brahms uses harmonic color to sustain the harmonic drive and to modify its local directions. The very opening is arresting. Two towering chords, neither of which have a conventional opening ring—a first inversion of the D-minor triad and an open fifth on A—unique representations of a tonic-dominant progression in D minor. Especially telling are the ringing open fifths that inhabit the upper registers of each chord, D–A and A–E. Then, as if to compromise D minor further, the main theme outlines an F-major triad, its C natural negating the functional aspect of D minor, the leading tone C-sharp, and giving an Aeolian-mode shading to the melody. The archaic-sounding open fifths and lowered seventh degrees provide a foil to the powerful authentic cadences that confirm D minor at measures 21 and 33.

While the second key area is solidly anchored in F major at both ends (mm. 106 and 197), it makes a wide sweep away from that key to F minor, returning to F major via a harmonic back door that momentarily touches on B minor (mm. 137–38). Thus both key areas are heavily shaded by shifts of harmonic focus that insert strange glints of chord color along the way to their eventual familiar goals.

Brahms substitutes an extended episode in slow tempo for the usual development. Still, his harmonic plan exemplifies traditional procedures in Classic development sections. Essentially, the path of keys takes us up the circle of fifths:

| | |
|---|---|
| A minor | m. 211 |
| E minor | m. 243 |
| B minor | m. 247 |
| F-sharp minor | m. 251 |
| C-sharp minor as V of F-sharp minor | m. 263 |

These keys are stations along the ascent by fifths; while they do not embody a balance of phrases, periods, or cadences, they do point to a clear harmonic direction of the sort we find consistently in Classic development sections.

When the music arrives at C-sharp major, the V of F-sharp minor, we have come to the point of furthest remove in the harmonic trajectory of the piece. Brahms here executes a stunning tactic. With a deceptive cadence to D, he arrives immediately at the key of the rhyme in the recapitulation and begins the rhyme itself with the material that articulated the shift from D minor to F major in the exposition. Much the same tactic for returning—the arrival at the home key via V of III—was used earlier by Beethoven in the first movement of his Symphony No. 2 in D Major, Op. 36 (1802), and even earlier by Haydn in the finale of his Symphony No. 104 in D major (1795). And as Haydn and Beethoven do, Brahms dramatizes the deceptive cadence by dropping the dynamics down sharply and using sustained tones to articulate the half-step shift.

While harmony is the basic support for the form, Brahms's melody articulates the action and contributes to the overture's expansiveness. The melody's broad sweep and tight convolutions convey a sense of great consequence. This melodic manner adapts itself well to the nineteenth-century concept of sonata form, in which thematic groups are the principal constituents of the form.

Each of the principal segments of the form—Key Area I, the shift to the second key, Key Area II, the development, and the recapitulation—is set off by sharp melodic contrast from its adjacent segments. The form takes shape as a series of linked episodes, separated from one another by rhetorical gulfs that slow the motion and throw the thematic contrasts into high relief. Such a process of separation, often found in Romantic sonata form but practically never in Classic sonata form, provides the opportunity to stage the appearance of the so-called "second theme"; this theme, which embodies and stabilizes the second key, typically provides the form with the songlike element, which A. B. Marx characterized as the "feminine" melodic component. Thus each segment of the form is virtually an autonomous piece of music in its own right. In this work, however, Brahms retains a Classic element; he pits two contrasting affects against each other within key areas—a songlike legato manner and an incisive march style—while maintaining the large-scale separation of segments.

Rhythm and texture enhance the harmonic-melodic action of this work in a manner typical of Brahms. His rhythm draws from traditional syntax, while his texture offers a climate of sound based on nineteenth-century innovations in scoring. Brahms maintains a remarkable consistency in measure groupings in pairs and by fours throughout the work. With pleasant, neatly trimmed melodic material, such regularity could cause the form to flatten out, or to extend itself by simple addition. On the other hand, this regularity can become the basis for an exponential treatment of measure rhythms, especially when there is counterrhythmic action within measures and measure groups, as is characteristic of Brahms's declamation. The regularity piles up the momentum, builds powerful drives against the local displacements, and shapes broad key areas. Measures 3–24, illustrated in Example 13-7, embody this rhythmic process.

The climate of sound that supports the portentous action—the broad harmonic trajectories, the eloquent melodies, the powerful rhythms—has a typical Brahmsian layout, an amplification of eighteenth-century continuo

EXAMPLE 13-7. Scansion of mm. 3-24. Brahms, *Tragic* Overture, Op. 81, 1880.

texture: strongly active bass polarized against an active melody, with enrichment of harmony and color in the middle voices. Example 13-8 again (see also Exs. 4-4 and 4-5) illustrates the characteristic texture and color of Brahms's orchestra—substantial doublings by mixed choirs that pit two active lines against each other.

Brahms's scoring—full, layered, with frequent doublings in unisons, octaves, thirds, and sixths—supports the breadth of action in other aspects of his declamation: harmony, melody, rhythm. Indeed, it is the sound itself that enables the declamation to make sweeping gestures, to prolong a phase of action, and to articulate segments of the form. While every figure in this work, every progression, every rhythm clearly demonstrates an application of traditional syntax, each detail is colored and transformed by the setting in which it moves. The result is a form in which broad key areas intensively explore distinctive affective stances and in which key areas are sharply set off from one another, as though they were individual pieces or episodes.

# Adaptations

In the two movements next to be examined some drastic adaptations of the traditional layouts and procedures appear. We can recognize features that are prominent in sonata form—key and thematic contrasts, cadences, developments—the critical points along the sonata-form trajectory. However, the placement of these points and the musical action between them lack the

EXAMPLE 13-8.   Textures and doublings. Brahms, *Tragic* Overture, Op. 81, 1880.

Brahms, Tragic Overture, Eulenburg Edition. Used by kind permission of European American Music Distributors Corporation, agent for Eulenburg Editions.

direct forensic control that cadential harmony provides, a control that carries the argument from one harmonic station to the next. Expressively, both these works, the first movement of the Symphony No. 2 in C Minor, 1894, by Gustav Mahler and the Sonata in B minor by Franz Liszt, cover enormous gamuts of feeling. Their intensity is supported by, and often arises from, their deployment of sound, texture, and harmony.

Sonata-form configurations are set out boldly in the first movement of Mahler's Symphony No. 2 in C Minor (1894). Striking textures and sharp contrasts place in sharp relief the harmonic and melodic stations that locate keys and themes. Distant tonalities and contrasting themes—a vigorous C minor and a singing E major—distinguish the exposition's two key areas. The counterparts of these components in the recapitulation exhibit the same contrasts. The recall of the opening theme at the beginning of the recapitulation has all the dramatic impact associated with this moment in sonata form. Toward the end of the movement, the ostinato figure of measures 392–400 rhymes its earlier appearance (mm. 97–108), now at the fifth below, G answered by C. Exactly at this point, measure 392, Mahler begins the final confirmation of his home key, C minor.

These stations provide landmarks for the listener in this huge movement, 445 measures in length. However, these stations represent sonata-form features that articulate a line of action with the tangents of the fantasia rather than the direct harmonic argument of the sonata. Many changes in affective stance, in topic, and in tempo combine to create an episodic continuity in the movement.

Mahler's deployment of sound is critical to this episodic structure. Sound validates the striking gestures, the sudden shifts, and the explosions and subsequent collapses that characterize Mahler's intense declamation. His scoring and harmony both share responsibility for generating the idiosyncratic qualities of sound that infuse his syntax.

Mahler rivets our attention immediately with the opening sound—a powerful concitato on Gs in octaves, to be performed by at least forty to forty-five violins and violas. This concitato, maintained for twenty-four measures, embodies some typical features of Mahler's treatment of sound. It is a separate, isolated line that acts as a background for figures that enter and move at tangents to it and to each other. The scoring for these figures is lean—penetrating unisons and octaves, contrasts of timbre rather than the blending typical of Brahms's scores; spaces between lines of action, rather than amplification through rich chordal settings. Throughout these twenty-four measures, octaves and open fifths—G–G, C–G—shaded by E flat, dominate the harmony; indeed, the entire section is a drawn-out embodiment of the fifth C–G, with the hovering effect that comes from orienting the sound around the fifth, G, rather than the root, C. The only shift in harmonic meaning appears in measure 19, where tones from the supertonic triad replace those of the tonic in the theme given to the winds; this shift has something of the character of an ornament rather than of a functional process, since the harmony returns immediately to the tonic in the next measure. The spare scoring, with an edgy impact, along with a broad stretch of a single harmony anchored to a pedal point, creates a distinctive climate of sound, which will have a pervasive influence on the subsequent action in this movement.

Examples 13-9 and 13-10 illustrate some typical features of Mahler's scoring. Example 13-9, has the full orchestra spread-eagled on Gs five octaves apart. Two disparate melodic lines impinge upon each other, joined in the second measure of the example by still another figure in octaves. In Mahler's tutti passages, heavily doubled lines continually crisscross, often to create sharp dissonances. Notwithstanding the massive reinforcements at unisons and octaves, this texture has the open spaces and the give-and-take of significant figures that we associate with chamber music. Example 13-10 shows Mahler now in an elegiac mood, with minimum sound delicately disposed. Again we hear a sustained background pedal, this time on B, again widely spaced. Each participant in this poignant tracery is given a clear image, by spacing, by countertime, by contrast of timbre. On the other hand, the harmony remains static, suspended on B, that has the effect of a curtain against which the melodies move.

Mahler's treatment of harmony exerts a long-range effect on the movement's form. Though his harmonic vocabulary is traditional—triads and seventh chords—his usage alters the role of harmony in shaping form. Three idiomatic harmonic procedures stand out:

1. Long pedal points underlay the play of figures. Of the 445 measures, approximately 300 are fixed on pedal points or repeated tones over a number of measures.
2. Cadential action in the traditional sense of linked cadential formulas plays a minor role in the harmonic progress. Only about a half dozen authentic cadences occur, compared to the dozens of authentic cadences as well as traditional cadential formulas that create a chain of harmonic action in Brahms's *Tragic* Overture.
3. Harmonic shifts between tonic triads of significant keys are managed in a number of places by turning or pivoting on a pitch or pitches common to both triads. Example 13-11 illustrates several of these pivots.

Mahler's manipulation of the triad creates much of the sound climate of this movement. Ringing effects of pure triads, minor and major, juxtapositions of distantly related triads, superimpositions of disparate triads scored to highlight their contrast, biting dissonances against triads, all contrast to Wagner's saturation of tritone harmonies.

In each of the places cited in Example 13-11, as well as in a number of similar progressions throughout the movement, the half-step movement around a common tone acts as a turning point, a lever, to shift the harmony from one massive gesture to another. At the same time, the half-step motion

EXAMPLE 13-9.   Texture resembling chamber music. Mahler, Symphony No. 2 in C
Minor, 1894, first movement.

itself has the binding effect of a melodic leading tone, so that the connection
retains the essence of cadential action. Mahler rests an enormous rhetorical
weight on this connection, especially in view of the bold contrasts in affective
stance, scoring, key, and in many places, tempo itself.

Such harmonic shifts are staged effectively, often suddenly, by Mahler's
handling of figure and phrase. The march topic promotes a two-measure
melodic-rhythmic articulation; with the spun-out harmony (extended pedal
points and repeated figures), these two-measure groups can be strung along a

EXAMPLE 13-10.   Lyric E-major theme. Mahler, Symphony No. 2 in C Minor, 1894, first movement.

chain of action without being pulled to anchor by strong cadential gestures. They can also suddenly veer.

The effect of these characteristic scoring, harmonic, and rhythmic features on the form of the movement is to shift structural priorities away from the large-scale harmonic movement of traditional sonata form (although this form clearly was Mahler's model) to the individual shapes and local effects that seem to be Mahler's principal concern. The complementary aspects of sonata form, Classic key areas and Romantic theme contrasts, hold the form together, but they enclose the composer's unique adaptation of the two schemes.

From Classic usage, Mahler maintains the hegemony of the central key, C minor. He embodies it in a broad first key area, by a dramatic effect of recapitulation, and by a coda that confirms the home key. He also opposes the home key with a second key—not the traditional relative major, E flat but a remote key, E major.[13] Consistent with Classic practice, Mahler gives the second key an extended closing section (mm. 126–44). Also from Classic sonata form is Mahler's use of rhyme: ostinato on G minor (V of the home key) in measures 96–103 is rhymed in the coda in C minor, measures 392–99. The movement has a substantial development, typical of Classic sonata forms, and a powerful dominant approach to the recapitulation.

EXAMPLE 13-11. Turning points—turning on a note. Mahler, Symphony No. 2 in C Minor, 1894, first movement.

a. Link between first and second keys of the exposition—C minor to E major. Contrary half-step motion pivoting on E flat, mm. 45–46; chromatic rising half step, mm. 47–48. Note second inversion of E major.

b. Return to home key of exposition. G natural taken as interchange of mode, i.e., E-flat minor to E-flat major, then read as dominant scale degree of C minor.

c. Link between two sections of the development, each of considerable length. Half-step drop to B major, B natural to B flat, to form E-flat minor triad.

d. Harmonic link from E major to C minor; beginning of coda. Two quick interchanges of mode: G sharp lowered to indicate interchange from E major to E minor; E natural lowered to E flat to imply interchange from C major (VI of E minor) to C minor.

From Romantic usage Mahler introduces a distant harmonic color for the second key. E major lies remote from C minor, especially since the two tonic triads lack a common tone.[14] The second key suddenly appears as a short episode, dramatizing the opposition of first and second themes often found in Romantic sonata form (see Example 13-11a). E major is reached by a bit of harmonic legerdemain, instead of being staged as the climax of an extended cadential drive. The effect is a juxtaposition of highly contrasted harmonic color, rather than a deliberate, subtle shift of position.

Also, in contrast to the end of the exposition in Classic sonata form, where the confirmation of the second key is a powerful effect of conclusion, Mahler's E major lacks a peroration, an emphatic closing statement embodied in a powerful cadential section. Instead it is spun out on a drone fifth to serve as a closing gesture for the C minor–E major opposition, a dying-away often heard as a final effect in Romantic music. The sound reverberates, suspended in the air, after action has ceased.

Perhaps the most unusual treatment of key takes place in the final appearance of the lyric theme, measures 362–388, where Mahler has recalled it in E major, instead of the traditional C major, or even C minor. The unity of key in the recapitulation, essential to sonata form, gives way to the episodic color of the distant key, a recollection, rather than a resolution.

The following outline locates the Classic and Romantic procedures that Mahler employs in this movement as well as his individual modifications and adaptations.[15]

| Sonata form | Classic | Romantic | Mahler |
|---|---|---|---|
| Exposition, 1–73, 126–143 | Home key area, C minor, 1–41 | First theme (march) 1–41 | |
| | | | Short, abrupt transition to second key, 41–47 |
| | | Second theme; song; remote key, E major, 48–57 | |
| | | | Transition back to home key, 58–62 |
| | | | Short return to home key and first theme, 62–73 |
| | | | Development as a parenthesis in the key scheme, 74–116: A-flat major, 74–78; G minor, 79–116 |
| | | | Varied rhyme of second theme, C major, 117–125 |

| Sonata form | Classic | Romantic | Mahler |
|---|---|---|---|
| Development, 143–328 | Harmonic exploration, return to home key | March and song developed | |
| Recapitulation, 329–88 | Return to C minor, recall of first theme, 329–56 | Recall of first theme | |
| | | | Shortened verion of transition from 41–47, 355–61 |
| | | | Extended and varied recall of material from second theme, 362–88 in E major. |
| Coda, 388–445 | Rhyme of ostinato from 97–102, now in C, 392–98 | | |
| | Cadential confirmation, 398–445 | | |

The preceding survey has centered upon the important role that harmonic color plays in Mahler's adaptation of sonata form in the first movement of his Symphony No. 2. Harmonic color highlights the landmark moments in the form—important keys, salient themes, the instant of recapitulation. It also supports some drastic changes in proportion by striking shifts of key and scoring. By its contribution to the intensity of a gesture, a passage, or a broad section, harmonic color directs the listener's attention to the impact of the moment, rather than to the unfolding of a harmonic premise that grows steadily toward fulfillment as the movement progresses. Such immediate impacts are most effectively ordered as a series of clearly separated episodes. The tangents in the form are negotiated deftly by virtue of Mahler's handling of his mise-en-scène, his general climate of sound—a tendency toward clarity, spareness, separation of sounds, economical use of the bass register, clashes in the higher treble registers, much room in the middle registers, and exploitation of triad sounds as raw material for such effects.

Mahler's adaptation of Classic sonata form is a facet of his personal predilection for parody. His parodistic treatment of popular topics is familiar:

marches, waltzes, songs, chorales, and fanfares populate his music. The form of this first movement is itself a parody of sonata form; it retains many important configurations of the form, but puts them into odd places and proportions. Similarly, the melodic figures themselves have a familiar ring, but are placed into striking, often strange juxtapositions and are somewhat distorted so that their outlines represent comments on commonplace shapes. The familiar topics thus take on a substantive content not present in the trivial models. Indeed, Mahler's music, like that of no other composer, joins the popular and the bizarre, the common and the rare, in a manner that throws each aspect into high relief against the other. In this way Mahler reflects the bittersweet attitude that characterizes much of late nineteenth-century thought and expression.

Liszt's Sonata in B Minor, composed as a huge single movement, has attracted considerable attention in analytic writings on music, thanks to its unique deployment of features drawn from traditional sonata form. From Classic sonata form Liszt drew such elements as bold thematic and harmonic contrasts, opposition and reconciliation of keys, and firm melodic and harmonic recapitulation. In addition, the striking differences in affective stance that articulate this work suggest a multimovement layout—first movement, slow movement, scherzo, finale. Analysts of this work have made outlines of its melodic and harmonic features in the effort to reconcile its singular form with received ideas of traditional sonata form.[16] These outlines point to landmarks in the form—opening theme, "second themes," recapitulation of the principal themes, along with the opposition of keys and return to the home key—and some acknowledge the work's multi-movement aspect.

The landmarks taken from sonata form articulate a line of action that incorporates many changes of tempo and meter. The action is also interrupted by cadenzas and recitatives, by instants of suspenseful silence, and by occasional fermatas. Such changes in motion frame a series of varied affective stances—introspective, energetic, furious, grandiose, lyric, beatific. Like the first movement of Mahler's Second Symphony, the whole resembles a fantasia more than a Classic sonata form.

Liszt's deployment of keyboard texture and harmony validates both the fantasia and the sonata-form aspects of this work. Effects of keyboard sonority consistently provide sharp delineation and high relief to the juxtapositions of various affective stances. What in the keyboard works of Mozart and Haydn was a kaleidoscopic play of topic becomes in this piece a series of highly charged, often melodramatic stances, separated by silences, pauses, or elaborate lead-ins in which bold contrasts of keyboard texture reinforce changes in meter, tempo, or expression. Example 13-12, together with the excerpts from the opening and closing sections (see Examples 3-11, 3-12, 11-10, and 11-11), illustrates the sonata's great range of texture and affective stance, points up its vivid contrasts, and shows how pianistic effects nurture and validate the fantasia element. Such effects color and dramatize every change of stance, so much so that the listener's attention tends to be

EXAMPLE 13-12.   Contrasts in keyboard texture. Liszt, Sonata in B Minor, 1854.
a. Brilliant figuration; massive chords.

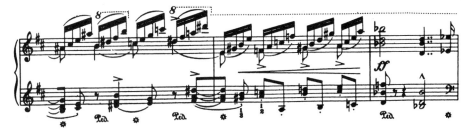

b. Full four- and five-part harmony; single-line recitative in lower register; song with interpolated arpeggio accompaniment figures.

fixed on local effects of color or virtuosity rather than the ongoing discourse of the sonata-form process.

In the complex, episodic continuity of this work, thematic material plays a profoundly important role in establishing coherence. The recall of thematic material from the first key area (mm. 32 et seq. recalled mm. 533 et seq.) and the rhyme of thematic materials from the D major and F-sharp major sections (mm. 105 and 600; mm. 335 and 711) represent the exposition and recapitulation processes typical of Classic sonata form. Thematic development and transformation constantly call the listener's attention to the principal melodic content of this piece; for all the prolixity of his declamation, Liszt is tightly efficient in the use of his principal themes. This aspect of his art reflects the later nineteenth-century tendency to assign ever-greater responsibility to thematic material for maintaining structural coherence, inasmuch as increasingly rich harmonies were gradually losing form-binding capacity.

Yet harmony, both as key and color, plays an important part in the unfolding of the sonata's form. Liszt's grand harmonic plan opposes two keys, D major and F-sharp major, to the home key, B minor, in broadly scaled sections; later, melodic materials heard in D major and F-sharp major are brought back to B major in the sonata form's characteristic process of rhyme

EXAMPLE 13-12.   *(continued)*

c. Recitative-like declamation in lower register; full four- and five-part chordal texture in middle and lower registers; song in higher register with light, figured accompaniment.

and reconciliation. Beyond the exploration of conventional key layouts, Liszt's treatment of the keys in this piece adds striking color value and formal definition to its continuity. One of the most amazing single features is that the home key, B minor, is not, *at any time,* personified by a clearly stated tonic triad. At most, we hear, in measures 32, 34, 533, and 535, arpeggiated B-minor triads that serve momentarily to establish the home key in the exposition and recapitulation sections. But B minor as a presence is stronger by implication than by explicit statement. Not so with the other keys: D major is ushered in with a long dominant pedal that resolves to massive D-major chords in chorale style. Later, the same figure is heard in C-sharp minor (m. 297) and in F minor (m. 301). F-sharp major is solidly established in measure 330. B, as the home key, is personified in the latter stages of the piece as a major key echoing the general cadential process that closed the extended F-sharp major section (mm. 395–454). Thus Liszt has used the color of keys and their embodiment in textures to create a long-range contour that runs alongside the thematic-harmonic processes. The effectiveness of this manip-

d. Cadenza; single line covering wide range in free rhythm; powerful full chords in six-part scoring in strongly marked march rhythm.

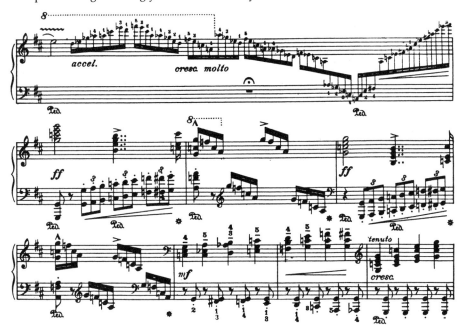

e. Recitative and "free" cadenza, accompanied by chords in middle register; eight-part scoring in massive chords, very low register, incisive rhythms.

ulation of color in keys rests solidly on the ability of Liszt's piano to project vivid, brilliant, resonant sounds, in whatever register, with whatever texture he may have specified.

Although we hear very little B-minor sound throughout the sonata, the home key is strongly implied by its diminished seventh, $VII^7$. The most salient theme of the sonata, heard at the beginning of the *allegro energico*, is harnessed to the diminished-seventh chord. During the course of the piece, diminished-seventh sounds appear often and prominently, straightforwardly

Example 13-12.  (*continued*)

f. Abrupt change of register, figuration, and tempo.

g. Extreme contrast in all parameters except harmony—rhythm, register, dynamics, melodic configuration, texture, affective stance; prolonged silence with strong dramatic implications.

or decorated. At least one-fifth of the entire duration of the work involves the sound of this harmony. Such a saturation of one kind of chord profoundly affects the sound values of the work as well as the construction of phrases and periods. Liszt sets this chord in high contrast to the stable major- and minor-triad sounds that interrupt the restless flow.

The diminished-seventh sound can be directed to opposing effects. Its tritones create a cadential urgency, so that the chord can participate in strong cadential drives (mm. 26–31, 101–2, 119–24, 226–38, 524–29, 737–43); at the same time, its colorful, restless, compact sound establishes an autonomous effect, one that can be isolated to set a mood, as at the beginning of the *allegro energico*. It also lies well to the hand, in compact or arpeggiated layouts, so that it can be managed brilliantly by the virtuoso pianist.

Two syntactical processes involving the diminished-seventh chord affect the unfolding of the composition's form. First, the mobility of the chord lends itself to the kind of sequential layout that pervades the entire sonata; this layout creates short-range complementary phrase groups, themselves arranged often in pairs (mm. 10–13, upbeats through mm. 17–22, mm. 45–50). Second, the chord's restless urgency promotes developmental procedures; in these the diminished-seventh chord operates with other unstable harmonies alternating with momentary triadic resolutions (mm. 18–25, 32 et seq., 191–97, and many other places). These phases of development are typically shaped as dynamic curves in which steady, deliberate rises in pitch levels, generally linked with crescendos, carry the music to a climax, effectively managed by the Romantic piano. (mm. 18–25, 45–55, 81–104, etc.).

Formally, the result of this deployment of texture and harmony is to incorporate development procedures throughout the work. Development alternates with stable episodes and themes to create a long-range rhythm of movement and arrival. The following outline gives a sketch of the three underlying processes: the sonata-form landmarks of key, recall, and rhyme; the episodic interpolations; and the continuity promoted by development procedures.

| Sonata | Episode | Development |
|---|---|---|
| *Exposition* <br> Key area I <br> B minor <br> mm. 1–32 | | |
| | | mm. 32–104 |
| Key area II <br> D major <br> mm. 105–71 | | |
| | | mm. 171–98 |
| | Recitative, cadenza <br> mm. 197–204 | |
| | | mm. 205–96 |
| | Pesante, recitative <br> mm. 297–330 | |
| Key area III <br> F-sharp major <br> I–V, mm. 331–47 | | |
| | Song, cadenza, pesante <br> mm. 349–94 (this episode <br> occupies the *x* phase <br> of a I–V, *x*–I form) | |

| Sonata | Episode | Development |
|---|---|---|
| I, mm. 394–453 | | |
| *Development* | | mm. 454–532 |
| *Recapitulation*<br>Return to key area I<br>recall of mm. 30–53<br>in mm. 531–54 | | |
| Rhyme of key area II<br>B major<br>mm. 600–636 | | mm. 532–99 |
| | Pesante, mm. 700–10<br>B major | |
| Rhyme of key area III<br>B major<br>mm. 711–28 | | |
| *Coda*<br>B major<br>mm. 729–59 | | |

For the listener, the immediate impression of this work is that of a fantasia. Liszt's brilliant compositional tactics carry us from one compelling mood to another, with bold contrasts that put each stance into high relief. His grand strategy, on the other hand, locates important stations in the form based on the traditional sonata-form rhetoric. Of these stations, the most securely anchored are those that accomplish closure for the two great harmonic arcs of the piece, those that end in F-sharp major and B major respectively.

These stations, mm. 394–453 (F-sharp major) and 711–759 (B major) respectively, are distinguished from the rest of the work in several salient respects. First, their songlike thematic material does not undergo thematic transformation; the song retains its affective integrity. Second, these two sections sustain their mood, an elegiac, reflective attitude, much longer than does any other section of the piece. Third, the harmonic color of these two sections has a purity of key sound (F-sharp major and B major) that contrasts vividly with the tritone-saturated, harmonically-shifting language of other sections; this purity of key sound, effectively projected with the nineteenth-century piano, acts to stabilize the harmony first in the dominant key, later to close the piece in the major tonic. Fourth, much of the extension of these sections involves a series of cadences that point to, yet evade a decisive act of final closure; eventually, closure is firmly achieved. Liszt here has drawn upon the harmonic periodicity that supports the rhetoric of Classic sonata form to shape and to close the circle of his form. In this sonata he has marshalled all the resources of the piano of his era, controlling them with what he chose to take from traditional sonata form.

# *Conclusion*

This study of Romantic music has taken as its point of departure the climate of sound generated by the improved and modified instrumentarium of the nineteenth century. The effects of this climate were all-pervasive, touching every aspect of Romantic musical composition and expression, from the smallest melodic detail to fully worked-out forms.

The appeal of the new sound values has long been recognized and appreciated. How these new sound values have affected musical forms of the Romantic era has not been specifically explored until now. This book has undertaken such an exploration.

In particular, this book has examined the interaction between new color values of sound and traditional processes of syntax with respect to Romantic musical form. We have seen how Romantic music could exploit the flow of sound, its sustaining power, its ability to make an impression on the listener without necessarily being tied to specific time values. We have also seen how punctuations and shifts in the line of action—the means by which musical time is measured—were used in Romantic music to articulate and focus the flow of sound. We have noted how sound can add color and thus enhance the symmetries of period structure. In turn, we noted how the points of articulation drawn from traditional periodic symmetries can harness the flow of sound. Thus sound and syntax establish polarities in Romantic music, working intensively and intimately with and against each other in the management of musical time.

The music chosen for analysis covered a wide range of usage. Some examples, representing a traditional orientation, colored Classic procedures with touches of new sound, thus suggesting subtly but unmistakably the effect of the new climate of sound. Other works moved boldly into the new world of sound, adapting traditional syntax to new lines of discourse generated to a great extent by innovative sound values.

The wide play of choices has provided the impetus to the modus operandi adopted here. First, sound values have been characterized to demonstrate the range of color and expression in the new climate of sound. Sound values then have been linked to traditional syntactical processes to show the interaction of sound and syntax on various levels of structure, from short, symmetrical periods to broadly scaled sonata forms.

By adding qualities of sound to the more familiar analytic criteria—melody, harmony, rhythm, form—this approach has done more than to coordinate sound and syntax. It has shifted the analytic perspective to focus attention on the individuality of a passage or work. This shift of attention reflects the role of sound as one of the most personal components of a composer's language. Indeed, we can often recognize a composer's style by the way in which that composer has deployed sound. Wagner's rich, closely spaced textures and restless, colorful harmonies; Schubert's gently pulsating accompaniments that support a gently flowing melody with luminous harmonies; Chopin's electrifying activation of the sound spectrum with vibrant figurations; Brahms's fullness of scoring and amplification of lines of action set in tangents against one another; Berlioz's and Mahler's leanness of texture—these and other qualities bespeak the power of sound to character-ize a musical personality. For performers, such characterizations can be valuable; they provide indications for the production of sound throughout a composition—timbre, balance, strength, fullness or lightness, articulation, accent. Thus they contribute to a convincing projection of affective content.

Beyond the scope of this book, the approach through sound values opens fresh lines of investigation. Among these are delineation of trends within the general climate of sound; the individual styles of composers in their use of sound and texture; the deployment of sound qualities and their relation to syntax in specific works and genres; and the role of sound qualities in representation—affect, topic, and description.

Also, sound can be used as a principal criterion in the style analysis of Western music. New light can be thrown on music rhetoric and expression and the effect of technologies—mechanical and electronic improvement and innovations. For example, in eighteenth-century music, emphasis was placed on action—the play of melody and rhythm, the thrust of harmony. Sound and texture accommodated this action discreetly, rarely drawing attention to themselves as primary values. Indeed, the sturdiness of that music, its clarity and firmness, accommodates alternate settings as well as huge scorings or electronic transcriptions. Yet this music retains its essential coherence and affective content, delivering its message directly and simply. As this book has shown, in nineteenth-century music sound comes to the fore, sharing equal attention with traditional syntax. The balance tips toward sound values in twentieth-century music when the actual sound intended by the composer is essential to the music's message. This condition becomes absolute in music generated by electronic means. In music composed during the middle and late twentieth century, traditional syntax appears only as a trace element or parodistic reference, if at all.

Finally, we recall the words of Alfred Einstein, quoted in the Preface of this book:

> The unifying principle that links all the composers from Weber and Schubert to the end of the neo-Romantic movement . . . is this: their relationship to the most direct and perceptible element of music, its sound.

This statement describes the basic premise of this book—sound as a feature of prime importance in Romantic music. Beyond the investigation of sound qualities, this book has endeavored to show how sound was a factor that influenced the way Romantic composers shaped their music.

# Notes

## Introduction

1. See Chapter 7 for a discussion of the traditional training of nineteenth-century composers.
2. Einstein, *Music in the Romantic Era*, p. 8.
3. Burckhardt, cited in Bukofzer, *Music in the Baroque Era*, p. 2.

## Chapter One. Sound as Criterion

1. Berlioz, *A Treatise upon Modern Instrumentation and Orchestration*, Introduction.
2. Marx, *Die Musik des neunzehnten Jahrhunderts*, p. 86.
3. *Allgemeine musikalische Zeitung*, vol. 10, No. 16, Jan. 14, 1807, p. 242 (hereinafter cited as AmZ).
4. Ibid.
5. Carl Maria von Weber, *Writings on Music*, May 13, 1817, p. 224.
6. Ibid., July 1818, p. 269.
7. Mendelssohn, *Letters*, Feb. 12, 1834, p. 93.
8. Liszt, *Letters*, July 9, 1856, vol. 1, p. 273.
9. Ibid., Jan. 8, 1858, vol. 1, p. 353.
10. Ibid., Oct. 2, 1876, vol. 2, p. 302.
11. Tchaikovsky, *Life and Letters*, p. 179.
12. Ibid., Feb. 27, 1889, p. 772.
13. Ibid., Jan. 20, 1888, p. 767.
14. Ibid., pp. 767–71.
15. Ibid., Jan. 12, 1883, p. 431.
16. Ibid., Jan. 20, 1879, p. 333.
17. Brahms, *The Herzogenberg Correspondence*, Oct. 30, 1888, p. 362.
18. Ibid., Dec. 16, 1890, p. 394.
19. Ibid., Oct. 30, 1885, p. 264.
20. Carl Maria von Weber, *Writings on Music*, Apr. 10, 1812, pp. 100–101.
21. Ibid., Apr. 20, 1821, p. 297.
22. Czerny, *School of Practical Composition*, vol. 3, p. 1.

23. Brahms, *The Herzogenberg Correspondence*, Feb. 3, 1886, p. 278.
24. Ibid., p. 277.
25. Tchaikovsky, *Life and Letters*, Jan. 23, 1883, p. 433.
26. Carl Maria von Weber, *Writings on Music*, Jan. 26, 1816, p. 161.
27. Ibid., Aug. 27, 1816, p. 193.
28. Eigeldinger, *Chopin*, Dec. 15, 1833, p. 312.
29. Ibid., 1877, p. 310.
30. Ibid., n.d., p. 104.
31. Curt Sachs, in *The Commonwealth of Art*, draws parallels between art, music, architecture, literature, and the dance throughout Western history. With reference to the late eighteenth century, he speaks of "nature, simplicity, feeling" as general motifs, p. 171.
32. Czerny, *School of Practical Composition*, vol. 3, p. 1.
33. Marx, *Die Musik des neunzehnten Jahrhunderts und ihre Pflege*, p. 134.
34. Carl Maria von Weber, *Writings on Music*, p. 11.
35. *AmZ*, vol. 12, No. 33, May 1810, p. 519.
36. Marx, *Die Musik*, p. 90.
37. Tchaikovsky, *Life and Letters*, Sept. 17, 1878, pp. 319–320.
38. Ibid., May 5, 1879, p. 345.
39. Ibid., Sept. 8, 1884, p. 462.
40. Carl Maria von Weber, *Writings on Music*, 1814, p. 127.
41. Berlioz, *Treatise*, p. 3.
42. Carl Maria von Weber, *Writings on Music*, July 1812, p. 109.
43. Ibid., Apr. 1816, p. 171.
44. Eigeldinger, *Chopin*, Mar. 30, 1832, p. 328.
45. Liszt, *Letters*, vol. 2, p. 426.
46. Brahms, *The Herzogenberg Correspondence*, Oct. 30, 1885, pp. 262–63.
47. Ibid., Nov. 14, 1881, p. 143.
48. The episode is translated in Schafer, *E. T. A. Hoffmann and Music*, pp. 145–48, and Charlton, *E. T. A. Hoffmann's Musical Writings*, pp. 131–36.
49. Helmholtz, *On the Sensations of Tone*, 1863.
50. Riemann, *Präludien und Studien*, vol. 1, p. 55.
51. Ibid., vol. 1, pp. 55–56.
52. Einstein, *Music in the Romantic Era*, p. 8.
53. Handschin, *Musikgeschichte*, p. 370.
54. Loesser, *Men, Women, and Pianos*, p. 340.
55. Dahlhaus, *Musik des 19. Jahrhunderts*, p. 202.
56. Kurth, *Romantische Harmonik*, p. 443.

## Chapter Two. Texture

1. Examples 2-1a and 2-1c illustrate the circle-of-fifths progression that later was taken by Schoenberg as the cornerstone of his *Harmonielehre* in 1911. Indeed, in his approach to harmony, Schoenberg represents a direct line of descent from Sechter through Bruckner.
2. Berlioz, *Mémoirs*, p. 15.
3. Tchaikovsky, *Life and Letters*, p. 309.
4. Typical treatises are Momigny, *Cours Complet* (1806); Koch, *Handbuch* (1811); Gottfried Weber, *Versuch*, 3d ed. (1830–32); Marx, *Lehre*; 2d ed. (1841–51); Sechter, *Grundsätze* (1854); Lobe, *Lehrbuch* (1858); and Fétis, *Traité* (1858).
5. Marx, *Die Musik*, p. 91.

6. Sections of the following works that deal with the strict style: Momigny, *Cours complet*, pp. 517–83; Koch, *Handbuch*, pp. 347–483; Logier, *System*, numerous examples in latter part of the book; Marx, *Lehre*, all of vol. 2; Czerny, *School of Practical Composition*, vol. 1, pp. 114–31; Lobe, *Lehrbuch*, all of vol. 2.

## Chapter Three. The Piano

1. Loesser, *Men, Women, and Pianos*; Harding, *The Pianoforte*; Good, *Giraffes, Black Dragons, and Other Pianos*; Newman, *The Sonata since Beethoven*; Schonberg, *The Great Pianists*; Bie, *A History of the Pianoforte*.
2. Loesser, *Men, Women, and Pianos*, p. 340.
3. Ibid., pp. 339–40.
4. Newman, *The Sonata since Beethoven*, pp. 88–89.
5. *Neue Zeitschrift für Musik* (hereinafter cited as *NZM)* 17 (1841), p. 200.
6. Czerny, *Briefe*, pp. 48–49.
7. Newman, *The Sonata since Beethoven*, p. 88.
8. Schumann, *On Music and Musicians*, p. 136.
9. Ibid., p. 253.
10. *AmZ* 15, (March 1813), p. 142.
11. Czerny, *School of Practical Composition*, vol. 2, p. 7.
12. Schumann, *On Music and Musicians*, pp. 82–83.
13. Newman, *The Sonata since Beethoven*, pp. 89–90.
14. *AmZ* 31 (March 1829), p. 175.
15. Eigeldinger, *Chopin*, p. 136.
16. Robert Winter, "The most unwitting foes of the Romantic piano may be those well-intentioned curators who lend their instruments for recording sessions" *Early Music* 12 (Feb. 1984), pp. 21–25.
17. Artis Wodehouse investigates twenty-four different performances of the Nocturne in F-Sharp Major by Chopin in her doctoral thesis, *Evidence of Nineteenth-Century Piano Performance Practice* (1977). She catalogues wide differences in a great many points of interpretation among such performers as Josef Hofman, Leopold Godowsky, Eugène d'Albert, Alfred Cortot, et al.
18. Among the important piano makers were the Erard brothers in Paris (Sebastian Erard, 1752–1831; Jean-Baptiste Erard, 1745–1826; and a nephew, Pierre Erard, 1796–1885); John Broadwood, 1732–1812; Muzio Clementi, 1752–1832; and Ignaz Playel, 1757–1831.
19. Among the most notable virtuosos were Franz Liszt, 1811–86; Daniel Steibelt, 1765–1823; Friedrich Kalkbrenner, 1785–1849; Carl Czerny, 1791–1857; Johann Nepomuk Hummel, 1778–1837; Ferdinand Ries, 1784–1838; Ignaz Moscheles, 1794–1870; Sigismond Thalberg, 1812–71; et al.
20. Among the most significant eighteenth-century keyboard tutors were C. P. E. Bach, *Versuch*, 1759–62; Marpurg, *Anleitung zum Clavierspielen*, 1755; Türk, *Klavierschule*, 1789; Löhlein, *Clavier-Schule*, 1765.
21. E.g., Czerny, *The Complete Theoretical-Practical Piano School*, Op. 500 (1839). The earlier editions of Löhlein's *Clavier-Schule* (1765, 1781) and Witthauer's adaptation (1791) give considerable attention to figured-bass realizations of typical music of the later eighteenth century. Fingering instructions focus on clarity and ease of articulation. A later edition of the *Clavier-Schule*, Müller (1804), eliminates most of the figured-bass and stylistic material and substitutes dozens of fingering exercises aimed at the development of dexterity.
22. Occasionally in late Classic music, a curtain precedes the entry of a distinctive

tune, as in the first movement of Mozart's Symphony in G minor, K. 550, 1788, the first movement of his Concerto in B-flat major, K. 595, 1791, and the second movement of Haydn's Symphony No. 101 in D major, *Clock,* 1794. These examples bespeak the orchestra's ability to use sound as a value in its own right, subtle yet distinctive, especially in the first movement of Mozart's G minor Symphony, often considered his most "Romantic" symphony.

23. *AmZ* 44 (Feb. 1842), p. 144.
24. Berlioz, *Mémoirs*, pp. 13–14.
25. Hoboken lists many Haydn symphonies in arrangements for pianoforte, two hands, as well as for small ensembles with or without pianoforte.
26. *AmZ* 42 (April 1840), p. 306.
27. Berlioz, *Mémoirs*, pp. 83–84.
28. Berlioz, *Treatise upon Modern Instrumentation*, p. 73.
29. Liszt quoted in Newman, *The Sonata since Beethoven*, pp. 87–88.
30. Berlioz, *Mémoirs*, pp. 266–67.
31. Eigeldinger, *Chopin*, p. 37.

## Chapter Four. The Orchestra

1. Details of the changes in scoring are provided in Adam Carse's studies in the history of orchestration: *The Orchestra in the Eighteenth Century* (1951), *The History of Orchestration* (1925, 1964), and *The Orchestra from Beethoven to Berlioz* (1948).
2. Berlioz, *Mémoirs*, p. 49.
3. For example, the Mannheim crescendo that Burney praised; the powerful tutti sections in the symphonies of Haydn, Mozart, and Beethoven.
4. Burney, *A General History of Music*, p. 866.
5. The indexes of *AmZ*, 1798–1848, list many performances of the symphonies, concertos, and operas of Classic composers, but mention no performance of any Classic sonata.
6. Carse, *The History of Orchestration*, Chapter 9, gives succinct information on the changes in instrumental construction in the nineteenth century.
7. Carse, *The Orchestra from Beethoven to Berlioz*, pp. 45, 51.
8. Liszt, *Letters*, vol. 1., p. 465.
9. Berlioz, *Treatise upon Instrumentation*, p. 241.
10. Ibid., p. 244.
11. Carse, *The Orchestra from Beethoven to Berlioz*, p. 21.
12. Daube, *Der musikalische Dilettant*, pp. 4–6.
13. Kollmann, *Essay on Practical Musical Composition*, pp. 87–100.
14. De Momigny, *Cours complet*, p. 585.
15. Michaelis, C. "Einige Bemerkungen über den ästhetischen Charakter, Werth, und Gebrauch verschiedener musikalischer Instrumente," *AmZ*, Jan. 14–21, 1807, pp. 241–50, 257–62.
16. Czerny, *School of Practical Composition*, vol. 2. Marx, *Lehre*, vol. 4. Lobe, *Lehrbuch*, vol. 2.
17. Berlioz, *Treatise upon Instrumentation*, p. 4.
18. Quoted in Carse, *History of Orchestration*, p. 221.
19. Berlioz, *Mémoirs*, pp. 367–68.
20. Czerny, *School of Practical Composition*, vol. 3, p. 23.
21. *AmZ* 48 (April 1846), p. 243.
22. Czerny, *School of Practical Composition*, vol. 3, p. 36.
23. Werfel, *Verdi*, p. 344.

24. Ibid., p. 345.
25. Charles Maclean, "Modern Sensationalism," *Proceedings of the Royal Musical Association* 24, (January 10, 1898) p. 47.
26. Hedley, Arthur, *Selected Correspondence of Fryderyk Chopin*, p. 45.
27. Kurth, *Romantische Harmonik*, p. 143.
28. Werfel, *Verdi*, p. 235.
29. Valve horns are specified in the first edition; see Carse, *History of Orchestration*, p. 265 n.
30. Originally, the score called for two ophicleides (keyed low brass instruments). The tone of these instruments was considerably rougher than that of the tuba. Example 4-15 is taken from the Dover reprint of the Complete Works Edition, edited by Charles Malherbe and Felix Weingartner, Breitkopf and Härtel, Leipzig, 1900, and reflects the current practice of using tubas in place of ophicleides. The original scoring is restored in the Norton Critical Score series; Edward T. Cone edited the symphony, which was published by W.W. Norton, New York, 1971.
31. Berlioz, *Mémoirs*, p. 326.
32. AmZ 29 (April 1827), p. 266.
33. Riemann, *Präludien und Studien*, vol. 1, p. 57.
34. J. Becker, "Ideen über Malerei und Musik," *NZM* 34 (October 24, 1840), pp. 133–34.

## Chapter Five. Chamber Music

1. *New Grove Dictionary*, Vol. 4, 1980, p. 117.
2. Marx, *Lehre*, vol. 4, p. 425.
3. Czerny, *School of Practical Composition*, vol. 2, p. 6.
4. AmZ, *Register (Index): 1829–1848*, (1849), pp. 18, 101–102, 164.
5. Kirkendale, *Fuge und Fugato* uses the term *pathotyp* (p. 137) to designate a subject in relatively long notes where the diminished seventh appears in alternation with the minor tonic triad. The order of notes is variable, but the affect is always pathetic.
6. Other chamber-music works involving groups of winds include the Octet in E major, Op. 32 for violin, two violas, cello, double bass, and two horns by Ludwig Spohr (1817); also his nonet in F major, Op. 31, for flute, oboe, clarinet, bassoon, horn, violin, viola, cello, and double bass (1813); the Serenade in E flat major, Op. 7, for two flutes, two oboes, two clarinets, four horns, two bassoons, and a double bassoon or tuba, by Richard Strauss (1881). Brahms's Serenade No. 2 in A Major for small orchestra, Op. 16, (1859) uses winds and strings in soloistic or paired voicing much in the manner of chamber music. This work stands between chamber music and orchestra in its texture. Its complement, five pairs of winds, violas, violoncellos, and string bass, make up a small orchestra, especially since Brahms indicated that the string group should have eight violas and four each of the low strings. This small string group, thanks to its low tessitura, is capable of projecting the rich, sombre tone colors that Brahms so often preferred in his music. The Serenade was a favorite of Clara Schumann's. She wrote a glowing response to him in 1859, in which she told of her reactions to the tone qualities in the Adagio: "And now, what am I to say about the adagio? . . . It is exquisitely beautiful. The bass moves so softly and yet with such dignity like a noble figure, the gait of Bach and the 2nd theme begins so sublimely, with such sadness (the mere sound takes hold of one) and then interweaves so marvellously with the other parts. And how magnificent the close of the first part is, with the pedal note coming in, in the middle! And then the ff is so fine, and the way it immediately quiets down again, and the whole transition into Ab major, the horn, the new theme, the liquid pedal

note, the entrance of the viola again, and the crescendo! Up to G major it is all beautiful, but from there it carries on to heaven." Litzmann, *Clara Schumann*, vol. 2, pp. 174–75.

7. Ulrich, *Chamber Music*, pp. 310–11.

## Chapter Six. Harmonic Color

1. See, for instance, for coloristic use of harmony in scoring: Ex. 3-5, Chopin, Prelude in E minor, Op. 28, No. 4; Ex. 3-6, Chopin, Etude in C Major, Op. 10, No. 1; Ex. 3-11, Liszt, Sonata in B Minor, coda; Ex. 4-6, Smetana, *The Bartered Bride*, Overture; Ex. 4-7, Berlioz, *Symphonie fantastique*, finale; Ex. 4-8, Verdi, *La Traviata*, Prelude; Ex. 5-2, Schumann, Quartet in A Major, Op. 41, No. 3, second movement; Ex. 5-7, Schubert, Quintet in C Major, Op. 163, first movement.

2. Richard Wagner, *Sämtliche Briefe*, vol. 4, pp. 385–86.

3. *NZM* 14 (June 1841), p. 203.

4. Fétis, in the *Traité*, 6th ed. (1858), in considering the harmonic practice of his time, designates it as the "omnitonic order." His concern is principally with modulations, especially those that involve altered chords and enharmonic readings. A critical point in his presentation is the various ways in which the chord B–F–G–D♯ can be read so as to lead to any of a dozen or more keys.

Louis and Thuille, *Harmonielehre* (1907, 1908, 1911, 1913), is a comprehensive treatise, rich with examples from many nineteenth-century composers, among them Bruckner, Brahms, Chopin, Liszt, Pfitzner, Schubert, Schumann, Richard Strauss, and Wagner. The work deals extensively with chromatic progressions with a great many illustrations, generally laid out in four-part chorale or keyboard textures.

Riemann, in *Handbuch der Harmonielehre* (1887), accounts for the rich harmonic vocabulary of Romantic music by assigning chords to one of three functions— tonic, subdominant, and dominant. Chromaticisms, alterations, and deceptive resolutions are considered to be substitutions in the basic functional formulas. Romantic harmony thus is seen as a variant of basic harmonic phenomena.

Schoenberg, *Harmonielehre* (1911), provides an exhaustive catalogue of chromaticisms and modulations between near and distant keys, all set in four-part note-against-note texture.

Kurth, *Romantische Harmonik* (1920), is the most important study to date on Romantic harmony. This work takes Wagner's *Tristan und Isolde* as the crucial stage in the evolution of harmony in the nineteenth century, centering much attention on the implication of the opening chord, the so-called Tristan chord— its voice-leading tendencies, its ambiguous harmonic sense, its various transformations throughout the music drama. Kurth examines antecedents of Wagner's harmonic language and discusses what came afterward—expressionism and impressionism. During the course of the book, Kurth refers to various aspects of harmonic color: *Klangverschleierung* (tone veiling or clouding), pp. 113ff; *Erhöhte Farbentonungen* (heightened color shadings), pp. 130ff; the effect of the minor subdominant, pp. 143ff; effects of individual chords, p. 301, etc. The section on impressionism, pp. 384ff, is of particular interest in that it directs attention to qualities of sound as special effects rather than as components of a harmonic progression.

5. Chopin achieves much the same closing effect by expanding the final tonic harmony over a great range and for a considerable length of time at the end of his Etude in A-Flat Major, Op. 25, No. 1 (1835–36). Other passages of extended

harmony may be found in: Example 3-11, Liszt, *Sonata in B minor,* final measures; Example 5-7, Schubert, Quintet in C major, first movement, opening measures; Example 5-8, Schubert, Quintet in C Major, second movement, opening measures; Example 9-6, Mendelssohn, *Hebrides* Overture, opening measures.

6. See Barzun, *Berlioz,* vol. 1, pp. 456–60, for an assessment of Berlioz's use of harmony.

7. Brahms, *The Herzogenberg Correspondence,* p. 184. The excerpt is taken from Grieg's song for baritone and small orchestra, *Der Bergentrückte* (The mountain thrall), Op. 32 (1877–78), mm. 1–2.

8. Kurth, *Romantische Harmonik,* p. 133.

9. Stein, *Form and Performance,* p. 36.

10. Brahms, *The Herzogenberg Correspondence,* p. 227.

11. In a somewhat comparable manner, the restless, unstable sound of augmented triads colors the opening measures of Liszt's *Eine Faust* Symphony (1857), a musical representation of the troubled introspection of Faust.

## Chapter Seven. Period Structure

1. Among these are Reicha, *Traité de haute composition* (1826); Gottfried Weber, *Versuch* (1817–21); Marx, *Lehre* (1841–51 and several subsequent editions); and Lobe, *Lehrbuch* (1850 and later editions).

2. To be sure, paired phrases, closing respectively with open and closed punctuations, appear early in Western music. Sequences and dances with paired phrases from medieval and Renaissance music are indeed periods, according to present definitions. The incorporation of such formations into the mainstream of Western musical composition, however, takes place much later.

3. Zarlino, *Istitutioni,* pp. 221, 226.

4. Walther, *Musikalisches Lexikon,* p. 472.

5. Rousseau, *Dictionnaire,* pp. 385–6.

6. Koch, *Musikalisches Lexikon,* p. 1149.

7. Reicha, *Traité de mélodie,* Text, p. 45, *Supplément,* pp. 22–23.

8. Koch, *Versuch,* vol. 3, p. 305.

9. Kollmann, *Essay on Musical Harmony,* p. 84.

10. Riepel, *Rhythmopoeia,* p. 23.

11. Sulzer, *Allgemeine Theorie,* vol. 2, p. 35.

12. Koch, *Versuch.* De Momigny, *Cours complet.* Daube, *Anleitung.* Reicha, *Traité de mélodie.*

13. Chastellux, *Essai sur l'union,* pp. 16–17.

14. Daube, *Der musikalische Dilettant,* p. 81.

15. Reicha, *Traité de Mélodie,* p. 70.

16. Ibid., p. 19.

17. Riemann, *Musik-Lexikon,* p. 997.

18. Gottfried Weber, *Versuch,* vol. 2, p. 103.

19. Quoted in Einstein, *Music in the Romantic Era,* p. 137.

20. Eigeldinger, *Chopin,* p. 70.

21. Richard Wagner, *Sämtliche Werke,* vol. 19, *Klavierwerke.* Mainz: B. Schott's Söhne, 1970.

## Chapter Eight. Rhetorical Reduction

1. Daube, *Anleitung,* pp. 9, 10.

2. Koch, *Versuch,* Vol. 3, pp. 226ff. Logier, *System,* p. 310.

## Chapter Nine. Symmetrical Arrangements

1. Leonard B. Meyer, in McMurrin, ed., *Tanner Lectures*, comments on the effect that sound qualities have on goal-oriented (periodic) syntax: "Only by expressly weakening the processive, goal-oriented aspects of experience can we be forced, as it were, to attend primarily to the qualities of sense experience—to the timbre of a particular instrument, the sound of a specific harmony" (p. 38). The reverse process also works in such situations; articulations and goals control and even reduce the effect of sense experiences.

2. Edward Cone, in *A View from Delft*, p. 251, cites this passage as an example of ascending thirds that outline the tonic triad of the piece; he then compares and contrasts the progression with the opening of the Prelude to Act I of Wagner's *Tristan und Isolde*, which carries out a similar pattern of ascending thirds, A, C, E, embodied, however, in highly unstable harmonies (see Ex. 6-19). Since Wagner's harmonies are saturated with tritone action, they still imply allegiance to cadential harmony; paradoxically, Mendelssohn's simple shifts of triads avoid cadential action and hint clearly at modal usage. In this light, Mendelssohn's progression is less orthodox than that of Wagner. Oddly enough, Wagner used the ascending progression B, D, F sharp, the same that Mendelssohn employed, in the opening measures of the "Ride of the Valkyries" from *Die Walküre*, Act III (1856). Both pieces portray elemental forces of nature.

## Chapter Ten. Modifications of Symmetry

1. Theorists of the late eighteenth and nineteenth centuries describe modifications and extensions of period structure. Specific references to these procedures appear in Koch, *Versuch* (1793), vol. 3, pp. 153–232; Reicha, *Traité de mélodie* (1814), p. 32; Logier, *System* (1828), pp. 310–46; Czerny, *School of Practical Composition* (1848), vol. 1, p. 18; Marx, *Lehre* (1841–51), vol. 2, pp. 47–52; Lobe, *Lehrbuch* (1858), vol. 1, pp. 294–96, 297–98; Prout, *Musical Form* (1893), pp. 102–50; and Goetschius, *Homophonic Forms* (1898), pp. 34–61, 72–87. These descriptions deal with melodic and harmonic modifications and extensions—deceptive cadences, repetitions, harmonic digressions, insertions of melodic material, cadential reinforcements, etc. Sound, as a means of modification or extension, is not considered in any of these works.

2. Wagner, in Act II, Scene 1, of *Tristan und Isolde*, employs the same separability of the lower and upper fifths of the dominant major ninth to suggest a polychordal effect. The scene depicts two parties of hunters, each with its own set of calls, one assigned the F–A–C triad, the other the C–E flat–G triad, each with its own separate scoring for brass instruments. While Schumann's sound is blended by the uniform timbre and figuration of the piano, Wagner's treatment creates a sharply defined separation of sound among the components of the harmony.

## Chapter Eleven. Extensions

1. In his *Das Lied von der Erde*, p. 40, Danuser cites this segment of the "Trinklied," describing it as a variant of the *Liedestrophe* type, consisting of two phrases closing with an emphatic cadence.

2. While F sharp is the more prominent tone in the second beat of measure 3, the D at the end of the second beat is the essential tone of the harmony and carries the line downward toward the leading tone, G sharp.

3. The melody was originally that of the song "Je vois donc quitter" composed ca. 1819; destroyed. This information is given by D. Kern Holoman, *Catalogue of the Works of Hector Berlioz* in *Hector Berlioz New Edition of the Complete Works*, vol. 25, Kassel, Basel, London, New York: Bärenreiter, 1987.

4. The reduction constitutes a single period but contains within itself the configuration of a small two-reprise form (see Chapter 12, p. 241). The first eight measures, closing on the dominant, represent the first reprise; the next four measures constitute a brief digression while the last four measures recall part of the opening melody to close the second reprise. Another reduction would deploy the opening melody in an antecedent-consequent phrase layout, taken from measures 3 and 28 respectively, to embody symmetrical period structure.

5. See Ratner, *Classic Music*, pp. 308ff.

6. See Haydn, *The Seven Last Words*, Op, 51, No. 1 (1787), mm. 99–104; Mozart, Sonata in F Major, K. 333 (1778), first movement, mm. 1–5; Bach, *The Well-Tempered Clavier*, book 1 (1722), Fugue in D Minor, mm. 43–44; and Beethoven, Sonata in A-flat Major, Op. 27, No. 1 (1801), third movement, mm. 2–4.

## Chapter Twelve. Small Forms

1. See Chapter 7, note 1. In addition we can list Czerny, *School of Practical Composition* (1848); Jadassohn, *Die Formen* (1889); Prout, *Musical Form* (1893); Riemann, *Grosse Kompositionslehre* (1902); d'Indy, *Cours de Composition* (1903); and Goetschius, *Homophonic Forms* (1898).

2. Reicha refers to two-part forms in *Traité de mélodie*, p. 36, and to three-part forms, p. 41. Marx discusses *Zweiteiligkeit* in *Lehre*, vol. 1, p. 184, and *Dreiteiligkeit*, p. 60. Czerny described themes of two parts or strains in *School of Practical Composition*, vol. 1, p. 9. The term *two-reprise* is used here as a reflection of the traditional concept of the two-part or binary form, a concept articulated in eighteenth-century writings. See the discussion of this point in Ratner, *Classic Music*, pp. 209–16.

3. See note 1 above.

4. Koch, *Versuch*, vol. 3, pp. 59–60, describes the simplest complete piece as sixteen measures in length. He quotes a minuet of Haydn that is built of two repeated sections or reprises.

5. See the discussion of this type of cadence in Ratner, *Classic Music*, p. 226. Also see p. 276 below for a similar type of progression. The drop of a third after a half cadence is a latter-day version of an ancient modal cadence described Francesco Gasparini in *L'armonico pratico al cimbalo*, 1708, p. 23, where the bass drops a third instead of a fifth.

6. Gavoty suggests that Chopin "conceived the idea of a modern sequel to Bach's *Preludes and Fugues*," adding that Chopin "had erected an undying monument to the modern piano" (*Frédéric Chopin*, pp. 60–61).

## Chapter Thirteen. Sonata Form

1. Marx, *Lehre*, vol. 3, p. 282. Koch, *Versuch*, vol. 3, p. 301. Kollman, *Essay on Practical Composition*, p. 5. Momigny, *Cours complet*, vol. 2, p. 397. Reicha, *Traité de mélodie*, p. 46. Czerny, *School of Practical Composition*, vol. 1, p. 33.

2. Portmann, *Leichtes Lehrbuch*, p. 50.

3. Kollman, *Essay on Practical Composition*, p. 5.

4. Portmann, *Leichtes Lehrbuch*, examples, pp. 39–56. Czerny, in *School of Practical Composition*, vol. 1, pp. 39–46, offers a paraphrase of the first movement of the Sonata in D Major, K. 381, for four-hand single keyboard by Mozart. Czerny's

version is a simplified two-hand piece that retains structural and harmonic features of the model, but makes complete changes in the melodic material.

5. Galeazzi, *Elementi*, pp. 251ff, refers to a "pazzo caratteristico" as a contrasting theme; Koch, *Versuch*, vol. 3, p. 364, describes a *"cantabler Satz"*; Vogler, *Kurpfalzische Tonschule*, vol. 2, p. 62, speaks of a gentler idea in contrast to a stronger one; Kollmann, *An Essay on Practical Musical Composition*, Preface, provides a complete movement in which a vigorous theme alternates with a cantabile subject.

6. Marx, *Lehre*, vol. 3, p. 201.

7. Dommer, *Kochs Lexikon*, pp. 780ff.

8. Marx, *Lehre*, vol. 3, p. 282.

9. The broad half cadence on G, the dominant, represents one typical Classic procedure—to arrive at the dominant as a chord that embodies a half cadence in the home key, then to continue with the dominant as a key to be established and confirmed throughout the remainder of the exposition. The first movement of Mozart's Sonata in D major, K. 576, 1789, deploys its harmony in this way.

10. Both Mozart's Sonata in F Major, K. 332, second movement, and Beethoven's Concerto in G Major, Op. 58, first movement, digress to minor-mode harmony as a foil to the arrival at the major dominant key.

11. See the discussion of chromatic third relations in Chapter 6.

12. Ratner, *Classic Music*, pp. 226–27.

13. Mahler originally conceived the lyric theme in E-flat major, a traditional relationship of keys (C minor to E-flat major) in a sonata exposition. His decision to shift the second key area to E major introduced an effect of harmonic color contrast that highlights the extreme contrast of affect between the opening theme and the lyric theme (Vill, *Vermittlungsformen*, p. 252).

14. Beethoven employed a third-related key scheme, C–E, in the first movement of the Sonata in C major, Op. 53 (1804), the *Waldstein*, and in the *Leonore* Overture no. 3, Op. 72a, (1806). In these works the two keys are connected by a common tone, E; in each case the approach to E from C is made by powerful cadential drives, very different than Mahler's sudden slip into E via a C–B drop in the bass.

15. Vill, *Vermittlungsformen*, pp. 248ff, and Sponheuer, *Logik des Zerfalls*, pp. 108–9, locate the beginning of the development of this movement at m. 117, where the lyric theme appears in C major. According to the harmonic argument of sonata form, the reappearance of the lyric theme in C major should take place in the recapitulation, where it acts as a reconciliation of the harmonic contrast of the exposition, in the process of the final confirmation of the home key. Presumably, this reconciliation would take place at m. 362. From a harmonic point of view, the appearance of the lyric theme in C major can be seen as a premature recapitulation rather than the beginning of the development. On the other hand, the broad extension of the E-major sound in mm. 126–44 confirms the long-range opposition of E major to C minor and acts as a powerful gesture of closure. Thus, in the harmonic view, the exposition ends at m. 144, and the development begins with an interchange of mode to E minor in the following measure. The effect of these harmonic manipulations is to throw key contrasts into sharp relief, highlighting their individual colors.

A comparable strategy was employed by Chopin in the first movement of his Concerto in E Minor, Op. 11 (1830). For the solo exposition, Chopin introduced the lyric theme in E major, instead of the traditional G major. No change of tonal center takes place between the first and second key areas of the exposition. The opposition of keys basic to a sonata-form exposition is put aside in favor of a striking change of harmonic color. G major makes a belated appearance in this movement, to frame the rhyme of the lyric theme. Here, the tonic-relative major opposition of keys loses its structural force; the effect is that of an episode, with striking local contrast of key color.

Chopin's scheme:

| Solo exposition | | | Recapitulation | | | |
|---|---|---|---|---|---|---|
| E minor | mm. 139–221 | | Recall | | E minor | mm. 486–572 |
| E major | mm. 222–332 | | Rhyme | | G major | mm. 573–621 |

16. Newman, in *The Sonata since Beethoven*, p. 375, charts the form of the sonata along five different lines: one-movement sonata form; four-movement cycle; main tempos and meters; main tonal centers; main thematic elements. Searle, in *The Music of Liszt*, pp. 58ff, suggests a four-section division, including a slow movement, and quotes main theme and "second subject" (m. 153). Dömling, in *Franz Liszt und seine Zeit*, pp. 123ff, makes two great sections of this work, an exposition, mm. 1–346, and a reprise, mm. 460–728, separated by a slow movement. Finally, Kentner, in Walker, *Franz Liszt*, pp. 82ff, refers to first and second subjects, then continues with a running account of events in the piece without offering an overview of its form.

# Selected Bibliography

ABRAHAM, GERALD. *Chopin's Musical Style.* London: Oxford University Press, 1941.

————. *A Hundred Years of Music.* 3d ed. Chicago: Aldine, 1964.

*Allgemeine musikalische Zeitung.* Leipzig, 1798–1848.

*Allgemeine musikalische Zeitung, Register (Index) 1829–48.* Leipzig: Breitkopf and Härtel, 1849.

BACH, CARL P. E. *Versuch über die wahre Art das Clavier zu spielen.* Berlin, 1759–1762. (Eng. tr., William J. Mitchell tr. & ed., New York: Norton, 1949).

BARZUN, JACQUES. *Berlioz and the Romantic Century.* 3d ed. 2 vols. New York: Columbia University Press, 1969.

BERLIOZ, HECTOR. *Memoirs of Hector Berlioz from 1803 to 1865, Comprising his Travels in Germany, Italy, Russia, and England.* Translated by Rachel Holmes and Eleanor Holmes and edited by Ernest Newman. 1932. Reprint. New York: Dover, 1966.

————. *A Treatise upon Modern Instrumentation and Orchestration,* Op. 10. Translated by Mary Cowden Clarke. 2d ed. London: Novello, Ewer, 1858.

BIE, OSKAR. *A History of the Pianoforte. . . .* Translated by E. E. Keller and E. W. Naylor. London: J. M. Dent, 1899.

BLUME, FRIEDRICH. *Classic and Romantic Music.* New York: Norton, 1970.

BRAHMS, JOHANNES. *The Herzogenberg Correspondence.* Edited by Max Kalbeck and translated by Hannah Bryant. New York: Da Capo Press, 1987.

BUKOFZER, MANFRED. *Music in the Baroque Era.* New York: Norton, 1947.

BURNEY, CHARLES. *A General History of Music.* 1789. Edited by Frank Mercer. 1935. Reprinted New York: Dover, 1957.

CARSE, ADAM. *The History of Orchestration.* 1925. Reprint New York: Dover, 1964.

————. *The Orchestra from Beethoven to Berlioz.* Cambridge: Heffer, 1948.

————. *The Orchestra in the Eighteenth Century.* Cambridge: Heffer, 1940.

CHARLTON, DAVID, ED. *E. T. A. Hoffmann's Musical Writings: Kreisleriana, The Poet and the Composer, Musical Criticism.* Cambridge: Cambridge University Press, 1989.

CHASTELLUX, FRANÇOIS J. *Essai sur l'union de la poésie et de la musique.* Paris, 1765.

CONE, EDWARD T. *Music; A View from Delft.* Edited by Robert P. Morgan. Chicago: University of Chicago Press, 1989.

CZERNY, CARL. *Briefe über den Unterricht auf dem Pianoforte.* Wien: Diabelli, [1850?].

———. The Complete Theoretical-Practical Piano School, Op. 500, 3 vols. London: R. Cocks, [1839].

———. *School of Practical Composition.* 3 vols. Translated by John Bishop. London: Robert Cocks, 1848.

———. *Schule der Geläufigkeit auf dem Pianoforte,* Op. 299. Wolfenbüttel: L. Holle, [18-]

DAHLHAUS, CARL. *Musik des 19. Jahrhunderts.* Wiesbaden: Akademische Verlagsgesellschaft Athenaion, c1980.

———. "Satz und Periode: Zur Theorie der musikalischen Syntax." *Zeitschrift für Musiktheorie* 2 (1978): 16–26.

———. "Wagners Begriff der 'dichterisch-musikalischen Periode.'" In *Beiträge zur Geschichte der Musikanschauung,* edited by Walter Salmen, 179–94. Regensburg: Gustav Bosse, 1965.

DANUSER, HERMANN. *Das Lied von der Erde.* Munich: Wilhelm Fink, 1986.

DAUBE, JOHANN FRIEDRICH. *Anleitung zur Erfindung der Melodie.* Wien: Christian Gottlob Täubel, 1797.

———.*Der musikalische Dilettant: Eine Abhandlung der Komposition.* Wien: Von Trattner, 1773.

DÖMLING, WOLFGANG. *Franz Liszt und seine Zeit.* Laaber: Laaber, 1985.

DOMMER, ARREY VON. *H. C. Kochs musikalisches Lexikon.* 2d ed. Heidelberg: J.C.B. Mohr, 1865.

EIGELDINGER, JEAN-JACQUES. *Chopin vu par ses élèves.* Neuchatel: à la Baconnière, 1979. Translated as *Chopin, Pianist and Teacher, As Seen by His Pupils.* Translated by Naomi Shohet with Krysia Osostowicz and Roy Howat. Cambridge: Cambridge University Press, 1986.

EINSTEIN, ALFRED. *Music in the Romantic Era.* New York: Norton, 1947.

FÉTIS, FRANÇOIS J. *Biographie universelle des musiciens et bibliographie générale de la musique.* 2d ed. Paris: Firmin-Didot, 1878–84.

———. *Traité complet de la théorie et de la pratique de l'harmonie. . . . 6th ed.* Paris: Brandus, Dufour, 1858.

———, ed. *Revue musicale,* 15 vols. Paris: 1827–35.

FREDERICK, EDMUND. "The 'Romantic' Sound in Four Pianos of Chopin's Era." *19th-Century Music* Vol. 3, no. 2, Nov. 1979 150–53.

FRISCH, WALTER. *Brahms and the Principle of Developing Variation.* Berkeley and Los Angeles: University of California Press, 1983.

GALEAZZI, FRANCESCO. *Elementi teorico-pratici di musica.* Rome: Pilucchi Cracas, 1791–96.

GASPARINI, FRANCESCO. *L'armonico pratico al cimbalo.* Venice: Bortoli, 1708.

GAVOTY, BERNARD. *Frédéric Chopin.* Translated by Martin Sokolinsky. New York: Scribner, 1977.

GOETSCHIUS, PERCY. *The Homophonic Forms of Musical Composition.* New York: G. Schirmer, 1921.

———. *The Larger Forms of Musical Composition.* New York: G. Schirmer, 1915.

GOOD, EDWIN. *Giraffes, Black Dragons, and other Pianos.* Stanford, Calif.: Stanford University Press: 1982.

GUTMAN, ROBERT W. *Richard Wagner: The man, His Mind, and His Music.* London: Secker and Warburg, 1968.

HANDSCHIN, JACQUES. *Musikgeschichte im Überblicke.* 2d ed. Lucerne: Raber, 1964.

HARDING, ROSAMUND. *The Pianoforte: Its History Traced to the Great Exhibition of 1851.* Cambridge: Cambridge University Press, 1933.

HEDLEY, ARTHUR. *Selected Correspondence of Fryderyk Chopin.* London, Melbourne, Toronto: Heinemann, 1962.

HELMHOLTZ, HERMANN VON. *On the Sensations of Tone.* Translated by Alexander Ellis. 2d ed. 1948. Reprint. New York: Dover, 1954.

HINDEMITH, PAUL. *The Craft of Musical Composition.* 2 vols. Translated by Arthur Mendel. Rev. ed. New York: Associated Music Publishers, 1945.

HOBOKEN, ANTHONY VON. *Joseph Haydn: Thematisch-bibliographisches Werkverzeichnis.* Vol. 1. *Instrumentalwerke.* Mainz: Schott, 1957.

HOLOMAN, D. KERN. *Berlioz.* Cambridge: Harvard University Press, 1989.

———— "Catalogue of the Works of Hector Berlioz" in *Hector Berlioz, New Edition of the Complete Works,* issued by the Berlioz Centenary Committee London in Association with the Calouste Gulbenkian Foundation, Lisbon. Kassel, Basel, London, New York: Bärenreiter, 1987.

INDY, VINCENT d'. *Cours de composition musicale.* 2 vols. Paris: Durand, 1902–3, 1909.

JADASSOHN, SALOMON. *Die Formen in der Werken der Tonkunst.* Leipzig: Breitkopf und Härtel, 1923.

KALKBRENNER, FRIEDRICH. *Méthode pour apprendre le piano-forte.* Paris: I. Pleyel, 1830.

KIRKENDALE, WARREN. *Fuge und Fugato in der Kammermusik des Rokoko und der Klassik.* Tutzing: Hans Schneider, 1966.

KOCH, HEINRICH CHRISTOPH. *Handbuch bey dem Studium der Harmonie.* Leipzig: Hartknoch, 1811.

————. *Musikalisches Lexikon.* Frankfurt am Main: August Hermann, 1802.

————. *Versuch einer Anleitung zur Composition.* Leipzig: Adam Friedrich Böhme, 1782, 1787, 1793.

KOLLMANN, AUGUST F. C. *An Essay on Musical Harmony.* London: J. Dale, 1796.

————. *An Essay on Practical Musical Composition.* London: Privately printed, 1799. Reprint. New York: Da Capo Press, 1973.

KOURY, DANIEL. *Orchestral Performance Practices in the Nineteenth Century.* Ann Arbor, Mich.: UMI Research Press, 1986.

KRAMER, LAWRENCE. "The Mirror of Tonality: Transitional Features of Nineteenth-Century Harmony." *19th-Century Music* 4, no. 3 (Spring 1981): 191–208.

KURTH, ERNST. *Romantische Harmonik und ihre Krise in Wagners "Tristan."* 1923. Reprint. Hildesheim: Georg Ulm, 1968.

LISZT, FRANZ. *Letters of Franz Liszt.* Edited by La Mara [Marie Lipsius] and translated by Constance Bache. 2 vols. London: H. Grevel, 1894.

LITZMANN, BERTHOLD. *Clara Schumann: An Artist's Life.* Translated by Grace Hadow. 4th ed., abridged. New York: Vienna House, 1972.

LOBE, JOHANN CHRISTIAN. *Lehrbuch der musikalischen Komposition.* 2d ed., Vol. 1. Leipzig: Breitkopf und Härtel, 1858.

————. *Lehrbuch der musikalischen Komposition.* Revised by Hermann Kretschmar, 6th ed., 1900.

LOESSER, ARTHUR. *Men, Women, and Pianos.* New York: Simon and Schuster, 1954.

LOGIER, JOHANN B. *System der Musik-Wissenschaft. . . .* Berlin: Heinrich Adolph Wilhelm Logier, 1827.

LÖHLEIN, GEORG SIMON. *Clavier-Schule.* 5th ed. Edited by J. G. Witthauer. Leipzig: Fromanns Erben, 1791.

LONGYEAR, REY. "Liszt's B Minor Sonata." *Music Review* 34 (1973): 193–209.

————. *Nineteenth-Century Romanticism in Music.* 3d ed. Englewood Cliffs, N. J.: Prentice-Hall, 1938.

LORENZ, ALFRED. *Das Geheimnis der Form bei Richard Wagner.* Reprint of the 2nd ed., Vol. 2. Tutzing: Hans Schneider, 1966.

LOUIS, RUDOLF, and LUDWIG THUILLE. *Harmonielehre*. 6th ed. Stuttgart: Grüninger, [191-].

MCMURRIN, STERLING M., ed. *Tanner Lectures on Human Values*. Salt Lake City: University of Utah Press, 1985.

MARCUSE, SIBYL. *A Survey of Musical Instruments*. 1st ed. New York: Harper and Row, 1975.

MARPURG, FRIEDRICH. *Anleitung zum Clavierspielen*. Berlin: Haude und Spener, 1755.

MARSH, JOHN. *Hints to Young Composers of Instrumental Music.* . . . London: Clementi, Hyde, Ranger, Collard & Davis, 1800.

MARX, ADOLPH BERNHARD. *Die Lehre von der musikalischen Komposition*. 2d. ed. 4 vols. Leipzig: Breitkopf und Härtel, 1841–51.

———. *Die Musik des neunzehnten Jahrhunderts und ihre Pflege*. 2d ed. Leipzig: Breitkopf und Härtel, 1873.

MENDELSSOHN, FELIX. *Letters*. Edited by Felix Moscheles. Boston: Ticknor, 1888.

MEYER, LEONARD B. *Music, the Arts, and Ideas*. Chicago: University of Chicago Press, 1967.

———. *Style and Music*. Philadelphia: University of Pennsylvania Press, 1989.

MOMIGNY, JÉRÔME-JOSEPH DE. *Cours complet d'harmonie et de composition*. 3 vols. Paris: Privately printed, 1806.

MOYER, BIRGITTE. *Concepts of Musical Form in the Nineteenth Century with special reference to A. B. Marx and Sonata Form*. Ph.D. diss., Stanford University, 1969.

*Neue Zeitschrift für Musik*. Leipzig, 1834–.

NEWCOMB, ANTHONY. "The Birth of Music out of the Spirit of Drama," *19th-Century Music*, 5, no. 1 (summer 1981): 38–66.

NEWMAN, WILLIAM. *The Sonata since Beethoven*. Chapel Hill: University of North Carolina Press, 1969.

PAISIELLO, GIOVANNI. *Regole per bene accompagnare il partimento.* . . . St. Petersburg: 1782.

PLANTINGA, LEON. *Romantic Music*. New York: Norton, 1984.

PORTMANN, JOHANN G. *Leichtes Lehrbuch der Harmonie, Composition, und des Generalbasses.* . . . Darmstadt: J.J. Will, 1789.

PRIMMER, BRIAN. "Unity and Ensemble: Contrasting Ideals in Romantic Music." *19th-Century Music* 6, no. 2 (Fall 1982): 97–140.

*Proceedings of the Royal Musical Association*. London, 1874–.

PROUT, EBENEZER. *Musical Form*. 3d ed. London: Augener, 1893.

RATNER, LEONARD G. *Classic Music: Expression, Form, and Style*. New York: Schirmer Books, 1980.

REICHA, ANTON. *Traité de haute composition*. Paris: Zetter et Cie, 2 vols., 1826.

———. *Traité de mélodie*. Paris: Privately printed, 1814.

RETI, RUDOLPH. *The Thematic Process in Music*. New York: Macmillan, 1951.

RIEMANN, HUGO. *Grosse Kompositionsfehre*. 3 vols. Berlin: W. Spemann, 1902–13.

———. *Handbuch der Harmonielehre*. Leipzig: Breitkopf and Härtel, 1887.

———. *Musik-Lexikon*. 1882. 6th ed. Leipzig: Hesse, 1905.

———. *Präludien und Studien*. Reprint. 3 vols. Hildesheim: Georg Ulm, 1967.

RIEPEL, JOSPH. *Rhythmopoeia*. Vol. 1 of *Anfangsgründe zur musikalischen Setzkunst.* . . . Regensburg: Bader, 1752.

RIMSKY-KORSAKOV, NICOLAI. *Principles of Orchestration*. Edited by Maximilian Steinberg and translated by Edward Agate. New York: Kalmus, 1933.

ROUSSEAU, JEAN-JACQUES. *Dictionnaire de musique*. Paris: Duchesne, 1758.

SACHS, CURT. *The Commonwealth of Art*. New York: Norton, 1946.

SADIE, STANLEY, ED. *The New Grove Dictionary of Music and Musicians.* London: Macmillan, 1980.

SCHAFER, R. MURRAY. *E. T. A. Hoffmann and Music.* Toronto: Toronto University Press, 1975.

SCHENKER, HEINRICH. *Neue musikalische Theorien und Phantasien.* 3 vols. Stuttgart: J. G. Cotta, 1906–35.

SCHOENBERG, ARNOLD. *Harmonielehre.* 3d ed. Wien: Universal Edition, 1922.

SCHONBERG, HAROLD. *The Great Pianists.* New York: Simon and Schuster, 1987.

SCHUMANN, ROBERT. *On Music and Musicians.* Translated by Paul Rosenfeld and edited by Konrad Wolff. Berkeley and Los Angeles: University of California Press, 1983.

SEARLE, HUMPHREY. *The Music of Liszt.* London: Williams and Norgate, 1954.

SECHTER, SIMON. *Die Grundsätze der musikalischen Komposition.* 3 vols. Leipzig: Breitkopf und Härtel, 1853–54.

SOLIE, RUTH. "The Living Work: Organicism and Musical Analysis." *19th-Century Music,* 4, no. 2 (Fall 1980): 147–56.

SPONHEUER, BERND. *Logik des Zerfalls.* Tutzing: Hans Schneider, 1978.

STEIN, ERWIN. *Form and Performance.* New York: Knopf, 1962.

STOWELL, ROBIN. *Violin Technique and Performance Practice in the Late Eighteenth and Early Nineteenth Centuries.* Cambridge: Cambridge University Press, 1985.

STRUNK, OLIVER, ED. *Source Readings in Music History.* New York: Norton, 1950.

SUBOTNIK, ROSE R. "Romantic Music as Post-Kantian Critique: Classicism, Romanticism, and the Concept of the Semiotic Universe." In *On Criticizing Music,* ed. Kingsley Price, 74–98. Baltimore: Johns Hopkins University Press, 1981.

SULZER, JOHANN G. *Allgemeine Theorie der Schönen Künste.* 2 vols. Leipzig, 1771–74.

TCHAIKOVSKY, MODEST. *The Life and Letters of Peter Ilich Tchaikovsky.* Translated and edited by Rosa Newmarch. London: John Lane, The Bodley Head, 1906.

TÜRK, DANIEL G. *Klavierschule.* 1789. Reprint. Kassel: Bärenreiter, 1962.

ULRICH, HOMER. *Chamber Music: An Intimate Art.* 2d ed. New York: Columbia University Press, 1966.

VILL, SUSANNE. *Vermittlungsformen verbalisierter und musikalischer Inhalte in der Musik Gustav Mahlers.* Tutzing: Hans Schneider, 1979.

VOGEL, MARTIN. *Der Tristan-Akkord und die Krise der modernen Harmonielehre.* Düsseldorf: Orpheus, 1962.

VOGLER, GEORG J. *Kurpfälzische Tonschule.* Mannheim: in commission bei Herrn C. F. Schwan, 1778.

WAGNER, RICHARD. "Über das Dirigieren." In *Gesammelte Schriften und Dichtungen von Richard Wagner.* 2d ed. 8; 261–337. Leipzig: E. W. Fritzsch, 1888.

———. *Sämtliche Briefe.* Vol. 4. Edited by Gertrud Strobel and Werner Wolf. Leipzig: VEB Deutscher Verlag für Musik, 1967.

WALKER, ALAN. *Franz Liszt: The Virtuoso Years, 1811–1847.* Rev. ed. Ithaca, N.Y.: Cornell University Press, 1987.

WALTHER, JOHANN G. W. *Musikalisches Lexikon.* 1732. Reprint. Kassel: Bärenreiter, 1953.

WATSON, DEREK. *Liszt.* New York: Schirmer Books, 1989.

———. *Richard Wagner.* New York: Schirmer Books, 1981.

WEBER, CARL MARIA VON. *Writings on Music.* Translated by Martin Cooper and edited by John Warrack. Cambridge: Cambridge University Press, 1981.

WEBER, GOTTFRIED. *Versuch einer geordneten Theorie der Tonsetzkunst.* 4 vols. 3d. ed. Mainz: B. Schotts Söhne, 1830–32.

WEBSTER, JAMES. "Brahms's *Tragic* Overture: The Form of Tragedy." In *Brahms,* ed. Robert Pascall. Cambridge: Cambridge University Press, 1983.

————. "Schubert's Sonata Form and Brahms's First Maturity." *19th-Century Music* 2, no. 1 (July 1978): 18–35; 3, no. 1 (July 1979): 52–71.

WERFEL, FRANZ, ED. *Verdi: The Man in His Letters.* New York: L. B. Fischer, 1942.

WINKLHOFER, SHARON. *Liszt's Sonata in B Minor.* Ann Arbor, Mich.: UMI Research Press, 1980.

WINTER, ROBERT. "The Emperor's New Clothes: Nineteenth-Century Instruments Revisited." *19th-Century Music* 7, no. 3 (April 1984): 251–55.

————. "The most unwitting foes of the Romantic piano may be those well-intentioned curators who lend their instrument for recording sessions." *Early Music* 12, no. 1 (Feb. 1984).

————. "Performing Nineteenth-Century Music on Nineteenth-Century Instruments." *19th-Century Music* 1, no. 2 (Fall 1977): 163–75.

WODEHOUSE, ARTIS ANN. "Evidence of Nineteenth-century piano performance practice found in recordings of Chopin's Nocturne, Op. 15, No. 2, made by pianists born before 1900." DMA thesis, Stanford University, 1977.

WOLF, ERNEST WILHELM. *Musikalischer Unterricht.* Dresden: Hilcher, 1788.

ZARLINO, GIOSEFFO. *Le istitutioni harmoniche.* Venice: Granesco sense, 1562.

# Index to Names
# and Works

## A

# Index to Subjects

J1